LAND, PROTEST, AND POLITICS

M.S.T
MOVIMENTO
SEM TERRA
QUEREMOS PLAN

Gabriel Ondetti

LAND, PROTEST, AND POLITICS

**THE LANDLESS MOVEMENT AND THE STRUGGLE
FOR AGRARIAN REFORM IN BRAZIL**

The Pennsylvania State University Press
University Park, Pennsylvania

Library of Congress Cataloging-in-Publication Data

Ondetti, Gabriel A.
   Land, protest, and politics : the landless movement and
   the struggle for agrarian reform in Brazil / Gabriel
   Ondetti.
         p.   cm.
Summary: "Analyzes the development of the movement for
agrarian reform in Brazil, and attempts to explain the major
moments of change in its growth trajectory, from the late
1970s to 2006"—Provided by publisher.
Includes bibliographical references and index.
ISBN 978-0-271-03354-9 (pbk : alk. paper)
1. Movimento dos Trabalhadores Rurais sem Terra (Brazil).
2. Land reform—Brazil.
3. Agricultural laborers—Brazil—Political activity.
I. Title.

HD1333.B6053 2008
333.3'181—dc22
2007048616

The Pennsylvania State University Press is a member of the
Association of American University Presses.

It is the policy of The Pennsylvania State University Press
to use acid-free paper. This book is printed on stock that
meets the minimum requirements of American National
Standard for Information Sciences—Permanence of Paper
for Printed Library Material, ANSI Z39.48–1992.

Page xx: Map of Brazil showing the states and major regions.
From *A History of Brazil*, 3d ed., by E. Bradford Burns.
Copyright © 1993 Columbia University Press. Reprinted with
permission of the publisher.

Frontispiece courtesy of José Francisco Borges.

To **Indira**

CONTENTS

LIST OF TABLES, FIGURES, AND MAPS

Tables

Figures

Maps

LIST OF ABBREVIATIONS

Acronyms

ARENA	National Renovating Alliance
ASPLANA	Association of Sugarcane Planters of Alagoas
ASSESSOAR	Association for Rural Studies, Consultation, and Technical Assistance
ATES	Program for Technical, Social, and Environmental Advising
CAT	Agricultural and Environmental Center of the Araguaia-Tocantins
CCA	Central Agricultural Cooperative
CEAPA	State Center for Settler Associations and Smallholders
CEB	ecclesial base community
CENTRU	Center for Rural Worker Education and Culture
CNA	National Confederation of Agriculture
CNBB	National Conference of the Bishops of Brazil
CONCRAB	National Confederation of Agrarian Reform Cooperatives of Brazil
CONTAG	National Confederation of Workers in Agriculture
CPA	Agricultural Production Cooperative
CPMI	Bicameral Congressional Investigating Commission
CPT	Pastoral Commission on Land
CUT	Unified Workers' Central
FAEA	Agricultural Federation of the State of Alagaos
FAEPA	Agricultural Federation of the State of Pará
FARSUL	Agricultural Federation of Rio Grande do Sul
FASE	Federation of Organizations for Social and Educational Assistance
FETAG-AL	Federation of Workers in Agriculture of the State of Alagoas

FETAGRI-PA Federation of Workers in Agriculture of the State of Pará

FETAPE   Federation of Workers in Agriculture of the State of Pernambuco

IBGE   Brazilian Institute of Geography and Statistics

IMF   International Monetary Fund

INCRA   National Institute for Colonization and Agrarian Reform

IPEA   Institute for Applied Economic Research

ITESP   Land Institute of the State of São Paulo

MASTER   Movement of Landless Farmers

MASTRO   Movement of Landless Rural Workers of Western Paraná

MBST   Brazilian Landless Movement

MDA   Ministry of Agrarian Development

MEC   Ministry of Education

MDB   Brazilian Democratic Movement

MLT   Struggle for Land Movement

MLST   Movement for the Liberation of the Landless

MST   Movement of Landless Rural Workers

MST-SMT   Landless Movement of Southern Mato Grosso

MT   Workers' Movement

NERA   Center for Studies Research, and Projects on Agrarian Reform

OAB   Organization of Brazilian Attorneys

NGO   nongovernmental organization

PCR   First Rural Command

PDS   Democratic Social Party

PFL   Party of the Liberal Front

PL   Liberal Party

PMDB   Party of the Brazilian Democratic Movement

PNAD   National Household Survey

PNRA   National Agrarian Reform Plan

PPB   Brazilian Progressive Party

PROCERA   Special Credit Program for Agrarian Reform

PRONAF   National Program for Strengthening Family Agriculture

PSDB   Party of Brazilian Social Democracy

PSOL   Party for Socialism and Liberty

PT	Workers' Party
PTB	Brazilian Labor Party
SCA	Settlers' Cooperative System
SMO	social movement organization
STR	union of rural workers
UDR	Democratic Rural Union

Abbreviations of State Names

AL	Alagaos
CE	Ceará
DF	Federal District
MG	Minas Gerais
PA	Pará
PB	Paraíba
PE	Pernambuco
PR	Paraná
RN	Rio Grande do Norte
RS	Rio Grande do Sul
SC	Santa Catarina
SE	Sergipe
SP	São Paulo

PREFACE

The past two decades have generally not been kind to the Latin American Left. Although the import-substitution regimes that had characterized most economies of the region since the 1940s often did little to undermine social hierarchies, leftists realized that an activist state was a necessary condition for achieving greater equity. The dominant interpretation of the profound economic crisis that struck the region in the 1980s, however, called for a dismantling of the state apparatus. Under the influence of neo-liberalism, Latin American governments set about cutting social programs, selling off state enterprises, and taking down protective tariff walls. The collapse of European communism in the early 1990s was another powerful blow, signaling what seemed to be, at least to some influential observers, the definitive triumph of economic liberalism and the demise of the uto-pian dream of socialist revolution.

Until relatively recently, resistance to state retrenchment in most coun-tries of the region was limited to isolated outbursts of protest. Sustained mass mobilization in favor of redistributive reforms was hard to find. Within this general context of popular quiescence, the struggle for agrarian reform in Brazil increasingly stood out. The key organization within this movement, the Movement of Landless Rural Workers, or MST, had been formed in the mid-1980s, but in the 1990s it achieved national and even international recognition and established itself as one of the most impres-sive examples of grassroots political organizing in Latin America. Its bright-red flag and its trademark encampments—vast agglomerations of wooden shanties covered with black plastic sheeting—became icons of popular re-sistance to oppressive social conditions, not only for Brazilians but also for progressives all over the region and beyond.

I began graduate school at the University of North Carolina, Chapel Hill, in the fall of 1995, just as the MST was emerging as a major actor on the Brazilian political stage. Although I had not originally intended to focus my research on social movements (or even on Brazil), I was seduced by this organization, with its unusual combination of massive numbers, disruptive tactics, and strong internal discipline. Its success in mobilizing poor farm laborers and other traditionally hard-to-organize sectors of Brazilian society to exert pressure on authorities for land redistribution seemed to offer solutions to some of the central challenges faced by the Latin American Left. I spent a year in Brazil in 1997–98, during which I visited MST camps and settlements in four states. I returned for a year and a half of in-depth field research in 1999 and 2000 and made additional, briefer visits in 2003 and 2005.

This book is the fruit of my decade-long engagement with the MST and the broader social movement of which it is part. It traces the movement's evolution from its origins in the late 1970s through 2006. In the end, the book projects a less romantic image of the movement than the one many of its admirers probably have in their heads, or the one I had in mine when I first decided to embark on this study. In particular, I have endeavored to show how some of its achievements in terms of mobilizing workers and gaining concessions from the state were in part a function of contextual conditions over which activists had little control. I have also been at least implicitly critical of certain tactical decisions made by the MST. Nevertheless, I believe that, taken as a whole, the book reaffirms both the tremendous skill and determination of the movement's activists and the importance of their struggle for Brazilian society.

I had many wonderful experiences and made a number of lasting friendships as a result of my work on this project. It is partly for this reason that the debts I accumulated are truly immense. It is not possible to recognize all the people and organizations who helped, but I will try to cite a few of the most important.

I should probably start by expressing my gratitude to Evelyne Huber and Kurt Weyland, who have provided especially generous and valuable assistance. Evelyne has been a crucial source of advice and support since the very beginning of my research on this topic. Her persistent belief in my work is greatly appreciated. Kurt also made a number of fundamental contributions to this project. I thank him, in particular, for his incisive comments on an earlier version of this manuscript and his encouragement at key moments in the project's development. Jack Hammond, Jonathan Hartlyn, Wendy Hunter, Anthony Oberschall, Lars Schoultz, and John Stephens have also been valuable intellectual and professional mentors.

My debts to friends and colleagues in Brazil are also great. Lúcio Flávio

Rodrigues de Almeida provided me with food and lodging on many occasions. What I am most appreciative of, however, are our many stimulating conversations on Brazilian politics and history. Salomão Mufarrej Hage has been a dedicated friend and helped me greatly with my research in the state of Pará. Angela Schwengber and Antonio Eleilson Leite were generous in sharing with me both their experiences as former MST activists and their home in São Paulo. Other friends and colleagues who aided my research efforts in Brazil include Cloves Barbosa, Maria Lúcia Barbosa, Claudemir, José Luiz Augusto da Cruz, Ivete Dias, Bernardo Mançano Fernandes, Renata Gonçalves, Volnei Manfron, Zander Navarro, Ariovaldo Umbelino de Oliveira, José Vaz Parente, Salvador Sandoval, Maria Aparecida Alves de Souza, Dimas Tavares, and Carlos Wagner.

Of course, I must also thank the many people who sat through interviews or otherwise aided my data-gathering process. Among these were dozens of MST activists, who, despite their deep antipathy toward the policies of the U.S. government, were quite open to the prying questions of an American researcher and unstintingly generous with their time. Some of the conclusions I have reached here may contradict their own views on the struggle for land, but I am deeply grateful for their help and cooperation, without which this study would have been impossible.

Also critical to my research efforts was the generous financial support of the Social Science Research Council; the Fulbright-Hays program of the U.S. Department of Education; the Institute for the Study of World Politics; and the Graduate School of the University of North Carolina, Chapel Hill. I should also thank Frank Einhellig of the Graduate College at Missouri State University for allowing me to count my work on this book as part of my Summer Faculty Fellowship.

Two anonymous reviewers provided exceedingly thorough and insightful critiques of my manuscript. Whatever its remaining flaws, this book is a much better piece of scholarship because of their efforts. Chris Strunk also provided valuable assistance by reading the final proofs of the manuscript.

Finally, I must express my thanks to the people closest to me. These include my parents, Josephine Ondetti and the late Miguel Ondetti, who were a tremendous source of encouragement and practical assistance throughout the different stages of this project. I deeply regret that my father was not able to see it completed. I must also thank my wife, Indira, who has supported me through thick and thin and whose detailed comments on every chapter of the manuscript allowed me to identify and (hopefully) solve some important problems. With her insight and unflagging optimism, she has made a fundamental contribution to this book and for that reason I dedicate it to her.

Portions of this book appeared earlier and in somewhat different form in "Repression, Opportunity, and Protest: Explaining the Takeoff of Brazil's Landless Movement," *Latin American Politics and Society* 48, no. 2 (2006): 61–94, and "An Ambivalent Legacy: Cardoso and Land Reform," *Latin American Perspectives* 34, no. 5 (2007): 9–25.

RORAIMA

AMAPÁ

AMAZONAS

NORTH

PARÁ

MARANHÃO

CEARÁ

FERNANDO
DE NORONHA

RIO GRANDE
DO NORTE

PARAÍBA

PIAUÎ

PERNAMBUCO

ACRE

RONDÔNIA

TOCANTINS

NORTHEAST

ÁLAGOAS

SERGIPE

MATO
GROSSO

BAHIA

CENTER-WEST

GOIÁS

MATO
GROSSO
DO SUL

MINAS
GERAIS

SOUTHEAST

SÃO
PAULO

ESPÍRITO SANTO

RIO DE JANEIRO

PARANÁ

SOUTH

SANTA CATARINA

RIO GRANDE
DO SUL

PACIFIC
OCEAN

ATLANTIC
OCEAN

0   1000 km.

0   500 mi.

Brazil: States and regions

Introduction

By the end of the 1980s, agrarian reform seemed all but dead in Brazil. The return to civilian rule in 1985, following two decades of conservative military dictatorship, had widely been seen as an opportunity to finally restructure the country's rural landholding system, one of the most unequal in the world. But President José Sarney had granted land to only a tiny percentage of the country's landless and land-poor families. Worse still, the Sarney years had brought a constitutional reform that substantially restricted the conditions under which private farmland could be expropriated, effectively removing many of the country's larger farms from consideration. In October 1989 Brazilian voters had put what seemed to be the final nail in agrarian reform's coffin by selecting as their next president Fernando Collor, scion of a wealthy family from one of Brazil's most conservative states and an avowed champion of state-reducing "neoliberal" reforms.

Predictions of agrarian reform's final demise proved to be premature, however. About six years after Collor's electoral triumph, land reform abruptly reemerged as a major national issue, filling the newspapers and television news programs and inspiring one of the most successful *telenovelas* of recent decades. Land reform policy output also increased rather dramatically. During his first term in office (1995–98), President Fernando Henrique Cardoso implemented easily the largest land redistribution in Brazilian history, expropriating more than five million hectares of private farmland and granting small plots to some 250,000 families, an amount probably more than that of all the previous presidents combined.

At the same time as land reform was exploding as a public issue and a state policy, grassroots protest for land redistribution was expanding at an unprecedented pace in the Brazilian countryside. Land occupations, the major tactic of the movement for land reform, had been growing gradually in number since the early 1990s. In 1996 they multiplied almost threefold and continued to grow gradually in subsequent years. By the late 1990s more than fifty thousand families were said to be gathered in makeshift encampments on occupied land or at the margin of public roads, awaiting settlement by the federal government.

At the center of protest activity was an organization called the Movement of Landless Rural Workers (MST). Created in 1984 in southern Brazil, the MST had expanded gradually across the country during the following decade, becoming an actor of national scope, although one known to relatively few Brazilians. During the second half of the 1990s, with the explosion of protest and media coverage, the MST emerged as a major political force, and it became virtually a household word. For progressive political activists, both in Brazil and abroad, it became a symbol of popular resistance to oppressive social conditions and rejection of the neoliberal program of state retrenchment.

The dramatic resurgence of the agrarian question in Brazil in the second half of the 1990s underscores two important aspects of the dynamics of social movements. One is the ability of a well-organized popular protest movement to keep an issue from disappearing from the national political agenda, despite the best efforts of powerful elites. Through their determination and innovative tactics, the landless managed to keep the flame of land reform alive despite the crushing defeats of the late Sarney years and the indifference and repression of the conservative Collor government. The aggressive pressure they exerted on President Cardoso also forced him to make good on at least some of his promises.

The rise of the agrarian question, however, also underscores another, equally important theme. That is the crucial influence that changes in the broader political context have on the intensity and impact of protest activity. The explosive growth of land occupations and the ascension of the MST to the status of high-profile political actor were products, not only of the movement's persistence, but also of changes in the larger political environment over which activists had little control. These included a shift in national governing coalitions toward less conservative, more urban-based forces in the early 1990s, and a rapid transformation in the Brazilian public's perception of the urgency of the rural land problem, brought on mainly by two acts of shocking violence against land reform protestors in the Amazon basin in the middle of the decade.

In this book I trace the evolution of the Brazilian landless movement from its birth during the twilight of the military dictatorship in the late 1970s through the first Workers' Party (PT) government, which ended in December 2006. Like other discussions of the landless movement, this one illustrates the first of the two themes mentioned above: how the MST and other landless groups have used mass protest as a political resource to sustain pressure on Brazilian authorities to implement land reform. Much more than other analyses, however, it also gets at the second theme: how the landless movement's development has itself been shaped in fundamental ways by the larger national political environment. Far from being static, as I demonstrate, this environment has changed repeatedly over the course of the movement's history, sometimes constraining and other times facilitating its growth. By underscoring the two-way interaction between the landless movement and its broader political environment, I seek to provide a richer and more accurate account of the forces shaping its development.

The book fills an important gap in the academic literature. As one of the most influential grassroots social movements in the less developed world, the landless movement has attracted a great deal of attention, both within Brazil and abroad. Yet there are few studies of the movement in English. Their other merits notwithstanding, the two book-length treatments that do exist (Branford and Rocha 2002; Wright and Wolford 2003) do not explicitly relate the movement's development to the rich body of theory about social movements that has developed during recent decades. By applying theory to this case, I hope both to strengthen our understanding of an important contemporary movement and to contribute to our broader theoretical comprehension of the dynamics of social protest.

The main empirical focus of this study is on explaining the major moments of change in the movement's growth trajectory: its initial emergence in the late 1970s and early 1980s, its explosive expansion in the mid-1990s (described briefly above), its sharp crisis in the early 2000s, and its resurgence beginning in 2003. In addition, I try to account for the anomalous fact that the landless movement continued to grow during the decade following the end of the military regime in the mid-1980s, while virtually every other major social movement that emerged during the democratic transition declined.

From a theoretical angle, I seek primarily to contribute to the ongoing debate regarding the "political opportunity" perspective on social movements. The central idea of this vein of theorizing is that movements rise and (at least in some versions) fall as a result of shifts in the vulnerability or receptivity of the larger political system, over which activists have little or no influence (McAdam 1982; Tarrow 1994). This notion has had a strong impact on movement scholarship during the past two decades. However, it has come under increasing fire in recent years. Critics have questioned the empirical validity of political opportunity theory. Social movements, they argue, often rise in the absence of expanding opportunities and collapse even when the prospects for successful protest seem bright (Kurzman 1996; Goodwin and Jasper 1999). The critics have also attacked this perspective on conceptual grounds, citing the diverse ways the "political opportunity structure" has been defined or operationalized, the theory's inattention to subjective or cultural processes, and the tendency to neglect or underestimate how movements shape their political contexts through their own actions (Goodwin and Jasper 2004; Hobson 2003).

This debate has injected a healthy dose of conflict and pluralism into social movement theory. What is still missing are rigorous empirical tests of the political opportunity thesis. Several scholars have sought to demonstrate its effectiveness in explaining the evolution of particular movements (Meyer 1990; Costain 1992; Smith 1996). Yet few have actually pitted it against competing explanations in a systematic fashion (Meyer 2004). In this study I undertake such a test. Moreover, I seek to address some of the conceptual objections that critics of the political opportunity perspective have raised by setting out a definition of the political opportunity structure that is both unambiguous and narrow enough to make the theory readily falsifiable.

The landless movement lends itself well to the task of testing political opportunity theory. In almost three decades of existence, it has experienced major fluctuations in intensity of protest and important changes in its economic, social, and political context, providing variance on both the dependent and independent variables. In addition, existing analyses (Fernandes 1996, 2000; Veltmeyer and Petras 2002; Wright and Wolford 2003) would seem to position this movement as a challenging case for political opportunity theory to explain. The central emphasis of these works is on how the skill and determination of activists has allowed it to survive and achieve success in the face of a hostile political system. The idea that the Brazilian state has at some times and in some ways facilitated the movement's growth is, at most, downplayed.

In emphasizing the role of variation in the political vulnerability of the state in shaping the landless movement's development, this book generally strikes a strong blow in favor of political opportunity theory. I confirm the critical importance of changes in the broader political environment in explaining the growth and decline of movements over time. I also show that political opportunity structure can be an influential factor in determining why movements that arise in the same broad wave of protest activity subsequently experience different growth trajectories.

At the same time, I do not offer an unmitigated endorsement of this theoretical perspective. In particular, my empirical analysis provides support for suggestions put forward by the critics of political opportunity theory, including the need to recognize how subjective or cultural factors not stressed by mainstream analyses can influence the political opportunity structure for protest, and the need to focus more attention on the idea that movements can shape their own political opportunity structures.

In addition to contributing to the current debate on the political opportunity perspective, this book also speaks to the long-standing controversy surrounding economist Mancur Olson's (1965) theory of collective action and its relevance for social movements. Movement scholars have often disagreed with Olson's emphasis on the role of material "selective" incentives for promoting collective action. However, they have at least implicitly accepted his assumption that movements inherently pursue public or collective goods—ones that cannot be feasibly denied to individuals who do not contribute to their provision—and must therefore somehow overcome what he called the "free-rider" problem. Based on my analysis of the landless movement, I argue that this assumption is unwarranted.

Research Design and Data Sources

This is a book about a social movement. By that I mean a collective effort to pressure relevant authorities for a desired change through the use of protest (or "social protest"). The latter consists of tactics that are both highly public and are not explicitly legitimated by existing political institutions. Thus, for example, marches, demonstrations, sit-ins, road blockages, and land occupations are forms of protest, but voting, lobbying legislators, making campaign contributions, and writing letters to public officials are not.[1] Nonprotest actions have played a significant role in forwarding the

1. A related term is *mobilization*. When I use this I will be referring to the process through which people initially get involved in a social movement.

cause of land reform in Brazil in recent decades. For the most part, however, in this book I will discuss such actions only to the extent that they have influenced the intensity of protest activity.

The empirical focus of this book is somewhat broader than that of most studies of protest for agrarian reform in contemporary Brazil. Existing works generally focus exclusively on the MST, which is easily the most important, but by no means the only, group active in this struggle. The topic of my study, in contrast, is the totality of attempts to pressure authorities for land reform and supporting policies (for example, credit, housing) through protest since the revival of social movement activity in Brazil in the late 1970s.[2] This is what I refer to as the landless movement.

I set out to explore here two fundamental issues regarding the movement's development. One is variation in the intensity of mobilization and protest over time. More specifically, how can we explain the four major changes in the movement's strength, namely, its initial emergence as a significant actor during the democratic transition of the late 1970s and early 1980s; its rapid takeoff under the Cardoso government in the middle of the 1990s; its abrupt, but ultimately temporary, decline during Cardoso's second term in office; and its strong resurgence under the PT government headed by legendary former union activist Luiz Inácio Lula da Silva?

The second issue has to do with the landless movement's exceptional trajectory relative to other social movements that arose during the democratic transition period. Why did this movement continue to grow following the resumption of civilian rule in 1985, while virtually every other major movement was fading? Since the first issue can be broken down into four specific questions (one for each episode of change), I deal mainly with five empirical research questions. I use a broad theoretical framework that synthesizes the existing literature on social movements to guide and discipline my investigation of these questions. For each, I evaluate the plausibility of an answer oriented by each of what I see as the four basic theoretical perspectives on social movements. Which of these perspectives, I ask, provides the most convincing answer to the question at hand?

The data on which the book is based were gathered mainly during two extended periods of field research in the late 1990s and 2000. I made two additional research trips in the summers of 2003 and 2005. All told, I spent

---

2. I use the terms *land reform* and *agrarian reform* interchangeably to mean the redistribution of land resources by the state with the intention of creating a more equitable landholding system.

about two and a half years conducting research on the landless movement in Brazil. My fieldwork was conducted mainly in four states: Alagoas, Pará, Rio Grande do Sul, and São Paulo. In selecting these states, I sought to capture as much of Brazil's regional diversity (discussed further below) as possible, especially with regard to the rural sector. Rio Grande do Sul represents the relatively equitable, family-farming economy of southern Brazil; Pará the changing frontier economy of the Amazon region; São Paulo the highly modernized commercial farming of the industrialized Southeast; and Alagoas the typical northeastern blend of labor-intensive plantation agriculture, subsistence farming, and extensive cattle-ranching. I also conducted a smaller but significant amount of research in two other northeastern states, Pernambuco and Paraíba. Finally, I did about three weeks of research in the national capital, Brasília.

Much of my fieldwork involved formal interviews. I interviewed 128 activists directly engaged in organizing the grassroots struggle for agrarian reform. Most, but not all, of them were linked to the MST. I conducted an additional 60 interviews with people involved in the struggle over land reform in some other way. These included state and national legislators, leaders of a wide variety of nongovernmental organizations, and officials in the federal agrarian reform bureaucracy. Unlike many students of the landless movement, I spoke to those opposed to, as well as those in favor of, agrarian reform. My interviews included twelve with representatives of landowner organizations and five with legislators known for their opposition to land reform.

My research also benefited from numerous informal conversations with movement leaders and months of participant observation in the landless movement's camps, settlements, and offices. I ate and drank with activists, slept in their homes and tents, rode in their cars and on the backs of their motorcycles, and got to know their spouses and children. This gave me a privileged view of the movement's internal workings.

I also tapped a variety of other primary sources of information, including media coverage and documents published by the MST, state and federal governments, nongovernmental organizations, labor unions, and political parties. Finally, I was aided by the existence of a large number of published and unpublished studies of the landless movement by Brazilian authors. These works gave me insight into specific aspects of the movement and helped to extend the geographic scope of my knowledge of the movement beyond the states in which I was able to conduct field research.

Theoretical Perspectives on Social Movements

What tools does the literature on social movements offer to analyze the landless movement's development? I address this question more systematically in the following chapter, drawing on examples from the literature on rural movements to illustrate my discussion. Here, for the purposes of laying out the key arguments of the book, I briefly outline what I see as the four major theoretical perspectives on social movements, each of which focuses on a particular variable, broadly defined. These are discontent/grievance, organizational capacity, activist strategy and political opportunity.

The discontent/grievance perspective includes a broad variety of theoretical approaches, all of which see movement activity as a more or less direct reflection of the felt needs of the people involved in protest. Discontent can arise from a variety of sources, including socioeconomic changes and political dislocations. It may result from absolute declines in welfare or from conditions that make people feel that they are worse off than they should, or deserve to, be. It may also result from a reorientation of priorities, which causes people to be concerned about issues they once ignored. Discontent, or grievance-based, theories have focused mainly on explaining why movements initially emerge, but the logic behind them can be applied to other questions as well. I include in this category Marxist approaches to social protest, post–World War II "collective behavior" theories, and contemporary European "new social movements" theory.

In contrast to the discontent/grievance perspective, the organizational capacity perspective focuses, not on needs, but on the capacity of social groups or communities to organize and sustain mass protest. A major concern of this approach to social movements are the grassroots organizational structures that exist prior to or independent of social movement activity. Researchers working within this perspective tend to see the density of such "indigenous" organizational structures, including churches, clubs, labor unions, and friendship networks, as the key determinant of a community or social group's capacity to organize a social movement. These networks provide a number of resources, including leadership, communications, normative incentives, and a reduction of the uncertainty that can undermine the potential for collective action. Although it focuses mainly on indigenous organizational structures, the organizational capacity perspective also looks at the human and material resources made available by external actors and how they affect the possibilities for creating and sustaining social movements.

Social movements are sometimes influenced by structural and contextual forces that are largely beyond the power of activists to control. But the literature that comprises what I call the "activist strategy" perspective shows that movement development is also affected by the particular strategic choices made by movement activists. Especially since the 1970s, movement researchers have examined how the decisions taken by top movement activists shape the fate of the movements they lead. In particular, they have highlighted four key types of decisions, regarding (1) the structure of the organizations they create or adapt to coordinate their struggles; (2) the tactics they use to pressure authorities; (3) the basic goals they adopt; and (4) the rhetorical/symbolic "framing" strategies they employ to appeal to actual or potential supporters, the media, and the state. Although some scholars place these different types of decisions in separate theoretical categories, I treat them together because they all pertain to the question of how the choices made by movement activists matter.

Finally, the political opportunity perspective sees variation in the intensity of protest activity as a function of the degree of political vulnerability or receptivity of authorities to pressure for change. Although some researchers have applied political opportunity to explain variations in protest between polities, work in this perspective has concentrated mainly on explaining change over time. Political opportunity theorists have seen the rise and decline of social movements and broader "cycles" of protest as largely a reflection of the opening and closing of the "political opportunity structure." In outlining the relevant aspects of that structure, researchers working in this vein have tended to emphasize institutional structures and alliance patterns, focusing on shifts such as regime transitions and partisan realignments. These are shifts that are, for most part, beyond the capacity of activists to influence, at least in the short term.

These four basic perspectives constitute the theoretical framework that will guide my analysis of the landless movement's development. I will use this empirical case, in turn, to assess the explanatory power of each perspective. Later in this introduction I provide an overview of my major findings. Below, I lay the necessary empirical groundwork for that discussion by talking about the issue of rural land inequality in Brazil and the evolution of struggles for agrarian reform. I begin with a synthetic historical analysis of the issue of rural land inequality and what should be done about it (what Brazilians refer to as the "agrarian question") before the rise of the landless movement. Then I discuss the landless movement's trajectory in somewhat greater detail.

The Agrarian Question and Struggles for Land Before the Landless Movement

Brazil inherited from the colonial era an extremely unequal structure of rural landholding, in which a relatively small number of wealthy landowners controlled much of the good, accessible farmland (Guimarães 1981). Upon arriving in what is now Brazil at the beginning of the sixteenth century, the Portuguese established an economic system dominated by vast sugarcane plantations, initially based in the coastal areas of the Northeast. Much of the population, including the millions of slaves brought forcibly from Africa, remained landless. The small farms that existed were relegated to land that was poor or located in remote areas. As colonial society expanded, this basic structure was reproduced in new regions. The indigenous groups that inhabited the areas taken over by the colonists were either subjugated or driven progressively farther into the interior.

Independence from Portugal in 1822 did little to change this landholding system, since agricultural elites retained or even increased their influence in politics. In fact, the Land Law of 1850 was meant to limit popular access to land on the frontier and thus ensure a plentiful supply of cheap plantation labor (Silva 1996).[3] The abolition of slavery in 1888 also failed to affect the landholding structure, since the freed slaves were not granted land. The only significant exception to the rule of extreme land concentration was Brazil's South. In the late nineteenth and early twentieth centuries, authorities sought to stimulate European migration to this region, mainly for the purpose of defending the country's southern frontier, leading to the establishment of a substantial class of solid smallholders in the states of Rio Grande do Sul, Santa Catarina, and Paraná. These *colonos*, or "colonists," as they were called, were mainly of Italian, German, and Polish origin.

By the late nineteenth century, the sugar elite had been displaced by

3. In this sense, the Land Law was almost the opposite of the 1862 Homestead Act in the United States. The latter sought to promote, rather than limit, the establishment of small family farms.

the coffee planters of São Paulo as Brazil's dominant social group. In 1930, however, the *paulista* coffee "barons" were defeated in a political confrontation with an alliance of army officers and regional elites, led by Getúlio Vargas. Under Vargas, who ruled as the elected or de facto president until 1945, the political system became more centralized and industrialization and urbanization accelerated (Skidmore 1967). Although no leftist, Vargas sought to incorporate the urban working class into his coalition through labor reforms. These changes reduced the economic and political weight of agricultural elites. The latter, however, were by no means vanquished. Symptomatic of their continued influence was the fact that Vargas's labor reforms excluded rural workers.

The fall of Vargas's dictatorial Estado Novo (New State) in 1945 led to the establishment of a limited democracy.[4] Although the new parties sought to mobilize workers, appeals to class were initially relatively muted (Weffort 1980). Policies that would undermine landowner power in the countryside did not enter the political agenda. The 1946 Constitution held that land had to be used in a manner that promoted social well-being and could be expropriated from private owners if it did not (Welch 1999, 244–46). The principle that even private farmland has an inherent "social function" and must thus be put to productive use reflected the conviction of some intellectuals that the acute maldistribution of farmland created obstacles to Brazil's economic and political modernization. Yet it remained little more than words on a page.

Agrarian reform would emerge as a major political issue for the first time in the 1960s. Grassroots protest for land reform played a major role. In the late 1950s a movement called the Peasant Leagues arose among poor tenant farmers in the sugarcane zone of the northeastern state of Pernambuco. By the early 1960s the movement had spread to a number of other states and attained national prominence. The leagues demanded a "radical" agrarian reform and vowed to make it a reality "by law or by force" (Azevêdo 1982; Bastos 1984). Protest for land also arose in other regions. Most prominent was a movement that emerged in Rio Grande do Sul, at the southern tip of Brazil. Centered on an organization called the Movement of Landless Farmers (MASTER), it was supported by populist governor Leonel Brizola and had a heterogeneous social base (Eckert 1984). By 1964, however, these groups

4. The political regime in place between 1946 and 1964 limited democracy in a number of senses, including the exclusion of illiterates from the suffrage and the occasionally assertive political role played by the military.

were being overtaken by a union movement led by two rival organizations, the Brazilian Communist Party and the Catholic Church, that also supported agrarian reform but were more concerned with incremental changes (Pereira 1997).

Elite politics combined with social movement activity to put land reform on the national political agenda. In 1961 the unexpected resignation of conservative president Jânio Quadros brought a left-leaning populist and Vargas protégé, João Goulart, to the presidency. In a context of increasing popular mobilization, ideological polarization, and economic crisis, Goulart sought to break the political deadlock by pressing for major social and political reforms, especially agrarian reform. His drive to extend the right to unionize to rural workers was successful, resulting in the Rural Worker Statute of 1963. However, his push for agrarian reform was blocked by Congress. Goulart's subsequent attempts to intimidate or go around the legislature only served to accelerate the mobilization of conservatives against him, culminating in a military coup d'état, initiated on March 31, 1964.

The coup would have major consequences for the rural sector. With few exceptions, progressive activism in the countryside was quickly crushed. Instead of redistributing land, the new authorities aggressively promoted the technical modernization of agriculture and the growth of commercial crop production. This emphasis tended to erode popular land access in the core agricultural regions. The military governments also accelerated the demographic and economic penetration of remote areas of the country, especially in the Amazon basin, that had previously been populated mainly by indigenous peoples.

Although it did not engage in significant agrarian reform, the military regime did bring about an important change in the legal framework concerning this policy. Rather surprisingly, the idea of redistributing private farmland was embraced by General Humberto Castello Branco, the regime's early leader (Cehelsky 1979). His sponsorship led to the approval of the Land Statute, a law that could potentially provide the basis for an extensive program of land redistribution. A constitutional amendment approved at the same time allowed the state to compensate expropriated landowners with twenty-year bonds, rather than cash, a change Goulart had sought in vain. Elite resistance proved too great and agrarian reform did not go forward. However, the Land Statute's acknowledgment of the need for land redistribution would eventually—once the political context permitted open dissent—provide activists with a justification for pressuring the state to implement agrarian reform. In addition, the law provided important legal instruments that could make this policy viable, given a political will to carry it out.

Trajectory of the Landless Movement, 1978–2006

Organized protest for land reform was rare during the first fifteen years of the military regime. At the tail end of the 1970s, however, land occupations and other forms of protest began to intensify. These actions were part of larger wave of social protest that occurred amid mounting indications that the military regime was loosening its repressive grip on society. The movement emerged in various regions, intensifying and diffusing geographically during the early 1980s. It took on its most massive and organized expression in the smallholder-dominated areas of southern Brazil, reviving the social identity of the *sem terra*, or landless rural worker, created by the MASTER. Over time, this term would come to be applied to all rural workers with little or no land of their own who struggle for land redistribution through protest.

During the 1970s, a powerful progressive movement had emerged within the Brazilian Catholic Church, pushing the historically conservative church to the left. Catholic clergy and lay activists inspired by liberation theology played a critical role in the landless movement, providing leadership, ideological support, and access to material resources. Protest tactics, pressure from the church, and the intensification of land-related violence in frontier areas all helped to push agrarian reform tentatively back to the political front burner in the early 1980s, though policy initiatives in this area were quite timid. Catholic activists played an instrumental role in the creation, in 1984, of the MST. Although intended to lead the struggle for land at the national level, this loose organizational network was initially based mainly in the South.

Agrarian reform reemerged as a key national issue in 1985, when new civilian president, José Sarney, announced a major land redistribution program. The announcement helped accelerate the pace of landless protest, but also provoked a massive landlord counteroffensive, which crushed the program. Protest for land continued to grow gradually during the late 1980s and was increasingly dominated by the MST. Building on the movement's earlier experiences in the South, the MST made the massive, highly orga-

nized land occupation its core tactic. When expelled from an occupied property, MST families would set up their shanties at the side of a road or other
public place, waiting to be settled by federal or state authorities or to
mount a new occupation.

Protest for land reform stagnated somewhat under the following president, conservative Fernando Collor, but accelerated moderately in 1993 and
1994, after Collor was removed from office on corruption charges. By the
end of 1994, although the landless movement was still not well known to
the national public, protest for land reform had arguably reached levels not
seen since the 1960s. The MST had expanded far beyond the South and
become a truly national organization, with a centralized leadership structure, a large corps of activists, and a strong collective identity. Despite the
slow pace of land reform, tens of thousands of MST "campers" had gained
land. Although it still had strong ties to the church and other progressive
entities, the MST was an independent organization. In fact, its fierce defense of its autonomy often created friction with other leftist groups.

Perhaps the most striking aspect of the landless movement's development during the 1985–94 period was the fact that protest persisted, and
even intensified, despite a general trend toward movement decline. The
broad wave of social protest that had emerged in Brazil as the military
regime decayed had already begun to decline by the time Sarney came to
power. Collor's 1989 electoral victory brought a definitive end to it. Popular
quiescence was interrupted only briefly, in August 1992, by large demonstrations for Collor's impeachment in some cities. The landless movement
was the only major democratic transition–era social movement to clearly
buck this general trend.

After growing gradually during the preceding years, in late 1995 and
1996 land occupations intensified dramatically. The state of São Paulo was
the key area in late 1995, but in 1996 occupations multiplied in every major
region of the country. Occupation activity continued to grow at a slower
pace through 1999. Although the movement was truly a national phenomenon, during the second half of the 1990s, the coastal sugarcane areas of
the poor Northeast and parts of the Center-West experienced particularly
intense activity. The magnitude of the movement's growth is suggested by
the fact that the number of land occupations in 1999 was close to five times
the 1994 total.

The landless movement's takeoff began not long after Fernando Henrique Cardoso, a well-known intellectual and leader of a centrist political

party, donned the presidential sash. Cardoso had won the election mainly on the strength of his success in controlling inflation as finance minister under interim president Itamar Franco. Although known as a progressive thinker, Cardoso had not made land reform a major element of his campaign, and the strong presence of conservative forces in his coalition seemed to bode ill for this policy. Nevertheless, as I mentioned at the beginning of the introduction, during his first term in office (1995–98) the agrarian question once again became a crucial national issue. Media coverage and public debate on this question intensified enormously, and Cardoso implemented undoubtedly the largest land redistribution program in Brazilian history, although the actual magnitude of the program was the subject of heated debate between leftist forces and the government.

As protest for land grew, the MST's share of total occupations diminished. Nevertheless, this organization continued to be easily the most visible actor within the movement, in part because the MST, in its quest to find more effective ways to pressure authorities, increasingly made use of high-profile alternative tactics. Although its tactical repertoire had never been limited to land occupations, during the late 1990s the MST increasingly resorted to marches, occupations of government offices and highway toll plazas, and even looting. Effective in provoking media coverage and harassing authorities, some of these tactics were at the same time quite controversial and met with widespread public disapproval.

By the end of the 1990s, the landless movement had undoubtedly become the largest rural movement in Brazilian history. At least fifty thousand landless families—perhaps two hundred thousand people—were actively engaged in the struggle. Cardoso's second term (1999–2002), however, would bring hard times. In 2000 land occupations dipped sharply in number. The decline continued the following year, bringing occupation activity in the Brazilian countryside back down to a level comparable to that of 1995. Although other types of protest activity seem to have at least maintained the intensity of earlier years, the decline of occupations was a major blow, and activists began to ask how much longer the movement would last. Mobilization failed to revive in 2002, but activists were heartened by the success of the leftist PT—traditionally a staunch defender of land reform and one of the MST's key allies—in the October national elections. Lula captured the presidency, becoming the first leftist and the first person of humble, lower-class origins ever elected to that office.

The movement's crisis proved to be only temporary. In 2003, Lula's first year as president, protest for land experienced a strong resurgence nation-wide. Land occupations more than doubled in number relative to the previous year and other tactics seem to have intensified as well. Landless camps grew in size and number. Mobilization and protest for land reform continued to grow in 2004, leveling off in 2005. By 2006, some 150,000 families were said to be gathered in the movement's land occupations and roadside encampments. Although Lula's first term brought an intensification of protest for land reform, actual policy results were modest, leaving activist groups disappointed. The MST promised to continue pressuring Lula for greater progress in land redistribution during the PT president's second term, beginning in 2007.

Major Findings

As mentioned above, in this book I ask what the case of the landless movement suggests about the causes of two basic types of variance: temporal variance in the intensity of protest activity within a given movement, and variance in the growth trajectories of different movements that emerge during the same cycle of protest. With regard to the first, the findings clearly support political opportunity. All four episodes of change in movement intensity examined in this study—the movement's initial emergence near the end of the military regime, its takeoff in the early Cardoso years, its decline during Cardoso's second term, and its resurgence under Lula—were caused largely by political shifts that affected the receptivity or vulnerability of authorities to pressure for land distribution and, as a consequence, activists' expectations about the probable outcome of protest.

The national political context of democratic opening, which diminished the threat of repression and increased the possibility that authorities would respond positively to grassroots pressure for land redistribution, was a central factor behind the movement's rise in the late 1970s and early 1980s. Similarly, in the mid-1990s, land occupations and other forms of protest accelerated when it became clear that the Cardoso government would be more responsive to grassroots pressure for land reform than were past governments. Land occupations declined in 2000–2002 because, after years of tolerating or even implicitly encouraging these actions, Cardoso reversed course, taking pains to make clear that occupations would no longer be rewarded with concessions. Finally, the revival of landless protest beginning in 2003 resulted from the rise of the center-left PT government and, especially, its decision to ignore the anti–land occupation measures adopted during Cardoso's second term in office.

Factors rooted in each of the other three theoretical perspectives also played a role in one or more of these episodes of rapid change. Rising grievances were critical in the initial appearance of the movement and played a significant part in its expansion in the mid-1990s. Increasing organizational capacity also contributed to the movement's emergence. Changes in activist strategy, finally, were an important factor in the movement's temporary decline in the early 2000s. Overall, though, political opportunity is clearly the most effective perspective for explaining the landless movement's ups and downs.

Thus, my findings lend further support to the political opportunity perspective's claims to superiority in explaining social movement development over time. Nevertheless, they also contribute important qualifications, which support elements of the contemporary critique of this theoretical model. First, they suggest a need to pay more attention to the subjective aspects of the political context. As I noted earlier, political opportunity theory has focused largely on the impact of relatively concrete institutional, alliance, or electoral shifts in producing or closing down opportunities for protest. My analysis of the landless movement's takeoff in the second half of the 1990s, however, shows that the political opportunity structure for protest can also be shaped by particularly jarring or noteworthy events that affect the beliefs or priorities of the general public and civil society.

With the fall of President Collor in 1992, Brazil came to be governed by party coalitions with a stronger base in the moderate urban middle class of the Southeast and South. Although this shift created a more favorable political context for the landless movement, these coalitions also had a strong conservative component closely tied to rural landowners. Not surprisingly, the Cardoso government initially emitted very ambivalent signals about land reform. What tipped the political scales in favor of increased land distribution was the impact of two particularly large and visible police massacres of land occupiers that occurred in the Amazon region in late 1995 and 1996. Because they shocked public opinion and the media and galvanized progressive groups, these incidents forced the government to show that it was serious about land reform. They also made it riskier for state-level authorities, who control police forces, to repress the movement. These changes, in turn, provoked a major upsurge of landless protest.

Second, my findings underscore that, beyond the emergence phase, the political opportunity context for protest is not altogether independent of a movement's own actions. While political opportunity theory has some-times paid lip service to this notion, it has not really explored it in any depth or with much rigor. This idea is illustrated by two episodes analyzed in this book. One is the landless movement's takeoff in the mid-1990s. As noted earlier, the structure of political opportunities facing the movement underwent a crucial expansion as a result of the two big massacres of the mid-1990s, which took place in the Amazon *municípios* of Corumbiara and Eldorado do Carajás.[5] Landless activists could not have foreseen and cer-tainly did not actively seek to provoke these incidents, which together took more than thirty lives. Nevertheless, these events were partly a prod-uct of the threat the movement's aggressive protest tactics seemed to pose to the interests of landowning elites and their allies within the state.

The decline of protest for land reform in the early 2000s also illustrates how movements can shape their own political opportunity structures. As discussed, the abrupt drop-off in land occupations was a product of the declining receptivity of authorities to these actions. Nonetheless, Cardoso's decision to crack down was itself partly a response to the increasing aggres-siveness and disruptiveness of MST protest actions, beginning in the late 1990s. These both embarrassed the government and, because they were quite controversial, made it politically easier to take a hard line. Although the MST's options were quite limited, a different strategic tack, one more attentive to the conditional nature of public support for the movement, might well have avoided the crackdown.

The second issue dealt with in this book is why individual movements that arise as part of the same cycle of protest subsequently experience different growth trajectories. More specifically, how can we explain the landless movement's striking failure to follow the general trend toward the decline of social protest in Brazil after 1985? The activist strategy perspec-tive provides part of the explanation, I argue. In particular, the decision by movement activists to prioritize the land occupation as a pressure tactic played a critical role in its continued growth. This is the case because the

---

5. A *município* is roughly the equivalent of a county in the United States. It usually has one principle urban area, which serves as the administrative center, but it may also have a large rural hinterland.

way in which authorities responded to these actions, by granting concessions only to those people actually involved in them, greatly reduced what
Olson (1965) called the free-rider problem in collective action and thus
made the movement less dependent on the normative or idealistic incentives on which social movements usually rely to overcome this problem. As
a result, this movement was less vulnerable than other social movements
to the decline of such incentives for protest activity that occurred following the end of Brazil's military dictatorship.

The MST played a particularly important role in diffusing this tactic nationally. Its creative use of land occupations and the resulting roadside
camps were also critical to the movement's survival and expansion. In particular, MST leaders employed the camping process as a space for ideological
indoctrination and identity formation, leading some campers to eventually
become full-time activists and many others to continue to contribute time
and money to the movement even after gaining land.

Nonetheless, the movement's exceptionalism was not simply a product
of superior strategy. The possibility of using the occupation as a pressure
tactic was simply not open to other social movements to the same extent.
Some goods Brazilian movements sought, such as the protection of women's
rights or greater freedom in labor union organizing, were simply physically
impossible to occupy. However, others potentially could have been occupied. What set the farmland apart was its unique constitutional status, as
the only type of private property that readily can be subject to expropriation on the basis of its underutilization by the owner. This difference made
authorities politically vulnerable to the land occupation strategy. Hence,
my account of the landless movement's exceptional trajectory also provides
support for the political opportunity perspective.

A Note on Brazil's Regions

It would be useful before proceeding to say something more about Brazil's
geographical regions, since I will refer to them repeatedly during the course
of the book. Brazil is a vast country with great regional diversity. Official
terminology divides the national territory into five major regions: Center-
West, North, Northeast, South, and Southeast (see the map at the beginning of the book). Each has fairly distinct characteristics. The Southeast is
the most industrialized and urbanized region. It is dominated by the state

of São Paulo, Brazil's wealthiest and most populous. The South has traditionally been the second-most-developed region. Although not as industrialized as the Southeast, its solid smallholder heritage makes it the least
socially polarized region. Both these regions are characterized by relatively
modern, highly capitalized agricultural sectors.

The other three regions have traditionally been much less developed and
urbanized. The Northeast is poor and highly unequal. Its coastal areas boast
a substantial commercial agricultural sector, dominated by sugarcane, but
this sector has generally been characterized by relatively low technology.
The North, which contains most of the Amazon River basin, and the Center-
West were historically sparsely populated and economically backward frontier regions, dominated by subsistence farming and crude extractive activities. The advance of commercial agriculture and mining in the past few
decades has changed parts of these two regions dramatically. Today, the
Center-West has a farm sector that rivals those of the South and Southeast
in its technological development and emphasis on export-oriented mono-
crop production.

In political terms, the less developed regions of Brazil have tended to be
more conservative. The Northeast, in particular, is known for providing the
electoral base for the country's major conservative parties. During the period discussed in this book, however, signs of change began to appear. In
particular, the PT made major headway in some of the less developed states.

Chapter Layout

In the first chapter I flesh out the study's theoretical framework, laying
out the four major perspectives in greater detail and discussing how each
has been, or potentially could be, applied to explain the basic issues addressed in this book. As part of this discussion I evaluate some of the conceptual criticisms that have been leveled in recent years against political
opportunity theory. I also provide some examples of how these general
perspectives have been employed in studies of rural social movements. Also
addressed in this chapter is the long-standing debate about Olson's theory
of collective action and its relevance for social movement activity.

The five chapters that follow trace the landless movement's development
between 1978 and 2006. The focus of each is on solving a specific question
regarding the movement's growth trajectory. In each chapter I try to pro-

vide enough information about its internal organizational processes, tactical initiatives, and external socioeconomic and political environment to rigorously evaluate the competing theoretical perspectives.

In Chapter 2, I analyze the landless movement's emergence, between 1978 and 1984. Why, I ask, did a substantial social movement for land reform arise after years of conservative quiescence in the countryside? The discussion in Chapter 3 is of the movement's evolution between 1985 and 1994 and why it persisted, and even grew, despite the general trend toward movement decline in Brazil. Since the MST gelled as an organization during this period, this chapter includes a close analysis of its internal development.

In Chapter 4, I explain the rapid "takeoff" of landless protest during the second half of the 1990s, which transformed the landless movement into easily the most important grassroots social movement in contemporary Brazil. In doing so, I also shed light on the causes of two other important changes related to the agrarian question that occurred during this period: public and media attention to this issue intensified greatly and the Brazilian state's agrarian reform efforts reached unprecedented levels. In Chapter 5, I discuss the 2000–2002 period, when land occupations, traditionally the landless movement's core tactic, declined sharply, calling into question the movement's future. Finally, I analyze in Chapter 6 the movement's resurgence between 2003 and 2006, under the first PT government. Although the movement grew under Lula, the rise to power of a historical ally has presented the MST and other agrarian reform activist groups with new strategic challenges, which I discuss in this chapter.

In the book's conclusion, I take on three tasks. First, I briefly summarize the major findings of the preceding chapters. Second, I discuss some of the broader implications of these findings for social movement theory. In particular, I touch on what the results mean for the utility of political opportunity theory as a tool for explaining movement growth and decline, as well as on the validity of the notion that the free-rider problem may not always be relevant to social movement activity. Third, I shift gears a bit and talk about agrarian reform as public policy and a tool for socioeconomic change. I try to answer a number of questions: How much agrarian reform has been accomplished in Brazil since the landless movement's rise? What have been the results of this effort in terms of the welfare of settler families? Finally, what can we realistically expect agrarian reform to contribute to Brazilian society in the foreseeable future?

ONE Theoretical Perspectives

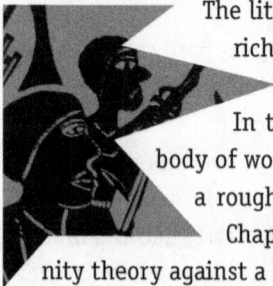

The literature on social movements and protest offers a rich array of explanatory strategies for answering the empirical questions addressed in this study. In the present chapter I attempt to distill from this body of work a theoretical framework that can both serve as a rough guide for my analysis of empirical variation in Chapters 2–6 and allow me to test political opportunity theory against a number of established alternatives. An important aspect of this task is evaluating the major conceptual criticisms that have been directed at the political opportunity literature. Because it is relevant to the empirical argument I will develop in Chapter 3, I also examine the long-running debate about Mancur Olson's theory of collective action and its applicability to social movements.

The voluminous literature on social movements has been parsed in different ways. It can be most usefully divided into four major approaches, or perspectives. Each of these focuses on a particular explanatory variable, broadly defined, in order to explain all kinds of variation in movement activity. These perspectives, as stated in the Introduction, are discontent/grievance, organizational capacity, activist strategy, and political opportunity. I should note that scholars who have formulated some of the general theories of social movements, such as Smelser (1963), Oberschall (1973), Tilly (1978), McAdam (1982), and Tarrow (1994), do not concentrate exclusively on one perspective. However, most can be seen to emphasize one, or possibly two, over the rest.

It is important to point out that my approach differs from many contemporary attempts to create a framework for understanding the social movement literature. First, authors often downplay or simply dismiss the literature that focuses on discontent/grievance (McAdam, McCarthy, and

Zald 1996; McAdam, Tarrow, and Tilly 1997). The typical justification for this is that discontent, the focus of much of the pre-1970 research, is essentially constant, while other factors vary. The evidence, however, is not strong enough to allow us to ignore grievances as a major cause of movement activity. Second, I place "framing" theory, which is often treated separately, in the same perspective as other issues related to strategy. I do this because I view all these factors as constituting aspects of activist agency. As such, they ought to be grouped in the same category, one that is distinct from structural or contextual variables.

Finally, unlike some authors, I do not parse the theories according to whether they focus on "structure" or "culture." Each of these four basic perspectives incorporates, or at least is capable of incorporating, both objective and subjective explanations of protest. Along the same lines, some readers may feel I give short shrift to the research that focuses on collective identity and demands for cultural recognition. My reasons for not devoting more attention to this literature are two. First, many of the groups analyzed by these works (for instance, countercultural movements and utopian communities) do not make demands on authorities and thus do not fall under the definition of *social movement* that I set out in the Introduction. Second, to the extent that it does address groups that fit my definition, this literature focuses on predominantly middle-class movements that have emerged mainly in wealthy societies and address "postmaterial" issues such as nuclear energy and gay rights. Its empirical focus makes this literature less relevant to my study than other bodies of social movement research.

My emphasis here is on discussing what the existing theoretical perspectives say about the factors that influence variation in movement intensity over time, the basic issue involved in four of the five empirical research questions I am asking. Political opportunity theory has made the strongest claim to explaining both surges and declines in movement activity, accounting for both within a simple causal model. To the extent that they address temporal variation in protest intensity specifically, other perspectives have tended to focus on initial emergence, rather than on subsequent fluctuations in the pace of collective action. As I argue below, though, each of these perspectives offers potential explanations of both movement growth and movement decline.

The other issue I explore in this study is why social movements that emerge as part of the same wave of protest within a particular polity subsequently experience different growth trajectories. This question focuses on change both over time and across individual movements. There is, to my knowledge, no extant work that addresses this particular issue and, hence, no perspective that can claim hegemony in understanding it. Nevertheless, as I discuss below, each theoretical perspective suggests potential explanations.

Most of the chapter is devoted to laying out the four broad theoretical perspectives and discussing some of the more specific arguments associated with each. Since the major theoretical purpose of this book is to test the explanatory power of political opportunity, I devote particular attention to this concept and the debates surrounding it. Where they are available, I illustrate my discussion with examples of how each theoretical perspective has been applied to rural social movement activity, particularly in the developing world. In doing this I hope to give the reader a better idea of how they may be applied to my specific case. It should be understood, however, that these examples by no means exhaust the ways in which these concepts can potentially be operationalized.

In addition to laying out a basic theoretical framework, in this chapter I discuss the long-standing controversy surrounding Olson's (1965) theory of collective action with regard to its relevance for social movements. It is important to address this issue, not only because of the centrality of Olson's theory to debates about social movement activity, but also because the theory serves as part of the foundation for the argument I offer in Chapter 3.

Perspectives on Social Movements

Grievance/Discontent

Although this approach has generally fallen out of favor in recent decades, especially in the United States, most theories of why social movements appear focus in one way or another on rising discontent or social grievances. There are a number of major movement theorists who adopt some version of this basic logic. Virtually all advance theories of movement emergence, saying relatively little about how movements evolve over time. However, there would seem to be no logical reason why this perspective cannot be applied to explain postemergence stages in a movement's growth trajectory.

Marxism views worker protest largely (although not exclusively) from this perspective. Social struggles are a response to the intensified exploitation of workers by the capitalist class, as well as increased consciousness of that exploitation. Post–World War II U.S. social movement theory, often referred to as the "collective behavior" school, also tended to see protest as a product of grassroots discontent arising from broad, disruptive social changes. However, unlike Marxist theory, which takes social class as its unit of analysis and views protestors as pursuing instrumental goals arising from concrete social needs, this current focuses on the individual psychological states generated by social change and tends to view protest as an irrational or spontaneous acting out of internal tensions.

One of the earliest versions of collective behavior theory in the United States is Kornhauser's (1959) "mass society" theory, based mainly on an analysis of European fascism and communism. The author argues that movements arise from situations that promote social isolation. Rootless individuals not immersed in "intermediate structures," such as social networks and associations, tend to develop feelings of frustration and anger, which, if intense and widespread enough, can boil over into extreme types of activism. Smelser's (1963) theory of social movements is broader than Kornhauser's. Although he outlines a number of necessary conditions for the emergence of a movement, Smelser addresses mainly the impact of broad social changes that produce "structural strain" and, consequently, psychological stress and tension. Smelser is not specific about what kinds of changes produce structural strain, allowing that both socioeconomic shifts, such as urbanization and industrialization, and political changes, such as war, can play this role.

In the late 1960s and early 1970s U.S. movement researchers developed "relative deprivation" theory (Gurr 1970; Davies 1962). The basic idea of this school is that what stimulates movement activity is not rising absolute need, but the growth of feelings among a social group that it is not getting the treatment or rewards it merits. Subjective feelings of deprivation can arise from a number of conditions, including abrupt declines in welfare following longer-term increases that raise a group's expectations; situations in which people rank high on one indicator of social status, but low on others, creating "status inconsistency"; and the rise of a formerly downtrodden social group, which threatens the sense of social superiority of other groups. Relative deprivation stimulates movement emergence by motivating people to change a system that they feel denies them, or threatens to deny them, what they in fact deserve.

Contemporary European "new social movement" theory can also be characterized as part of the discontent/grievance perspective, because it sees protest as responding to the rise of new needs. Studies in this vein have sought to explain the emergence in recent decades of movements that pursue noneconomic objectives, such as environmental protection and an end to nuclear power. Such movements have typically been seen as a consequence of advanced capitalist development (Offe 1985). By generating material prosperity, development shifted public priorities away from more immediate economic issues, the dominant concern of organized labor, toward new "postmaterial" issues.

Particularly in the United States, contemporary scholarship has tended to downplay the role of grievances in determining where and when movements will arise. However, the grievance/discontent perspective has not been totally absent even in the work of mainstream American scholars. For example, Tilly's (1978) concept of "threat," which refers to the extent to which a given group feels its interests will be harmed by changes that other groups are pressing for, undeniably involves an aspect of discontent.

The grievance/discontent perspective on social movements has often stressed the long-term structural forces shaping movement emergence, rather than more immediate provocations to protest. However, there is little reason to believe that grievance-generating changes cannot perform the latter role as well. Sharp dips in welfare after long-term gains have, as noted above, been associated with rising feelings of relative deprivation. Authors not working from a relative deprivation perspective have also discussed how sudden declines in social welfare, caused by food shortages or unemployment, can generate outbursts of protest (Rudé 1964; Piven and Cloward 1977).

The grievance/discontent perspective has been central to the study of rural movements. Wolf (1969), Migdal (1974) and Scott (1976) have seen peasant activism as a response to the penetration of market forces into agriculture, a change that threatens traditional strategies for ensuring subsistence. The sale or enclosure of communal lands and the erosion of elite practices of charity and ritual redistribution may expose small producers and landless laborers to higher risks of famine. Peasants may rebel in response to the consequences of market expansion or to the threat of proletarianization. Scott has emphasized that commercialization provokes protest not only by exposing peasants to hardship, but also by violating their belief in the legitimacy of local elites.

At times, the causal connection between capitalist development and rebellion is seen as less direct. Moore (1966) argues that peasant rebellion may result when backward landlords try to keep up with the pace of development in the larger society by intensifying the economic exploitation of their own peasants and workers, demanding higher rents, paying lower wages, and so on. Peasant discontent may also grow in response to state penetration of previously isolated rural areas, bringing new economic burdens, particularly increased taxation (Tilly 1964; Migdal 1974; Scott 1976).

Most of these analyses focus on long-term changes. However, Scott (1976) seems to acknowledge that it is not the capitalist penetration of agriculture per se, but the short-term famine that directly provokes peasant revolt. Some other authors also discuss how relatively conjunctural changes in socioeconomic conditions provoke mobilization. McClintock (1989), for example, argues that an acute subsistence crisis in Peru's central highlands, rather than longer-term structural changes, was behind the rise of the peasant-based Shining Path guerilla movement.

Theories of rural social movements have only occasionally referred to relative deprivation. Huizer (1972) argues that the emergence of peasant movements in Latin America has often resulted from instances in which development initiatives in backward regions raised the hopes of the rural poor without ultimately providing any real improvement in welfare. The frustration generated by these events leads peasants to begin organizing for real change. He also argues that mobilization can be generated by contact with the media, urban dwellers, and other manifestations of "modernity," because these contacts raise peasants' awareness of how badly off, in relative terms, they really are.

As mentioned earlier, grievance/discontent-based theories are mainly theories of emergence. Nevertheless, it stands to reason that, if movements are stimulated by rising discontent, subsequent fluctuations in the sources of discontent should, other things being equal, affect movement intensity. Good harvests, for example, may undermine movements triggered by famine. Discontent may also be reduced because of movement success; for example, movements for land reform may succeed in the retaking of ancestral lands and student movements may be demobilized by the granting of university autonomy.

What answers does discontent/grievance theory suggest to the question of why social movements that are born during the same general cycle of protest subsequently experience different growth trajectories? Although the literature does not address this specific issue, each of the various theoretical perspectives offers potential answers. From the viewpoint of discontent/grievance, the main one would seem to be that the sources of discontent motivating protest may evolve differently for different movements. Social or political problems that initially spurred collective protest may become less acute over time for some movements, perhaps because of the policy response of authorities to movement pressure, while remaining stable or deteriorating further in the case of other movements. Thus, variations in growth trajectory across different movements may be a product of differences in the evolution of discontent across social groups or issue areas.

Organizational Capacity

A second theoretical perspective on social movements focuses on the capacity of different groups to organize for protest. Its central idea is that the ability to organize and sustain social protest is facilitated by the presence of certain social structures and resources. These are generally indigenous to the social group that makes up the movement's mass base, but they can also be contributed by external actors. This perspective blossomed in the United States in the early 1970s as one of the central components of the "resource mobilization" school. Researchers associated with this school sought to distance themselves from the emphasis that postwar movement theory had placed on the grievances generated by social change. Grievances, they felt, were ubiquitous and thus could not explain the eruption of protest for change. The challenge was thus not to explain the origins of discontent, but to understand where and when discontented groups managed to mobilize politically.

A critical focus of the organizational capacity perspective are the grassroots institutions and social networks that exist prior to the emergence of a social movement. Directly contradicting Kornhauser's "mass society" theory, U.S. social movement researchers in the 1970s argued that movements are more likely to emerge when and where such indigenous secondary groups are strong (Oberschall 1973; Freeman 1973; Fireman and Gamson 1979). Far from being social isolates, those who engage in activism tend to be strongly integrated into their local civil societies. According to one influential version of this theory, the more homogeneous the population and the stronger the associative ties binding it together, the greater the capacity for engaging in collective rebellion (Tilly 1978).

Preexisting grassroots organizational structures, whether formal or informal, can facilitate movement organizing in various ways. Small-group contexts such as churches, clubs, neighborhood associations, and tribal groups create social incentives that can be a powerful impetus to movement participation (Oberschall 1973; McAdam, McCarthy, and Zald 1988). The feelings of group loyalty and desire for social approbation fostered in such contexts can help to overcome the rational disincentives to collective action identified by Olson (and discussed below). Some researchers argue that grassroots social networks also provide an environment in which problems experienced by individuals are more likely to be attributed to broad social forces than they are to personal failings (McAdam 1982, chap. 3). As a result, they help to promote an "insurgent" social consciousness that motivates participants to challenge the established order through protest. Finally, preexisting organizations can contribute to movement activity by providing experienced leadership, a membership base, and a communications network (McAdam 1982).

Indigenous organizational structures can be critical for explaining why some groups mobilize and others do not. However, in explaining changes in protest intensity over time, they are probably best seen mainly as a long-term background factor, rather than one that can account for relatively rapid shifts in the intensity of protest. This is because such structures tend to emerge only gradually, over the course of decades. Barring the effects of overwhelming repression, war, or natural disasters, they are likely to decline only gradually as well. Of course, activists can create new organizations during the life of a movement. Since these entities are a product of concrete decisions made by movement activists, I touch on them later in my discussion of activist strategy.

Organizational capacity need not depend wholly on the indigenous resources of a movement's mass base. It can also be influenced by external actors (Jenkins and Perrow 1977). This is particularly true when the movement's social base is constituted by a poor, uneducated group. Middle-class (or even elite) activists can help promote movement emergence by furnishing such resources as organizational skills and an ideological perspective that legitimates rebellion. The downside for popular groups is that the withdrawal of such resources, or their conditioning on the adoption of more institutionalized tactics, can bring movement decline (Piven and Cloward 1977). Typically, such fluctuations in the availability of external resources have to do with changes in the larger political context, but for reasons of conceptual clarity, it is useful to separate the question of capacity to engage in collective protest from the issue of how vulnerable authorities and elites are to pressure for concessions, which is the stuff of political opportunity, as I discuss further below.

Students of rural movements have sometimes used indigenous organizational capacity to explain differences in mobilization between social groups; Moore (1966), for example, argues that peasant communities that have not been affected by commercialization are more likely to rebel against authority because they retain traditional social bonds of group solidarity and loyalty. Nevertheless, in explaining changes in protest intensity over time, they have stressed influxes of external resources from elite or middle-class groups, frequently arguing that spontaneous peasant uprisings may occasionally occur without outside intervention, but are unlikely to take the form of a sustained movement in the absence of assistance from nonpeasant activists, such as party activists or middle-class intellectuals, or at least peasant leaders with urban experience (Wolf 1969; Landsberger 1969; Huizer 1972). Most rural lower-class groups, being extremely poor, uneducated, and subject to landowner domination, face too many resource deficits to organize a major, sustained movement on their own.

As the preceding discussion suggests, the organizational capacity perspective offers two basic solutions to the puzzle of why individual social movements that emerge as part of the same general wave of protest activity subsequently experience differing patterns of growth or decline. First, this difference may be a result of disparities in the strength of the indigenous organizational networks from which the movements originally arise. For example, a movement that arises within a community characterized by particularly robust social networks may be better able to persist in the face of state repression than one that is supported by weaker networks. The second way in which organizational capacity could explain differences in movement trajectory is through the availability of external resources. Specifically, some popular movements may enjoy the sustained support of relatively elite actors possessing human and material resources that are critical for mobilizing members and organizing protest events. In contrast, for any of various reasons, other movements may quickly lose much of their elite support and, as a result, find it increasingly difficult to maintain their intensity.

Activist Strategy

Variation in the intensity of protest may be a product of contextual conditions over which activists have little or no control, but it may also be a function of the wisdom and skill with which activists deal with the constraints and opportunities they encounter. This is another message of the resource mobilization literature. In addition to downplaying the role of grievances, resource mobilization theorists expressed disagreement with what they saw as the collective behavior school's tendency to characterize social protest as an irrational reaction to psychological strain. They conceived of protest in more strategic, political terms. Movements came to be seen as politics by other means, means generally chosen by groups lacking the material resources to exercise influence through electoral or lobbying channels (McCarthy and Zald 1973; Oberschall 1973; Gamson 1975). This change in perspective led researchers to pay greater attention to what activists actually do, and to what consequences their decisions have for the fate of their movements. The types of decisions most prominently represented in the literature have to do with organizational forms, pressure tactics, goals, and rhetorical/symbolic "framing" strategies.

Early on, a number of authors began to explore organizational form as a strategic choice. As described earlier, social movements generally emerge out of preexisting, nonmovement organizational structures, formal or informal. Once a significant movement has come into existence, though, new entities, sometimes referred to as "formal organizations" or "social movement organizations" (SMOS), are often created to lead it (Zald and Ash 1966). Since SMOS are created by activists themselves in the process of mobilization and protest, I regard decisions about their design as part of the activist strategy perspective.

Movement analysts have argued that the choice of organizational structure influences the prospects for movement survival and success; beyond this general assertion, there is little agreement. Some authors, particularly Gamson (1975), have claimed that relatively formalized and centralized structures are more effective. The idea behind this position is that, in order to succeed, movements must confront highly organized and sophisticated opponents, including the state and elite interest groups. To deal with these challenges a social movement must have a centralized organization that allows rapid decision making and a bureaucratic structure that permits activists to gather information and implement decisions efficiently on different fronts. For Piven and Cloward (1977) the opposite is true: anything but the most rudimentary and decentralized structure tends to deaden protest, pushing popular movements into institutional channels, where they are easily neutralized. Finally, Tarrow (1994, chap. 8) takes a middle-of-the-road position, asserting that organizations that allow for coordination between local groups without enclosing them within a hierarchical leadership structure are best.

These analysts have emphasized the role of formal organizations in relation to movement longevity and success in achieving objectives. It is not clear to what extent the choice of organizational structure helps us explain relatively rapid changes in the intensity of protest activity within a particular social movement, independent of contextual factors, such as discontent, opportunity, and access to external resources. To my knowledge, none of the authors who focus on organizational choice makes claims in this regard.

A number of researchers have also stressed the importance of tactical choice, most arguing that relatively disruptive and rowdy tactics are more likely to gain adherents and force concessions from authorities (Gamson 1975; Piven and Cloward 1977; McAdam 1982). A movement that relies on timid or conventional tactics can be easily ignored by authorities and will thus be regarded by potential supporters as innocuous. Conversely, tactics viewed as overly violent may eventually alienate a movement's supporters, dividing the movement and undermining its mass base. Disruptive tactics are also more likely to unite a movement's opponents and bring strong repression, which may end up destroying the movement. "Accordingly," writes McAdam (1982), "insurgents must chart a course that avoids crippling repression on the one hand and tactical impotency on the other. Staking out this middle ground is exceedingly difficult. Yet failure to do so almost surely spells the demise of the movement" (57).

Tactical choice would seem to provide somewhat more explanatory leverage on relatively rapid changes in the intensity of movement activity over time. Tactical innovations that catch authorities off balance and seem capable of provoking important changes may galvanize supporters, spurring outbursts of protest. McAdam (1983) has argued just that in the case of the U.S. civil rights movement. In contrast, tactical choices that overplay the movement's hand, alienating supporters, frightening the public, and pro-voking overwhelming repression, may result in movement collapse.

Another decision that movement activists must make involves goal selection (Gamson 1975). Gamson has recommended relatively narrow and modest goals, since movement organizations that focus on single issues and whose goals do not require the wholesale displacement of antagonist groups tend to be more successful. Making a similar case, McAdam (1982) cautions that groups that adopt radical goals tend to unify elites, pro-voking repression. These arguments, though addressing the question of how successful movements are in achieving their goals, can also be applied to the question of movement intensity. It is possible to envision situations in which a shift in the stated goals of major SMOs or top leaders affects the intensity of protest activity, either by energizing previously passive bystanders or by repelling existing activists.

Finally, a movement's development depends on its leadership's success in making rhetorical or symbolic appeals to actual and potential supporters and external actors, including the public, the media, and the state. This is the subject of a substantial body of literature developed since the 1980s on "collective action frames." Building on theoretical work from social psy-chology, the framing literature discusses how activists and their organiza-tions attempt to manipulate how others view their cause (Snow 1986; Snow and Benford 1988). The subjective frames they create, building on existing cultural understandings, seek to "underscore and embellish the seriousness and injustice of a social condition or redefine as unjust or immoral what was previously seen as unfortunate but perhaps tolerable" (Snow and Ben-ford 1988, 137). Movement framing does not go uncontested. The move-ment's opponents seek to challenge and refute the interpretations offered by activists, thereby generating competitive "framing contests." Thus, framing, like other strategic decisions activists make, is an ongoing process.

Framing theory has been formulated mainly as a characterization of *how* movements go about their business, rather than *why* they emerge, decline, or are successful in achieving their goals. Nevertheless, it is certainly possi-ble that frame innovation can influence the pace of collective protest over time. For proponents of the power of framing, frame innovation "creates the possibility that insurgents can *will* a movement into existence" (McA-dam, Tarrow, and Tilly 1997, 154). Conversely, an especially infelicitous frame may divide the movement or repel supporters.

Analysts of rural movements have not directed a lot of attention toward strategic issues. One exception is Keck (1995), who examined the struggle of rubber tappers in the Brazilian Amazon to protect their traditional tapping areas from deforestation. Keck demonstrates how the decision to frame the movement's struggle in environmental terms increased its influence, drawing in international allies. As this description suggests, however, the spotlight in Keck's analysis is on how strategic decisions affect success in achieving change, rather than on how strategy shapes the intensity of protest over time.

The activist strategy perspective would seem to offer several avenues for explaining differences in the growth trajectory of individual social movements that arise within the same protest cycle. Although choices about organizational structure may not readily explain rapid changes in protest intensity over time, they may help to elucidate why one movement survives whereas another that emerged during the same cycle declines. For example, one might argue (echoing Gamson) that an overly decentralized organization can render a movement helpless in the face of elite counterattacks, launched to turn national public opinion against the movement. Choices regarding tactics, goals, and framing strategies may also explain differences in the growth trajectory of different movements. Activists in one movement may be more creative or judicious in their choices in each of these areas, allowing them to galvanize potential supporters into action without provoking a countermobilization massive enough to swamp the movement.

Political Opportunity

During the past two decades, no perspective on social movements has been more influential than that of political opportunity. Despite substantial variation in how this concept is defined and operationalized, as I discuss below, Tarrow's definition of the political opportunity structure, as "consistent—but not necessarily formal or permanent—dimensions of the political environment that provide incentives for people to undertake collective action by affecting their expectations for success or failure" (Tarrow 1994, 85), is widely accepted. In other words, when relevant authorities are receptive or politically vulnerable to pressure on behalf of a cause, those interested in that cause become willing to devote more time, effort, and other resources to pushing for change. In contrast, when authorities are more likely to respond with indifference or repression than concessions, protest will languish, as only the most dedicated activists will be inclined to invest heavily in it.

Although elements of the opportunity perspective had never been altogether absent from social movement research, modern political opportunity theory began to emerge more forcefully in the late 1970s and early 1980s, largely as a result of seminal works by Eisinger (1973), Tilly (1978), and McAdam (1982). Like others associated with the resource mobilization current, these authors questioned the stress placed by earlier research on social grievances, but rather than focusing on organizational dynamics and internal movement resources, they began emphasizing how aspects of the larger political context shape movement activity. The political opportunity perspective seemed to achieve wider popularity in the early 1990s, in part because of the influential contributions made by Tarrow (1983, 1989, 1994), who highlighted the political roots and dynamics of broad "cycles" of social protest.

Like most other theoretical perspectives, political opportunity has focused mainly on explaining social movement emergence. Its proponents have made a strong claim to hegemony on this issue. According to McAdam (1982), "The generation of social insurgency presupposes the existence of a political environment increasingly vulnerable to pressure from insurgents. Specific events and/or broad social processes enhance the bargaining position of the aggrieved population, even as insurgent groups mobilize to exploit the expanding opportunities for collective action" (51–52). Tarrow (1994) is even more categorical: "Movements are created when political opportunities open up for social actors who usually lack them" (1).

Changes in the political opportunity structure vary along a continuum, from gradual shifts in basic structures of the political system to sudden conjunctural changes (Gamson and Meyer 1996). Opportunities can also be relatively narrow, affecting only one group, cause, or region, or quite wide, affecting the entire polity. The latter type of shift, theorists argue, is the key factor behind the emergence of broad national waves of protest, involving many movements. Tarrow (1994), outlining the internal dynamics of such protest "cycles," describes them as being set in motion when particularly well organized groups mount a successful challenge to authorities. Because they demonstrate the vulnerability of the political system to pressure, and offer lessons about what kinds of tactics and rhetorical appeals work, such "initiator" movements, or "early risers," tend to spur mobilization and protest among other, often less organized, groups (chaps. 5 and 9).

Researchers have identified numerous phenomena that they see as contributing to a movement's political opportunity structure (Meyer and Minkoff 2004). Some of the political shifts most often cited as being behind movement emergence include the opening of previously closed, authoritarian political regimes to greater participation; instances of alliance or electoral instability, when parties or elites are struggling over the allegiance of popular sectors; changes in the preferences of elite groups or organizations, which lead them to politically sponsor previously ignored popular causes; and defeats in interstate wars (Tarrow 1994, chap. 5; McAdam 1996). All these phenomena are seen as provoking protest because they suggest to activists that the potential rewards of protest are increasing, while the expected costs, in repression, are diminishing.

Just as movements emerge and grow in response to changes that make authorities more responsive to pressure, they decline, according to at least some exponents of political opportunity theory, mainly because of political shifts that make protest less effective or increase the intensity of repression. Tarrow (1994) is probably most emphatic on this point, arguing that "the frequent collapse of social movements that seemed well organized and brilliantly led suggests that both the sources of movement power, and their limits, are the results of political opportunity" (150).

By referring to conditions such as divided elites and alliance instability as "dimensions" of the opportunity structure, Tarrow (1994, chap. 5) and McAdam (1996) imply that decline occurs when the political situation that originally gave rise to a movement has changed. This may occur for reasons that have little to do with the movement itself. For example, intra-elite conflicts may give way to a new alliance structure, reducing competition for popular support. To a lesser extent, these authors suggest that the closing of the opportunity structure may have to do with changes in some way provoked by the movement itself. For example, groups threatened by a movement's demands may engage in countermobilization, repressing the movement themselves or forcing authorities to take a harder line against it (McAdam 1982, chap. 3; Tarrow 1994, chap. 5; Voss 1996).

Although scholars writing on the rise and fall of rural movements have typically not highlighted political opportunity, preferring to dwell mainly on grievances, they have sometimes incorporated a political opportunity dimension. In his study of peasant revolutionary movements, Wolf (1969) emphasizes the disruptive impact of capitalist development on peasant subsistence strategies while also noting that such movements cannot emerge without major dislocations that undermine the position of traditional elites, weakening the mechanisms of social control that normally hold the rural poor down. When the peasant "lights the torch of rebellion," he says, "the edifice of society is already smoldering and ready to take fire" (295).

Similarly, Zamosc (1986), writing on the peasant movement of the 1960s and early 1970s in Colombia, underscores the role of rising social discontent, but describes the movement's emergence as being provoked by the efforts of a new government to gain popular support for a land reform program that it hoped would create a broader domestic market for industry. A subsequent change in governing coalitions then brought about a fresh shift in policy toward a development model emphasizing exports over import-substitution. Zamosc argues that this change, combined with rising elite concern about mobilization in the countryside, led authorities to adopt a more repressive line, which contributed to the movement's eventual demise.

What explanation does political opportunity theory offer to the question of why movements that emerge during the same wave of protest activity experience different growth trajectories? If protest cycles respond directly to broad national political conjunctures, we should expect movements that arise during the same cycle to have similar trajectories, unless factors other than opportunity are at work. Still, it is possible that the various movements that make up the cycle may face somewhat different structures of political opportunity, as a result of the specific issues they seek to address, the actors aligned for and against them, and the policy preferences of governing elites.

Political opportunity–oriented analyses have been subject to much criticism in recent years, sometimes even by scholars who have used the concept in their own work. One aspect of the critique questions the empirical validity of the generalization that movements rise and fall in response to shifts in the opportunity structure. Critics have responded especially strongly to the bold assertion that expanding opportunities are a necessary precondition for movement emergence. They retort that protest often intensifies in the presence of hostile or unyielding authorities and fails to grow (or even declines) in settings where the prospects for success seem bright (Goodwin and Jasper 1999).

The explanatory power of the political opportunity perspective can be assessed only through empirical testing. Unfortunately, although numerous writers have used this perspective to elucidate specific cases, there have been few attempts to actually test it against alternative explanations (Meyer 2004). Some of those studies, furthermore, have examined dependent variables other than social protest, including violence, policy change, and coalition formation. Those tests that have focused on protest activity have yielded mixed results. Both Costain's (1992) study of the U.S. women's movement and Osa and Corduneaunu-Huci's (2003) comparative analysis of protest in nondemocracies find solid support for political opportunity. By contrast, neither Snow, Soule, and Cress's (2005) study of homeless protest in American cities nor Soule et al.'s (1999) study of the U.S. women's movement provide much backing for a political opportunity perspective. McCammon (2001) examines the formation of social movement organizations, which can be viewed as a precursor of protest; her study of the emergence of the American women's suffrage movement also offers little support for political opportunity.

The empirical chapters of this study will contribute to the debate on the explanatory power of the political opportunity perspective by pitting it against competing theories in the empirical case of the Brazilian landless movement. In the present chapter, however, it is important to deal with another aspect of the evolving critique of the political opportunity literature, which focuses on conceptual issues. In particular, I examine what I believe to be the three major conceptual criticisms of the political opportunity literature.

Probably the most commonly heard lament about the conceptualization of the political opportunity structure has to do with the range of phenomena seen as constituting it (Gamson and Meyer 1996; Goodwin and Jasper 1999; Meyer 2004). Individual works offer differing lists of the dimensions or elements of political opportunity, and empirical studies sometimes introduce new ones that do not always fit easily into any of the existing lists. The sheer scope and diversity of the conditions associated with the political opportunity structure, critics warn, threatens to reduce the concept to a useless tautology. If the trend continues, say Gamson and Meyer (1996), political opportunity may "become an all-encompassing fudge factor for all the conditions and circumstances that form the context for collective action. Used to explain so much, it may ultimately explain nothing at all" (275).

Although the dangers of conceptual stretching these authors point to are real, much of the diversity they criticize can be eliminated simply by applying in a consistent, disciplined manner the mainstream definition of the political opportunity structure I cited above. This definition clearly excludes various phenomena often viewed as aspects of political opportunity, allowing them to be placed in different theoretical categories. Below, I offer three examples from well-known texts to illustrate this argument.

In his analysis of peasant mobilization in Central America, Brockett (1991) portrays the consciousness-raising and grassroots-organizing work of progressive Catholic clergy in rural villages as positively influencing the political opportunity structure. If we take Tarrow's definition seriously, however, these phenomena do not constitute an aspect of the political opportunity structure, because their impact works through the peasants' sense of grievance and their capacity to mobilize, rather than through their estimation of the likelihood that authorities will respond positively to protest.

Smith's (1996) monograph on the movement against U.S. intervention in Central America during the 1980s offers an example of a different kind. One aspect of political opportunity that contributed to the movement's growth, according to the author, were President Ronald Reagan's aggressive foreign policy initiatives, including support for the contra insurgency in Nicaragua and repressive governments in El Salvador. These galvanized many normally apolitical Americans, prompting them to get involved in activism. Smith's empirical argument is convincing, but his classification of this phenomenon as political opportunity does not fit Tarrow's definition. Reagan's Central America policy prompted protest because it produced or inflamed grievances among people who felt the government should not be supporting actors involved in the indiscriminate killing of civilians.

A final example comes, ironically, from Tarrow himself. In his 1994 volume, he argues that social movements sometimes create political opportunity for their opponents. "When a movement's success threatens another group in a context of heightened mobilization," he says, "it can lead to outbidding and counter-protests" (97). While Tarrow is undoubtedly correct in asserting that movement activity can promote the rise of countermovements, the causal mechanism he is pointing to here is not a change in the countermovement's political opportunity structure. Rather, it is an exacerbation of the grievances felt by the social group it seeks to represent.

A disciplined application of Tarrow's definition thus substantially narrows the range of empirical phenomena that can be seen as constituting part of the political opportunity structure and makes political opportunity more readily falsifiable. A good deal of diversity remains, of course, in the kinds of political phenomena that can be seen as shaping a movement's opportunity structure. In my view, efforts to address this situation by defining a priori a short list of the "dimensions" of political opportunity are bound to fail, since they are necessarily arbitrary and ignore the rich complexity of political processes. My approach in this study, therefore, is to apply the mainstream definition of the political opportunity structure to the case of the landless movement in as disciplined and rigorous fashion as possible, without trying to restrict in advance of my empirical analysis what kinds of political phenomena I will find to be relevant.

The second broad criticism of political opportunity theory is that it ignores the more subjective aspects of the politics of protest, including perceptions, culture, and emotions. Scholars who pursue this angle actually make two rather different points. One is that political opportunity–based analyses too often take as unproblematic the relationship between the actual structure of political opportunities and its perception by activists (Gamson and Meyer 1996; Goodwin and Jasper 1999; Meyer and Migdoff 2004). In fact, they argue, the two may be quite different. It is thus critical to examine the process through which activists interpret, or "frame," their political environment. The second point has to do with the character of the political opportunity structure itself. Critics take political opportunity theorists to task for focusing excessively on certain types of political phenomena that are relatively concrete or tangible, such as regime change and alliance shifts. "Opportunity," Gamson and Meyer (1996) argue, "has a strong cultural dimension and we miss something important when we limit our attention to variance in political institutions and the relationships among political actors" (279).

With regard to the first of these points, I certainly agree that activists' perceptions of the political opportunity structure may be inaccurate, because of insufficient information, ideological bias, psychological predispositions, or other factors. It is also true that political opportunity analyses have not always acknowledged this. However, much of the appeal of the political opportunity perspective lies in its focus on how the external environment shapes protest. It is this focus that makes political opportunity theory useful in formulating predictions about when and where protest activity will occur. The concept of the political opportunity structure loses much of its analytical force if we simply equate it with what is in the heads of activists. Therefore, for conceptual reasons, the understanding of political opportunity theory I employ in this book focuses on the actual vulnerability or receptivity of the political system to a movement's demands.

On the second point, I agree that shifts in beliefs and perceptions among the general public or key organized groups can affect the state's vulnerability or receptivity to a social movement's pressure in crucial ways. This type of phenomenon, moreover, has been relatively neglected in political opportunity theorizing. At least one author explicitly urges that subjective changes not be considered part of the political opportunity structure (McAdam 1996). This, in my view, is a significant flaw of the political opportunity perspective. In Chapter 4, I underscore the potential importance of subjective factors in shaping a movement's political opportunity structure by demonstrating how a rapid shift in the Brazilian public's perception of the agrarian question in the mid-1990s helped provoke an upsurge in protest for land reform through its impact on state policies.

The third major critique of political opportunity theorizing has to do with its alleged "structural bias," or tendency to characterize as fixed or unchanging elements of the political environment that can be and often are affected by a social movement's own actions. Goodwin and Jasper (1999), in fact, suggest that the term *political opportunity structure* should be applied only in very restricted circumstances, since it refers to those aspects of the political context that are truly beyond activists' ability to control or alter.

Here again, there are really two separate issues involved in this critique. One is whether political opportunity theorists sufficiently recognize the fluid, reciprocal character of the causal relationship between social movements and their political environments. The second is whether the recognition of this reality should be seen as rendering the concept of political opportunity structure largely unusable.

It would be somewhat unfair to argue that political opportunity theory ignores the reciprocal causality between movements and their political contexts. McAdam (1982), for example, points out in his landmark study of the U.S. civil rights movement that once a significant movement has emerged, the political environment is not independent of that movement's initiatives: "Now the structure of political alignments shifts in response to movement activity, even as those shifts shape the prospects for future insurgency" (53). Nevertheless, as McAdam himself admits in a later publication (McAdam 1996), the impact that movements have on their political environment has received little attention from scholars.[1] Instead, the thrust of political opportunity–oriented theorizing and empirical analysis has been on how politics shapes protest.

If we recognize that the causal relationship between movements and their political environments is reciprocal and fluctuating, does this restrict the legitimate application of the term *political opportunity structure* to certain specific aspects of politics that can be considered essentially fixed and unchanging? This position strikes me as exaggerated. Nothing is structural in a permanent sense. What is unchangeable in the space of a few months may be more malleable over the course of years or decades. Thus, conditions that form part of a social movement's political opportunity structure in the present may be at least partially the product of its past actions and may eventually change as a result of its future initiatives. What we can reasonably label a "structure" therefore depends on what kind of variation in protest activity, short term or long term, we are trying to explain.

Two aspects of my empirical analysis in this book speak to the issue of reciprocal causality by illustrating how a movement's present political opportunity structure can be shaped by its own past actions. In Chapter 4, I argue that the expansion of the landless movement in the mid-1990s was in part a result of the political impact of two police massacres of landless protestors, which shocked Brazilians and forced the government to accelerate land reform. Activists did not plan the massacres and had little control over their interpretation by public and media once they occurred. The political impact of the massacres thus clearly represents a change in the movement's political opportunity structure. At the same time, these incidents were partially a product of the movement's own long-standing strategy of aggressive protest, which threatened local elites and their allies within the state, moving them to resort to violence.

Likewise, in Chapter 5, I contend that the reduction in land occupations in Brazil beginning in 2000 was the result of a decline in the receptivity of the state to these actions. Once it occurred, this change was essentially beyond the ability of activists to revert in the short term. In fact, it would

1. Some of the examples they offer of movements "creating" political opportunity, furthermore, are not very convincing. For example, Tarrow's (1994) discussion of how movements "create" opportunities focuses on how "early risers" in a protest cycle demonstrate the underlying vulnerability of the state to other groups. Rather than shaping the opportunity structure, they would seem merely to reveal it.

only be reversed two and a half years later, through a change in government. Nevertheless, the closing of the opportunity structure was itself partly a product of tactics adopted in the late 1990s and 2000 by the MST, which eventually made it politically easier for the government to crack down on protest.

Olson's Theory of Collective Action

There is an enduring debate in the social movement literature on the utility of Olson's rational choice theory of collective action, spelled out in his influential 1965 volume, *The Logic of Collective Action*. Although this theory was embraced by scholars who rejected explanations based on socioeconomic grievances, it is not really associated with any one of the perspectives discussed above, but, rather, cuts across these perspectives. It is rooted in a divide between those scholars who see pragmatic, material considerations as playing an important part in motivating movement activity and those who view protest as motivated mainly by more normative incentives.

Olson's theory is a critique of the assumption, present in Marxism and other contemporary bodies of social science theory, that individuals or firms that share a common interest in some government policy or other collective good will naturally join together to pursue that interest collectively. He argues that, on the contrary, especially among large groups, collective action is the exception rather than the rule because individual members normally do not have a rational incentive to contribute to it.

This is so for two main reasons. First, in a large group a single member's decision to contribute or not to the collective effort has essentially no discernible impact on the likelihood that the effort will be successful. Second, if the group's goal is achieved, all members will end up benefiting, whether or not they contributed. According to Olson (1965), this is because the benefits delivered by government generally take the form of "public goods," ones that "must be available to everyone if they are available to anyone" (14). Such things as public security, justice, and clean air cannot feasibly be denied to those who did not help to pressure authorities for their provision. As a result, there is generally a temptation to try to "free ride" on the efforts of others.

Small groups face fewer obstacles to collective action, largely because in such groups the relationship between individual participation and achievement of the collective good is stronger. For large groups, however, the obstacles to collective action may be insuperable unless a mechanism can be devised for selectively rewarding those who contribute or punishing those who do not. Groups that have succeeded in constituting strong organizations to promote their interests have done so by finding a way to provide such "selective incentives." According to Olson, large political pressure groups are generally "by-products" of organizations that provide private benefits to members. Thus, for example, the political influence of the U.S. labor movement is a by-product of the nonpolitical collective bargaining function of individual unions, while the power wielded by U.S. physicians is a result of the American Medical Association's success in using a combination of positive incentives (for instance, its prestigious professional journal) and subtle forms of coercion to gain members.

Olson allows that noneconomic incentives, including the desire for social approbation, avoidance of feelings of guilt, and promotion of self-esteem, can motivate people to act in group-oriented ways (60–65). The existence of social, psychological, or moral incentives, he says, is consistent with his theory, since they act as a form of selective incentive, motivating people to contribute to collective action though they lack a rational reason to do so. Nonetheless, Olson very clearly privileges material incentives, arguing that social incentives can only operate in smaller groups and that noneconomic incentives, in general, are unnecessary for explaining collective action. Moreover, his empirical discussions, including his extensive analysis of the American labor movement, exclude nonmaterial incentives altogether.

Scholars associated with the resource mobilization school generally embraced Olson's theoretical model early on (Oberschall 1973; McCarthy and Zald 1973; Gamson 1975; Tilly 1978). It was compelling to them in part because it shifted the focus of analysis from the origins of social grievances—an emphasis they rejected—to the conditions capable of transforming them into collective protest. All these scholars accepted the basic dilemma outlined by Olson. They also seemed to agree that, at least in some cases, the types of selective incentives he emphasized (namely, coercion and economic rewards) could be used to motivate social movement participation. However, there were some differences in how they understood the concept of selective incentives. Oberschall (1973), for example, embraced the idea that social incentives such as group loyalty and solidarity should be seen as just another kind of selective incentive. Meanwhile, Gamson

(1975) believed that this concept should properly be limited to more concrete phenomena. Otherwise, the theory would be reduced to the tautology
that people participate in movements when the incentives to do so out-
weigh the disincentives.

Since these works were published, discussions of Olson's theory in the
social movement literature have generally been more critical. Authors operating from a rational choice perspective have sometimes suggested that
Olson's model overstates the dilemma faced by larger groups. Oliver and
Marwell (1993), to cite the most prominent case among social movement
scholars, use formal modeling to contest the idea that larger groups are
necessarily at a disadvantage relative to smaller ones in terms of engaging
in collective action. They argue that this depends on other factors. In particular, they point to the distribution within the group of both interest in
the collective good and resources for obtaining it, as well as the good's
"jointness of supply," or the extent to which the cost of providing it remains constant regardless of how many members consume it.[2]

Nevertheless, by and large social movement scholars have not questioned the logic of Olson's analysis of the rational disincentives to collective action. Discussion has focused, rather, on how the obstacles to
collective action are ultimately overcome. In particular, scholars have criticized the theory's emphasis on material incentives, claiming that feelings
of group loyalty and adherence to principled beliefs are, as a rule, what
motivate participation in social movements (Fireman and Gamson 1979;
Tarrow 1994).[3] Individuals engage in collective protest because they feel a
moral obligation to the movement's cause or have affective ties to other
activists. They may also relish the sheer excitement of challenging authorities and established social norms. These normative or emotional incentives
can make engagement in movements its own reward (Hirschman 1982).
Material selective incentives of the kind emphasized by Olson, these authors contend, rarely play a significant role in motivating individuals to
participate in movement activism.

2. Specifically, Oliver and Marwell argue that large groups that are heterogeneous in interests and resources and seek a good with high jointness of supply are more likely to act
collectively.

3. Gamson changed sides in the debate over Olson's theory during the course of the 1970s.
While his influential 1975 volume *The Strategy of Social Protest* suggests that material selective
incentives play a significant role in motivating protest action, his later works, especially
Fireman and Gamson (1979), argue that such incentives are rarely available to social movements.

Criticism of Olson's theory with regard to social movement activity has thus focused principally on how movements solve the free-rider problem. This study will contribute to the debate in a different way. It will call into question another, arguably even more fundamental aspect of the theory: the assumption that collective action necessarily involves the pursuit of a public good.

As noted earlier, a fundamental building block of Olson's theory is the idea that organized groups pursue "public" or "collective" goods: ones that "must be available to everyone if they are available to anyone." This is critical to the theory because if a good can feasibly be provided only to those who contribute to its provision and not to others then there is no free-rider problem and selective incentives are not necessary to induce collective action. In such a situation, members of a group have a built-in incentive to participate in the collective action, because otherwise they will not receive the good in question. The remaining obstacles to collective action are those of coordinating effectively between individual members, not of overcoming a lack of incentives.

Discussions of Olson's theory in the social movement literature, be they complementary or critical, have almost always contained the assumption that social movements pursue what Olson termed *public goods*.[4] My analysis in Chapter 3 of the landless movement's exceptional growth trajectory following the transition to democracy in Brazil will show that this is not necessarily the case. The way that the Brazilian state responded to land occupations, by settling (at most) only those involved in the occupation, largely eliminated the free-rider problem with regard to a landless family's decision to join the movement. As a result, the landless movement was less dependent than other major social movements on the normative incentives that movements usually rely on to overcome the free-rider problem. I will argue in the book's final chapter, furthermore, that the landless movement is not an isolated case in this sense.

Conclusion

In this chapter I have attempted to lay out a coherent theoretical framework to guide my analysis of variation in protest activity in the rest of the

4. To my knowledge the only exception is Popkin (1979) in his analysis of peasant society in Vietnam. However, the examples he uses of collective actions in which the good sought is not a public good would not be considered social movement activity under the definition

book. I have divided the literature into four basic perspectives, each of which represents a particular way of explaining protest. Although this is certainly not the only legitimate way of parsing the stock of theories on social movements, I believe it is a useful one.

In elaborating this framework I have devoted particular attention to evaluating some of the conceptual criticisms of the political opportunity perspective, both because testing this perspective's validity is the central theoretical purpose of the study and because it has come under repeated attack in recent years. I have at least partially validated some of these criticisms, including the relative neglect of how subjective factors shape the political opportunity structure and how social movements influence their own political environments. However, I have broken ranks with the critics on other questions. I have argued that a mainstream, general definition of the political opportunity structure is narrow enough to be falsifiable, if applied in a disciplined and rigorous manner. I have also suggested that, if equated with the activists' perceptions of their political environment, as some critics would have it, the concept of political opportunity structure loses much of its utility. Finally, I have argued that accepting the idea that movements interact with their political environments in reciprocal and shifting causal relationships does not force us to abandon or greatly restrict our use of the term *political opportunity structure*.

In the chapters that follow, the theoretical perspectives outlined above will be tested against one another to assess their relative effectiveness in explaining different types of empirical variation in protest intensity. Although each perspective finds some support, the results will generally favor the political opportunity perspective. At the same time, they will also help to underscore the validity of some of the existing criticisms of how this perspective has been conceptualized, with regard to both the content of the political opportunity structure and how social movements interact with it.

In this chapter we have also looked at the controversy surrounding Olson's theory of collective action and its relevance to social movements. It was necessary to do so because this theory informs my empirical analysis in Chapter 3. Critiques of this theory in the social movement literature have focused mainly on the emphasis Olson places on the importance of material

---

adopted in this study, since they are mainly self-help projects, such as setting up an insurance scheme or a blood bank.

selective incentives in motivating collective action. Social movement scholars have almost universally accepted his assumption that collective action
inherently involves the pursuit of a collective or public good. The contribution of this book to this debate will be to show that this is not necessarily
the case.

TWO   Emergence, 1978–1984

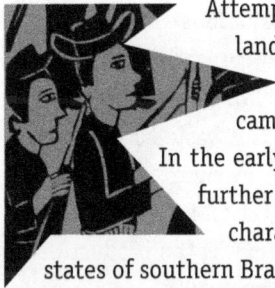

Attempts by landless workers to pressure authorities for land reform, never altogether absent in Brazil even during the height of the military regime, became much more common at the end of the 1970s. In the early 1980s, mobilization for land reform accelerated further and began to take on a more broadly organized character. This was particularly true in the three states of southern Brazil, where the movement was active in many *municípios* and quickly became a substantial political force. In 1984, activists formed the MST, an organization intended to lead the struggle for land at the national level. The movement emerged during a period of political effervescence, as Brazilians increasingly challenged the authority of the military regime. Protest helped to undermine the regime's legitimacy further and pushed its leadership to make good on their promise to turn over power to civilians, which they would do in early 1985.

In this chapter, using the theoretical framework outlined in Chapter 1 as an analytical guide, I attempt to explain why a substantial grassroots movement for land reform emerged in Brazil during the 1978–84 period. In turn, I ask what this episode suggests about the ability of each theoretical perspective to explain change in protest intensity over time and, in particular, initial movement emergence. In addition to analyzing the movement's emergence, I introduce some of the key political actors and government agencies that will affect its development in later years.

As suggested in Chapter 1, each of the theoretical perspectives offers a different strategy for explaining movement emergence. Grievance/discontent theory sees movement emergence as a product of changes, particularly socioeconomic ones, that increase either objective needs or subjective feelings of deprivation. The organizational capacity perspective would lead us to focus on the strengthening of grassroots organizational structures at the movement's social base or (more likely) the injection of external resources from other social groups or organizations. The activist strategy perspective, for its part, would expect emergence to result from strategic decisions, most plausibly in tactics or collective action frames, that galvanize people into action. For political opportunity theorists, finally, movements emerge because shifts in the larger political environment suggest to activists that the time is ripe to press for change.

This phase of the landless movement's development has been written about more extensively than any other. Studies have tended to highlight three factors, which roughly correspond to explanations of movement emergence offered by the grievance/discontent, organizational capacity and political opportunity perspectives (Wolford 2003). The analysis I develop in this chapter provides further support for this basic account, but diverges from the mainstream, as explained below, in my examination of the sources of social discontent encouraging mobilization for land reform.

The rise of a significant movement for land reform was the product of a convergence of several socioeconomic and political forces and it is difficult to say which one was most important. Rising social grievances played a substantial role. Existing accounts universally emphasize the negative impact on rural workers of the rapid "modernization" of agricultural production during the military years, which was in large measure a consequence of state policies (Wagner 1988; Navarro 1995, 1996a; Fernandes 2000; Wright and Wolford 2003). In particular, they underscore how technological change, rising land prices, and the expansion of commercial crops undermined access to farmland, making rural working-class people available for recruitment by land reform activists.

I agree with the central thrust of this argument, but it is too narrow an account of the generation of grievances, since it leaves out other socioeconomic forces affecting potential demand for agrarian reform. During the 1970s the negative welfare impacts of agricultural modernization were offset by other factors, including a strong urban job market, the robust growth of agricultural wage labor, and the opening up of new agricultural areas on the frontier. Had these trends continued into the 1980s, they would have made it more difficult for activists to mobilize rural workers to fight for agrarian reform. What ended up happening was that each of these trends either stalled or went into reverse, aggravating the social problems facing the rural or recently urbanized poor and making them more likely to consider the struggle for agrarian reform as an option.

Another important factor in the movement's emergence was the growth in organizational capacity among the landless and land poor. This, as analysts of the movement have asserted, was mainly a product of the rise of a strong progressive movement within the Catholic Church during the 1970s (Navarro 1995, 1996a; Fernandes 2000; Branford and Rocha 2002; Wright and Wolford 2003). Clergy and lay activists associated with this movement created various grassroots organizational structures designed to bring the church closer to the people and to provide vehicles for the diffusion of a new theological perspective, which called on Catholics to fight injustice in the here-and-now. All over Brazil, the progressive, or "popular," church movement played a critical role in mobilizing workers to struggle for land, organizing protest events, and linking together local activist groups to form a broader network. Among its achievements was the creation of the MST.

Finally, the emergence of the landless movement was quite clearly a reflection of an improved political opportunity structure, resulting mainly from the gradual opening of Brazil's military dictatorship beginning in the mid-1970s (Navarro 1995, 1996a; Stedile and Fernandes 1999; Wright and Wolford 2003). The regime's institutional liberalization and loss of political support encouraged social movement activity by lessening the threat of repression and increasing the prospects for concessions. It helped give rise to a broad national cycle of protest during the late 1970s and early 1980s, of which the landless movement formed part. Although the shift in political opportunity structure was incremental, the upsurge in protest began more abruptly in the late 1970s, in part because a major strike movement in the São Paulo industrial belt in 1978–79 drew national attention to the military leadership's hesitation to use the harsh repression employed earlier.

The only theoretical perspective that does not find support in this chapter is activist strategy. This is mainly a question of definition. The organizational structures and rhetorical appeals devised by the progressive church movement were clearly powerful innovations that helped to fuel the landless movement and many other social movements. However, the activist strategy perspective as I have defined it refers to the choices made by activists of the movement whose development one is trying to explain. The popular church's innovations precede the rise of the landless movement and thus are best thought of as part of the strategic action of an earlier movement within the Catholic Church.

I begin the chapter with two sections that discuss some of the major political and socioeconomic trends, respectively, in Brazil during the military dictatorship, particularly those that contributed to the emergence of the landless movement. Although protest for agrarian reform only began to intensify at the end of the 1970s, the causes of this change must be traced back somewhat earlier. I then discuss the formation of the movement itself, focusing mainly on what was going on in the South, where it emerged with greatest force and organizational solidity. I also talk about the state's response to protest for land and how it affected the movement. As will every empirical chapter in this study, this one ends with an analytical section in which I further develop the main arguments, linking empirical developments to the theoretical perspectives laid out in Chapter 1.

Regime Opening and Social Protest

The decade following the 1964 coup was characterized by deepening authoritarianism. Immediately after taking power, the military launched a campaign of repression aimed at destroying the Left. Many rural activists were killed, arrested, or forced into hiding. The MASTER and Peasant Leagues disappeared. Authorities arrested or exiled many politicians and prohibited others from participating in politics. Political freedoms were restricted and the powers of Congress curtailed (Skidmore 1988, chap. 2). In 1965 officials scrapped the existing parties and imposed instead a two-party system, featuring the pro-regime National Renovating Alliance (ARENA) and the opposition Brazilian Democratic Movement (MDB). In 1968, facing rising protest, a rebellious congressional opposition, and an incipient guerrilla movement, they cracked down harder. Under President Emílio Garrastazu Médici, who took power in 1969, civil liberties were curtailed further and Congress was temporarily closed (Skidmore 1988, chap. 5).

The progressive closing of political space after two decades of party competition and relatively broad civil liberties was undoubtedly resented by many Brazilians, but authorities justified it as necessary for restoring economic growth and addressing the threat of communist subversion. By the end of 1973 both rationales were starting to lose their force. Beginning in the late 1960s, the economy recovered rapidly, giving rise to a period of phenomenal growth known as the "economic miracle" (discussed below). By this time, moreover, leftist forces had been decisively crushed and the idea that Brazil was menaced by communism was becoming a harder sell. When General Ernesto Geisel assumed the presidency in 1974 he responded to this situation by promising a gradual process of political liberalization, or *distensão*. Throughout the rest of the decade, the military leadership would loosen the controls on political expression and competition, while also seeking to limit the scope and impact of the opening.

Their efforts to retain control over political activity were increasingly challenged by Brazilian society. Electoral support for the opposition MDB grew, despite institutional manipulations aimed at thwarting it. Congress was largely impotent, but the MDB's successes in legislative elections advertised the waning public support for military rule. Civil society also spoke out against the regime and its policies. Many groups were involved, from lawyers to artists, but the most influential source of opposition was the Catholic Church. Leftist groups in the church had existed prior to the 1970s, but they expanded greatly during this decade, making the Brazilian church perhaps the most progressive in the world (Mainwaring 1986). This shift would make the church, long a pillar of the status quo, a key source of opposition to the dictatorial regime and a critical ally of both rural and urban workers in their struggles for social reform.

The emergence of the popular church movement was in large measure a reflection of international trends. Since the late 1960s the Latin American church as a whole had been moving toward a more active role in promoting social justice. Following the lead of the Second Vatican Council, which had urged Catholic clergy to make the church more relevant to the lives of the faithful, the Latin American bishops met in Medellín, Colombia, in 1968 and issued a powerful declaration. The church, they said, could not be indifferent to worldly injustice and must struggle to improve the lot of the poor and oppressed in the here-and-now (CELAM 1968). During the late 1960s and 1970s, Latin American clerics developed liberation theology, which argued that the Bible itself demands that the faithful act against the "sinful structures" of social injustice.

The diffusion of these ideas among ordinary Catholics in Brazil and elsewhere was aided by organizational innovations intended to implement the Vatican II directive of bringing the church closer to the people. Thousands of grassroots Bible study groups, often known as "ecclesial base communities," or CEBs, were formed throughout the country. CEBs increasingly functioned as spaces for promoting a leftist worldview and fomenting social activism. The National Conference of the Bishops of Brazil (CNBB) created or strengthened a number of pastoral services, which sought to organize Catholics to tackle particular problems facing their communities. The guiding philosophy of the progressive church was to empower poor people to help themselves. Catholic activists were driven by a vision of grassroots democracy and popular participation, or *basismo*.

In the countryside one of the most important manifestations of the popular church was the Pastoral Commission on Land (CPT), an agency founded in 1975 to help rural workers defend their rights, particularly their right to farmland. Its creation was prompted largely by the military's rural development policies, especially in the Amazon basin. These initiatives, as I discuss below, led to the forcible eviction of many poor squatters. Although the CPT was largely an initiative of bishops based in the Amazon, chapters began to be formed in other regions during the second half of the 1970s by progressive priests and nuns. These, in turn, recruited religious lay people to support the effort, creating an expanding network of activism. Reflecting the church's *basista* philosophy, the CPT conceived of its role as principally that of advising and supporting attempts by rural workers to organize themselves. The CPT's emphasis on land access reflected not only the role of land conflicts in its foundation, but also a communitarian social vision, which saw in the smallholder village the ideal social context for the propagation of Christian values (Medeiros 1989, 115).

Another source of opposition to official policies in the countryside were the rural unions. Although not as important a political actor as the church, they are worth touching on here, both because of their rapid growth during the military years and because of the role they would play in future struggles for land. Goulart's 1963 Rural Worker Statute had called for the establishment of a rural union system made up of local unions, state labor federations, and a national confederation. In the late 1960s the leadership of the national entity, known as the National Confederation of Workers in Agriculture (CONTAG), developed a strategy of pressuring authorities to apply existing laws, particularly the Rural Worker Statute and the Land Statute (Maybury-Lewis 1994; Pereira 1997). It encouraged both the state federations and the local unions, known as "unions of rural workers" (STRS), to adopt this strategy in order to aid their members in conflicts with large landowners.[1] The STRS grew quite rapidly during the 1970s. By 1979 there were about twenty-three hundred local unions with a combined membership of some 6 million workers (Maybury-Lewis 1994, app. A).

Although the rural union system grew into a vast organizational network and clearly aided many workers, it was not a serious threat to the regime's political hegemony in the countryside. The CONTAG's political outlook was pragmatic and its tactics limited mainly to working through institutional channels, such as labor courts. Rather than reflecting an upsurge in activism, the growth of STRS was primarily a consequence of a new federal program, channeled through the unions, that provided medical and dental benefits, as well as modest pensions, to rural workers (Houtzager 1998). Although it was popular, the program arguably served to divert unions from their potential role as agents of class struggle by tying them more closely to the state. The strong federalism of the union structure also impeded the CONTAG from imposing a progressive direction on local unions. Most STRS remained rather conservative and were sometimes under the thumb of local elites.

Signs of discontent with military rule tended to increase gradually throughout the 1970s. There were factions within the military and its civilian support coalition who did not want to relinquish power. Proliberalization forces ultimately prevailed, however. Near the end of the decade the institutional opening deepened. In late 1978, as his term came to a close, President Geisel announced a number of liberalizing reforms, reducing the power of the executive, removing prior censorship on newspapers and radio, and reinstituting habeas corpus for political prisoners. His successor, João Batista Figueiredo, vowed to continue the process of democratization, moving from *distensão* to *abertura*, or "opening." In 1985, he promised, Brazil would inaugurate a civilian president.

Authorities continued to try to hamper the growth of opposition forces. With the electoral reform of 1979, which did away with the two-party ARENA/MDB system and allowed new parties to form, they sought to divide the opposition. However, Figueiredo did not reverse course. In November

---

1. The Rural Worker Statute uses the term *rural worker* to apply to any working-class person involved in agriculture, including independent farmers, tenant farmers, and wage laborers. I will use this term in the same sense in this study. Since there could only be one STR per *município*, local unions were supposed to represent a wide variety of demands. Some analysts have seen this characteristic as undermining their effectiveness.

1982, Brazil held its first gubernatorial elections since 1965, resulting in major gains for dissidents. Opposition candidates won eleven governorships, including the crucial states of São Paulo, Minas Gerais, and Rio de Janeiro. All but one of these victories was scored by the Party of the Brazilian Democratic Movement (PMDB), successor to the MDB.[2] Rejection of the military regime was encouraged by the sharp deterioration of the national economy, which I discuss below. In 1984, the parties began to maneuver for the indirect presidential election of January 1985 and the authoritarian coalition came apart.

This process of political opening at the elite level was accompanied by a broad wave of social protest, something largely absent from Brazilian politics since the late 1960s. The first major sign of this phenomenon appeared in mid-1978, when autoworkers in Brazil's industrial heartland, the "ABC" region of greater São Paulo, launched a series of strikes. They gained concessions and received substantial support from civil society and the media. In an important shift, military authorities failed to respond with strong police repression. The leader of this "new union" movement, Luiz Inácio da Silva, popularly called Lula, quickly became a nationally known figure. Popular mobilization intensified in many areas of Brazil in 1979, both urban and rural, as people protested not only for socioeconomic concessions but also for a return to democracy (Doimo 1995). The urban union movement expanded outward, as a series of strikes extended to fifteen states and many categories of workers (Keck 1992, 66). In Pernambuco, a focal point of rural activism in the 1960s, the rural union federation organized a massive strike of sugarcane workers (Pereira 1997, 53).

Protest continued to erupt throughout the country during the following few years. In the cities it involved a tremendous variety of groups, both popular and middle class. Leaders of these movements, particularly the new union movement, were the key force behind the creation, in 1980, of the PT. They sought to give Brazilian workers a political party of their own, breaking with the populist tradition of middle-class leadership of working-class parties (Keck 1992). In 1983, the new union movement founded a national labor confederation, the Unified Workers' Central (CUT). The creation of the CUT split Brazilian labor into two main camps: a more combative group associated with the CUT, and a more moderate one. The *cutista* union-

---

2. In Rio de Janeiro, Leonel Brizola, the former leftist governor of Rio Grande do Sul, came to office as the candidate of his new party, the Democratic Labor Party (PDT).

ism favored mass mobilization and reform of the corporatist legal structure tying unions to the state (Rodrigues 1995).

Significant movements also emerged among a broad variety of rural social groups. Sugarcane workers in Pernambuco and São Paulo engaged in major strike waves. In the South, smallholders demanded better prices for their goods and lower interest rates on credit. All over Brazil rural working-class people were involved in struggles over land. In some cases, particularly in the North and Northeast, these were defensive attempts by squatters or resident farmworkers to avoid expulsion by landowners or speculators. In others, they were offensive initiatives meant to pressure authorities for land reform. Since the latter category is the focus of this study, I will discuss it at much greater length later in the chapter. In many regions, rural activists sought to take control of local STRs and convert them into tools of class struggle. Although the combative, *cutista* unionism was primarily an urban movement, it had a substantial presence in the countryside (Ricci 1999; Houtzager 2005). The CONTAG leadership also claimed to espouse a progressive brand of unionism, but its tradition of legalism and largely conservative base of unions put it into conflict with the new, more leftist brand of unionism. The CONTAG thus opted to stay out of the CUT.

Catholic social activists were deeply involved in many of these movements, particularly those rooted mainly in popular sectors (Sader 1988; Mainwaring 1989; Doimo 1995). Many movement activists had got involved in activism by participating in the CEBS, youth groups, or other church-linked organizations. In the countryside, the CPT was particularly active and was a key force behind the union movement and struggles for land. Church leaders were in many cases also vigorous public defenders of social movements, giving them legitimacy and raising the political costs of repression.

Modernization and Economic Crisis

The years of military rule were a period of major socioeconomic changes. The late 1960s and 1970s brought a rapid economic expansion that elevated Brazil's international profile and led some to view it as a model of state-led industrialization in a less developed country. Although growth made Brazil richer, it deepened already profound social inequalities and set in motion jarring social transformations in both urban and, especially, rural areas. In the early 1980s, moreover, the years of rapid growth and job creation came to an abrupt halt with the onset of a brutal crisis characterized by economic stagnation, rising inflation, and a massive foreign-debt burden.

Besides eradicating the leftist threat, the major priority of new Brazilian leadership in 1964 was to revitalize the economy. Tough stabilization measures were the initial policy response, but gradually a longer-term strategy was elaborated that centered on expanding Brazil's industrial sector. Although this was to be accomplished, in part, by attracting foreign investment, the regime's economic planners were no liberals and state intervention deepened. Toward the end of the decade, as political space closed, the economy began to expand rapidly. During the "economic miracle" period of 1968–74 growth averaged more than 11 percent a year. The global oil crisis of 1973 sharply increased Brazil's import bill. Rather than adopting recessionary austerity measures, however, authorities chose to rely on foreign capital inflows. Despite some subpar years, the economy grew at an annual average of about 7 percent between 1975 and 1980 (Baer 1995, 382).

Growth brought economic and social change. Industry increased its share of the gross domestic product from 32.5 percent in 1964 to 39.5 percent in 1978. Despite a strong performance, agriculture's share shrank from 16.3 percent to 10.3 percent (Baer 2001, 462). Industry and service sectors also gained in their share of employment. Growth brought increasing prosperity. During the 1970s average family income increased by 89 percent (H. Hoffman 1989, 204). The poverty rate dropped by almost half. However, development was highly unequal and the concentration of income increased substantially (H. Hoffman 1989). In southern Brazil, where the landless movement would eventually erupt with greatest force, the rates of industrialization, income growth, and poverty reduction were all above the national average (H. Hoffman 1989; Baer 1995).

The agricultural sector and rural society underwent major transformations during the late 1960s and, especially, the 1970s. Although Castello Branco's agrarian reform initiative (described in the Introduction) ultimately failed, the regime's leadership accepted the critique of leftist and nationalist forces that Brazil's backward agricultural sector represented a barrier to industrialization (Sorj 1980). Outside São Paulo, productivity tended to be quite low. Brazil needed to increase agricultural exports, in order to boost foreign exchange earnings, and to increase domestic production of raw materials for industry.

These goals would be accomplished mainly by promoting more intensive land use through the incorporation of modern technologies, such as tractors and chemical fertilizers, and by promoting commercial crops. A series of new programs was introduced in pursuit of these ends. Clearly the most important involved subsidized credit. Government initiatives led to a threefold increase in total agricultural credit in the 1965–70 period and an additional fivefold increase during the 1970s. Credit was strongly skewed toward larger producers; the more developed regions; and certain crops, such as soybeans, wheat, and sugarcane.[3] The unequal distribution of credit was one of the central reasons why the distribution of agricultural income grew more concentrated during the 1970s (R. Hoffman 1988).

Technology incorporation advanced rapidly. The number of hectares of cultivated land per tractor dropped from 3,407 in 1960, to 1,483 in 1970, to 572 in 1980 (Graziano da Silva 1999, 93). Commercial crop production expanded swiftly in response to state incentives and strong international demand. Soybeans experienced the most impressive growth, with per capita production increasing from 3.9 kilos in the early 1960s to 103.4 kilos in the late 1970s (Martine 1987a, 82). Sugarcane also flourished. Its expansion had much to do with a federal program called Proálcool designed to ease adjustment to the 1973 oil shock by stimulating the production of ethanol-burning vehicles. After its launch in 1975, much of the sugarcane harvest was turned into ethanol.

In southern Brazil, where modernization was most intense, the major agricultural trend was the mercurial expansion of soybeans (Banck and Den Boer 1991). In 1965, soybeans accounted for less than 5 percent of total crop area in the region. By 1980, they occupied nearly 37 percent (Baer 2001, 360). In contrast, the proportion of crop area devoted to corn, beans, manioc, and coffee declined. Of the southern states, Paraná experienced by far the most rapid changes, as coffee and food crops quickly lost ground to soybeans and cattle (Carnasciali et al. 1987).[4] The South and Southeast continued to have the most modern agricultural sectors, but parts of the Center-West made gains, largely as a result of the soybean boom.

3. The overall concentration of credit is suggested by the fact that in 1975 only 14.4 percent of agricultural establishments received any official credit at all (Goodman 1989, 72).

4. Part of the reason for the dramatic changes in agriculture in Paraná was the severe frost of 1975, which devastated coffee trees and led many growers to turn (with state support) to soybeans or cattle.

While increasing the competitiveness of agriculture, these trends made access to farmland more difficult for people of modest means in the major agricultural regions (Graziano da Silva 1982; Goodman, Sorj, and Wilkinson 1984).[5] Technological change and the shift to commercial crops, which are generally less labor intensive, reduced the need for large permanent labor forces, accelerating the expulsion of resident wage workers and reducing the amount of land available to tenant farmers and sharecroppers.[6] Farm workers expelled from large *fazendas* often moved to nearby towns, where they continued to work at least part time as agricultural wage laborers (D'Incão e Mello 1975).[7] Federal policies also helped to limit land access through their impact on land prices. Plentiful credit, combined with strong demand for commodities, put upward pressure on the price of farmland (Reydon and Plata 1998). High land prices made it harder for rural people of modest means to purchase farmland for themselves or their children. The increasing commercialization of smallholder agricultural may also have helped to force some producers off their land by promoting unmanageable debt burdens (Goodman 1989).

Data from the federal government's agricultural census, displayed in Table 1, testify to these changes. In the most dynamic agricultural regions, the South and Southeast, the number of tenant farmers, sharecroppers, and squatters declined sharply. The number of independent (owner-operated) farms also shrank slightly. Wage labor, meanwhile, grew rapidly in every region. Wage workers boosted their share of the agricultural workforce from 15.0 percent to 23.3 percent. Larger farms came to control a bigger share of total farmland, bringing an increase in the Gini coefficient for landholding from 0.838 in 1970 to 0.852 in 1980 (Perz 2000).[8] The impact of modernization on land access contributed to an acceleration in

5. Two legal innovations, the 1963 Rural Worker Statute and the 1964 Land Statute, may have also contributed to these trends (Rezende 2006). By extending to resident workers certain legal rights, they inadvertently gave landowners an incentive to rely more heavily on nonresident labor.

6. Some traditional commercial crops, including coffee and cotton, also declined during this period. Ironically, these tended to be more labor intensive than the ones that expanded, especially soybeans.

7. The word *fazenda* refers to any large agricultural property.

8. The Gini coefficient is a measure of the level of inequality of the distribution of any good within a particular group. It ranges from 0, which represents perfect equality, to 1, which represents perfect inequality (i.e., one member of the group controls the entire supply of the good).

rural-urban migration.[9] The 1970s was the first decade since the national census began that the rural population fell in absolute terms. A decline in the fertility rate played a role in the decline, but it was mainly a result of migration. The number of people working in agriculture increased during the 1960s and 1970s, but at less than half the rate of the 1950s.[10] The slowdown occurred mainly during the second half of the 1970s.

As Table 1 shows, the South was the region most deeply affected by these changes, with every employment category but wage laborers suffering a decline. The South alone accounted for the entire net decline in sharecroppers at the national level and more than half the fall in tenant farmers. It was also the only region in which the number of independent farms fell. Wage workers, in contrast, grew in number and increased their share of the regional workforce from 9.8 percent to 15.9 percent. The Gini coefficient for land increased from 0.716 to 0.735 (Perz 2000). The South also experienced the most intense rural exodus (Goodman 1989, 66). The agricultural workforce grew more slowly than the national rate and actually shrank during the second half of the 1970s. These trends were driven mainly by Paraná, which lost 13.1 percent of its labor force in 1975–80. Ironically, rural Paraná had been Brazil's major agricultural frontier as recently as the early 1960s, attracting tens of thousands of migrants.

Despite increases in land inequality, social conditions in agriculture improved during the 1970s. R. Hoffman (1988), for example, finds a decline in the poverty rate among people active in agriculture from 81.4 percent

Table 1 Social changes in agriculture, 1970–1980 (%)

Region	Tenant Farmers	Sharecroppers	Independent Farms	Squatters	Wage Laborers
North	− 15.0	54.6	88.6	49.1	223.9
Northeast	3.5	12.0	15.1	5.5	110.5
Center-West	− 17.5	18.1	16.5	− 18.5	153.4
Southeast	− 28.5	− 18.2	0.8	− 12.1	55.1
South	− 27.3	− 35.6	− 1.8	− 13.9	69.1
Brazil	− 8.1	− 16.2	9.6	6.6	86.8

Source: IBGE 1970, 1980.

9. During the 1950s, the exodus had been equivalent to 24 percent of the 1950 rural population. For the 1960s, this figure was 36 percent; and for the 1970s, 42 percent (Merrick 1989, 40).

10. The rates of growth were 41 percent in the 1950s, 14 percent in the 1960s, and 20 percent in the 1970s (IBGE 1960, 1970).

to 59.5 percent (37). He also finds large increases in both the average and median incomes for all categories of workers, including employers, wage workers and family farmers. In southern Brazil, poverty in agriculture declined from 65.8 percent to 42.3 percent of the workforce, and both average and median incomes increased strongly for all categories (35–37). São Paulo, the state with the most modern agriculture, had similar outcomes (R. Hoffman 1993).

Why did "conservative modernization," as scholars termed the changes in Brazilian agriculture during the 1970s, not result in more unfavorable welfare impacts, especially in the regions where it was most intense? Perhaps the most important reason was the dynamism of the urban economy. With growth averaging close to 10 percent annually in a predominantly nonagricultural economy, the expansion of work opportunities in the cities during the late 1960s and 1970s absorbed many of the people marginalized from agriculture. The rural exodus, in other words, was driven by not only the push factor of agricultural change, but also the pull of urban jobs and the higher wages available in the cities.

Two other factors, both having to do with agriculture, were also important. One was the robust growth of wage labor, driven by the strong expansion of commercial farming, especially during the 1970s. Erstwhile tenants, sharecroppers, and squatters in many cases became permanent or seasonal wage workers. The average income among wage laborers also increased (R. Hoffman 1988). The other was the opening up of vast new agricultural areas, particularly in the Amazon basin. This phenomenon helped to compensate for diminished popular land access in older regions and largely accounts for the net increases in farms and, especially, squatter holdings during the 1970s.

The penetration of the Amazon deserves a bit more attention because of its centrality to criticisms of the regime's policies for the rural sector. Military authorities sought to accelerate the occupation of the Amazon basin in order to exploit its natural resources and solidify the country's claims to its massive share of this region.[11] Beginning in 1966 they offered generous tax incentives to those willing to invest in agriculture, mining, or industry in the North and neighboring areas of the Center-West and Northeast. Road-building efforts also accelerated, opening up access to the region. These initiatives helped provoke the rapid growth of large cattle ranches. In 1970

11. Military leaders were concerned that if Brazil did not occupy its part of the Amazon, foreign countries would try to seize it or place it under international control.

President Médici launched another Amazon initiative, aimed at settling landless people from other parts of Brazil in colonization projects on public land. The National Institute for Colonization and Agrarian Reform (INCRA), was created to implement it, and a new road cutting across the Amazon forest was built to facilitate it. The poetic motto of the program, "A land without men for men without land," contrasted with its prosaic reality. Public colonization efforts, which were never really massive, slowed after 1973. However, state-subsidized private colonization, mainly in the Center-West, accelerated toward the end of the decade.

Amazon colonization benefited a fairly limited number of people.[12] However, the government's rhetoric about land distribution, combined with its development initiatives, helped to provoke a flood of immigrants. More prosperous newcomers, mainly from the South, often sold small farms in their home states to buy much larger ones on the frontier.[13] Although some eventually returned home, discouraged by poor soils and infrastructure, many stuck it out and a few got rich, mainly by planting soybeans (Wagner 1995). Poorer immigrants from the Northeast and other regions worked as wage laborers or established squatter holdings on what they took to be public land. Combined, the North and Center-West experienced a 68.1 percent increase in their agricultural workforce and a 47.3 percent increase in the amount of land in farms during the 1970s (IBGE 1970, 1980).

At the same time as it provided a new source of land, the advance of the agricultural frontier brought conflict and violence (Martins 1981; Schmink and Wood 1992). Federal policies provoked a land rush in which poor squatters, known as *posseiros,* competed against large landowners or land-grabbers for control over public lands. These last two groups were assisted by hired gunmen, and their claims were generally favored by the state. In many cases, *posseiros* were unceremoniously evicted from their holdings. They did not necessarily take attempts to expel them lying down, and armed conflicts multiplied.

Foreign capital inflows had allowed the Brazilian economy to continue expanding rapidly throughout the 1970s. That expansion came to a crashing halt, however, in the early 1980s. The new global oil price spike of 1979 increased Brazil's import bill markedly and a sharp rise in international

12. In all, colonization directly benefited between 70,000 and 159,000 families through 1980 (Ozorio de Almeida 1992, 92).

13. Many other rural southerners went to Paraguay, where the government was advertising the availability of farmland (Wagner 1995).

interest rates raised the costs of making payments on its foreign debt. Fearing a default, foreign banks became hesitant to make new loans. Forced to service an enormous debt under adverse international conditions, Brazilian authorities adopted fiscal and monetary austerity. From 1981 to 1983, Brazil suffered through negative GDP growth, rising inflation, and massive unemployment (Baer 2001, chap. 6).

Agricultural-sector growth slowed from an average of 4.8 percent in 1971–80 to 2.4 percent in 1981–83 (Baer 1995, table A2), reflecting the impact of sharp cuts in the state's generous credit policy and sluggish demand. Despite these problems, growth in the agricultural labor force revived. The pace of expansion in 1980–85 was more than double the 1975–80 rate. Small farming operations accounted for most of the increase, with sharecropper holdings and independent farms increasing substantially in number. Although wage laborers increased slightly in absolute terms, their share of the total workforce declined from 23 percent to 21.5 percent (Umbelino de Oliveira 1991). A common interpretation of these shifts was that small-scale agriculture was serving as a kind of refuge for poor people of rural origin by absorbing labor released from other activities (Martine 1991).

Although agriculture's attractiveness relative to other sectors may have increased, social conditions in this sector did not. Indexes of overall land concentration remained stable or even improved because small farms increased their share of the total quantity of cultivated land. However, the influx of people into the small farming sector outstripped the increase in land held by this category. As a result, the average size of both small and very small holdings declined at a much faster rate than during the 1970s.[14] In other words, the renewed growth of the agricultural labor force provoked by the recession served to increase land scarcity among people of modest means. Poverty in the agricultural sector also grew, from 69.9 percent to 72.7 percent of the labor force between 1981 and 1984 (R. Hoffmann 1988, 46).[15]

In southern Brazil, social trends in agriculture mainly paralleled those at the national level: the workforce experienced renewed growth, with ten-

14. The average size of holdings under 50 hectares declined from 11.0 hectares to 10.9 hectares in 1970–80, then dropped to 10.3 hectares during the 1980–85 period. The average size of holdings of less than 5 hectares fell from 3.6 hectares to 3.5 hectares during the 1970s, dropping to 3.3 hectares in 1985.

15. These data do not include the North region.

ants, sharecroppers, and squatters all increasing in number. At the same time, the average size of small and very small holdings fell. The average small (< 50 hectares) holding, for example, dropped from 12.9 to 12.5 hectares in Paraná, from 14.7 to 14.1 hectares in Rio Grande do Sul, and from 15.2 to 14.2 hectares in Santa Catarina. In each state the reduction was faster than in the 1970s.

Like the economy, frontier expansion slowed in the early part of the 1980s. The amount of land in agricultural establishments in the North and Center-West combined increased by only 4.3 percent in 1980–85, compared with the 47.8 percent increase of the preceding decade. Much of the land made accessible by the feverish road construction and development initiatives of previous decades had already been occupied by cattle ranchers, small farmers, and land speculators (Schmink and Wood 1992; Perz 2000). One of the major escape valves for relieving land pressures was thus being closed.

Mobilizing for Land in the South

In many areas of Brazil, landless workers began mobilizing to pressure for land reform during the late 1970s and early 1980s, but it was in the South that landless movement activity was most intense, with larger protest actions and a much more extensive organizational network. In other regions, the movement tended to be more localized and spontaneous. It was the southern movement, moreover, that was primarily responsible for introducing an innovative tactical approach and providing the impetus behind the formation of the MST, which would play a central role in diffusing that approach nationally.

Protest for land reform in the South first showed signs of intensifying in Rio Grande do Sul, stimulated by a conflict between Indians and squatters. Activists linked to the Catholic Church sought to channel the resulting demands for land access into political activity. After some initial victories, their efforts resulted in a major showdown with authorities. Because it demonstrated the support available for those who would struggle for agrarian reform, the conflict at Encruzilhada Natalino helped to spark mobilization throughout the southern region. Church social activists were again at the forefront of these efforts, recruiting the landless, training potential activists, and knitting together local groups into a broader network. Although its social base was diverse, the movement arose mainly among the *colônias,* or smallholder communities established through European immigration.

Successful Land Occupations

In May 1978, residents of the Nonoai Indian Reservation, located in the Alto Uruguai region of northwestern Rio Grande do Sul, expelled about one thousand nonindigenous families who had been working their land for years. Two months after the expulsion, a group of these families occupied two adjoining *fazendas* in the Alto Uruguai owned by the state government but leased to private firms. The area had been the site of a conflict involving the MASTER during the 1960s, and some of the workers involved had been active in that movement (Wagner 1988, 58). The occupations were poorly organized and had little external support, and the families were forced off the property by police. Authorities eventually offered the Nonoai families land in colonization projects in distant Mato Grosso. About half accepted; the rest wanted land in Rio Grande do Sul. One group set up a camp in the state fair grounds near the capital, Porto Alegre. Authorities eventually responded by settling 128 families on state-owned property.

At about the same time, a group of activists linked to the CPT began to organize meetings with the families who remained, to try to find a solution to their problem. The group included a local parish priest, an employee of the state Secretariat of Agriculture, a PMDB activist, and a sociology professor. The state employee, João Pedro Stedile, would soon become part of the CPT's national leadership and, later, the most influential leader of the MST. The priest, Arnildo Fritzen, had helped found the Rio Grande do Sul CPT chapter in 1977 and was one of a number of clergy in the state who were implementing the mandates of Medellín by organizing CEBS and encouraging people to try to change their society (Carter 2002, chap. 2). The activists told the families that, contrary to what government officials were claiming, there was actually plenty of fallow land within the state that could be used for settlement. Authorities would not hand it over without a fight, though, so they needed to get organized (Torrens 1991).

In 1979, the families began a campaign to pressure authorities for land. In early September, about two hundred families entered the same two properties occupied earlier, the Macali and Brilhante, and erected a camp of wooden huts, much like those set up by the MASTER a decade and a half earlier. With the help of the CPT, the occupation had been orchestrated to attract media attention and gain public sympathy. Prior negotiations with authorities suggested that state government might respond positively (Wagner 1988). Police threatened to expel the families, but the women and children formed a protective cordon around the camps, and the police eventually backed off. State authorities promised to grant the families land of their own in short order.

Other, apparently less successful, occupations occurred in the region later in 1979 and 1980 (Torrens 1991; Fernandes 1999). The CPT continued its organizational campaign, and its meetings were beginning to attract people other than the Nonoai families. Working with CPT activists, the landless sought material support from local mayors, STRS, and churches and traveled to the capital to pressure the governor, the state legislature, and the INCRA (Torrens 1991, 11). In November, a group of landless from the Macali and Brilhante occupations set up a camp in the central square of Porto Alegre to demand that the state speed up settlement of the families. Authorities promised to do so and, by the end of 1980, these camps had become legal settlements (Wagner 1988, 63).

Protest for land reform spread north to the western end of neighboring Santa Catarina in 1980. In May, a small group of local landless families occupied a large *fazenda* known as Burro Branco, rumored to be the target of a future INCRA expropriation. Within a few weeks the number of families involved had swelled to more than three hundred. Although the original group of families had organized the occupation by themselves, CPT activists soon arrived to support them (Fernandes 1999). The progressive church was already strong in the region, largely because of Bishop José Gomes, based in the region's main city, Chapecó. Gomes had begun promoting participation in Bible study and youth groups years earlier. Catholic activists collected donations of food for the occupiers, helped them organize themselves, and accompanied them in negotiations with authorities. CPT lawyers fought against the landlord's attempt to have the landless expelled and applied political pressure on authorities to expropriate the property. In November, the INCRA did expropriate Burro Branco and promised to settle the families occupying it.

Encruzilhada Natalino

These initial gains helped to encourage continued activism for land in both states, but the scope and intensity of this process would increase as a result of a protest initiative that occurred in the Alto Uruguai in 1981. Early that year, encouraged by the CPT, landless families began setting up wooden huts at the intersection of two roads in the *município* of Ronda Alta, not far from Nonoai (Carter 2002). By the end of May, the number of families in the camp at Encruzilhada Natalino had swelled to around six hundred, or about two thousand people. Some were from the Nonoai group, but most were not. Counseled by the CPT, the families demanded land in their own state. Authorities said that in Rio Grande do Sul, with its modern agriculture, there was no longer any farmland to distribute. Instead, they offered them land on the frontier. The campers rejected the offer. Plenty of land could be found in their state. Moreover, they insisted, under the 1964 Land Statue, they had a right to it.

Clergy and lay activists began playing a central role in organizing and supporting the camp (Marcon 1997). Local priests came regularly to celebrate mass. Bishops linked to the CPT traveled from distant states to express their support. They told the campers to trust in their faith to see them through the ordeal. CPT activists and sympathetic clergy helped to organize material, political, and moral support for the effort in their parishes and among progressive groups in civil society. The CPT also played a central role in the internal organization of the camp, seeing to it that they reflected their own principals of broad participation and collective leadership (Zamberlam and Froncheti 1993). Following their advice, the families broke into small groups and elected a commission to serve as the camp's leadership. They also organized commissions to deal with specific issues, such as food, health, and prayer. Reflecting the influence of religion, a large wooden cross became the symbol of the camp's struggle.

Support for the camp was by no means limited to religious groups, however. Rio Grande do Sul is one of the most progressive states in Brazil, and all manner of activist groups, from labor unions to human rights groups, also began supporting the campers materially and politically (Marcon 1997). Out-of-state groups also offered support and encouragement. A committee was formed to support the camp, and a secretariat was set up in Porto Alegre, staffed by political activists, students, and seminarians. It began to publish a regular newsletter with articles on the camp and the land issue.[16] In July, some ten thousand people gathered for a rally at the camp.

16. Interview with Flademir Araújo, former editor of the newsletter called the *Boletim Sem Terra*, March 5, 1998, Porto Alegre, RS. Araújo, a PMDB activist and an employee of the

Press coverage referred to the families as the *colonos sem terra*, and sometimes characterized the camp as an extension of the old MASTER. It thus helped to revive a social identity, that of the *sem terra*, a rural worker struggling to return to the land. Although *sem terra* simply means "landless" and is commonly used to describe rural workers who do not have land of their own, the term had acquired a broader meaning in Rio Grande do Sul as a result of the MASTER. A *sem terra* is not just a rural proletarian, but a small farmer by origin and culture, who has been deprived of the one resource that is essential to his or her livelihood. In a sense, this term expresses the idea that rural workers should have land of their own and have the right to fight for it. The struggle in Ronda Alta helped to revive this concept and to disseminate it beyond Rio Grande do Sul.

Events appeared to take a turn for worse at the end of July, when military forces, led by an officer famed for his expertise in rural counterinsurgency, arrived to demobilize the camp. The soldiers physically isolated the campers and began using carrot-and-stick tactics to convince them to abandon the effort and, instead, accept land on the frontier. They also tried to intimidate local clergy who supported the campers, threatening to arrest them under the notorious Law of National Security (Wagner 1988).

However, the monthlong occupation did not bring the results desired by the authorities. Although many families did leave, most remained firm. Moreover, the military initiative backfired in terms of public relations, provoking an intensification of public support for Encruzilhada Natalino. The *gaúcho* bishops, who were initially somewhat divided over the camp, came together in solidarity with the campers (Goes 1997).[17] Other groups redoubled their efforts to help the landless. Media coverage of the effort broadened and news of Encruzilhada Natalino began to appear in the national media. The camp became, like the ABC strikes of the late 1970s, a symbol of resistance to the regime.

Authorities continued to refuse the campers' demand for settlement in Rio Grande do Sul. However, in early 1982, the state's bishops led a fundraising campaign that allowed them to purchase an agricultural property in Ronda Alta to serve as a provisional settlement. The state government would settle the families only in 1983 and 1984, but the church's action was a symbolically important partial victory for the landless cause.

State Assembly during the period discussed in this chapter, had been involved in the CPT's efforts to provide political support for landless workers since 1979.

17. *Gaúcho* is a term used to refer to people and things from Rio Grande do Sul.

Diffusion Accelerates

Encruzilhada Natalino helped accelerate the landless movement's diffusion in the South by forcefully demonstrating the support available in civil society and public opinion for those willing to struggle for land reform in their own state.[18] The episode galvanized the CPT and other groups interested in forwarding the cause of agrarian reform in the South. This was especially clear in Rio Grande do Sul, where the CPT redoubled its efforts to recruit activists, giving rise to a much broader and more intense process of organization and recruitment of landless families (Torrens 1991). The *gaúcho* CPT itself underwent important transformations during this period, benefiting from a major influx of new activists and greater support from the state's Catholic bishops, now more fully committed to the cause of land reform (Goes 1997).

Ruscheinsky suggests that Encruzilhada Natalino, more than the Burro Branco occupation, also pushed forward the process of organizing the landless movement in neighboring Santa Catarina (Ruscheinsky 1989). He quotes an activist involved in the movement during that period:

> It's beginning with Ronda Alta that the movement really begins to get structured. Earlier, there was the case of the Fazenda Burro Branco, but that did not provoke a process. Now, Ronda Alta, that unleashed a process of struggle for land in the South and showed that this was no paradise for smallholders, as was being argued. The South had land problems, which the government tried to send to Mato Grosso, and there also existed land conflicts and landless. This provoked the organization of the movement. (Ruscheinsky 1989, 68)

As a result, CPT activists, combative union leaders, and some of the settlers who had gained land on the former *fazenda* Burro Branco began to meet and map out a plan of organization and mobilization of landless families.

To the north, in Paraná, Encruzilhada Natalino also seems to have stimulated a process of mobilization. Paraná was colonized more recently than the rest of the South and in the 1970s its landholding structure was still not wholly consolidated. As a result, the state experienced more land con-

---

18. Interview with Carlos Wagner, veteran reporter for the Porto Alegre–based newspaper *Zero Hora*, September 4, 1999, Porto Alegre, RS.

flicts than Rio Grande do Sul or Santa Catarina. These conflicts usually involved attempts by squatters and tenant farmers to resist expulsion. Land occupations also occurred prior to the late 1970s, but these were usually small, isolated events lacking much prior organization or external support.

In southwestern Paraná, the CPT had been heavily involved since 1978 in aiding smallholders whose properties were being seized to implement the huge Itaipu hydroelectric dam project. Rural union activists were also involved in this campaign, which resulted in a substantial organizational network. In mid-1981, as Encruzilhada Natalino was attracting national attention, CPT leaders in this region decided to advertise on the radio to determine the level of local demand for land reform. The results were impressive: within days, hundreds of families had expressed interest. As a result, the CPT decided to dedicate itself to organizing landless families in the region to press for land reform.

CPT activists in the South did not limit their efforts to their own states. The leadership of the CPT's southern regional division, which brings together the three states of the South, plus neighboring Mato Grosso do Sul and São Paulo, began in 1982 to promote a broader, parallel process of organization at the regional and national level. This process would eventually result in the foundation of the MST, in 1984.

Social Base

In all three states of the South, the movement emerged mainly in "colonial" regions, where small, owner-operated farms predominate and much of the population is of Italian, German, or Polish extraction. Not surprisingly, many of the people who joined the movement were of *colono* stock (Stival 1987; Franco 1992; Zamberlam and Froncheti 1993). In some cases their families owned farms but did not have enough land to divide between all their children. Many of these were still living with their parents when they decided to enter the movement. In others cases, participants came from families that had already lost access to land. Members of both groups often worked as tenant farmers, sharecroppers, or agricultural wage laborers. Some had worked in urban areas, generally in blue-collar jobs, and a few had returned from colonization projects on the frontier.

Nonetheless, the movement was by no means wholly constituted by *colonos*. Studies of landless camps and settlements show that, at least in some areas, individuals and families not of traditional *colono* ethnic origin were present in large numbers. These people, often referred to as *caboclos,* or *brasileiros,* tended to be poorer and darker skinned and to lack a history of landowning. *Caboclos* generally occupied a rather marginal position in southern smallholder communities, often working as wage laborers, a type of employment smallholding families avoided if they could. They were basically the same class of landless and land-poor rural workers present in many areas of Brazil.

The largest surveys of the settlers and campers in the South during the 1980s indicate that about half the movement's social base was made up of *brasileiros.* One study of eight land reform settlements in Rio Grande do Sul found that 53.9 percent of the settlers characterized themselves as *brasileiros* (Zamberlam and Florão 1989, 34). People of German extraction were next, at 21.7 percent, followed by those of Italian origin, at 21.4 percent. In an extensive survey of several landless camps in western Santa Catarina, almost half (47.2 percent) of the heads of family identified themselves as *luso,* a synonym for *brasileiro* (Ruscheinsky 1989, 128). Given that the movement was based mainly in smallholder-dominated areas, these data suggest that non-*colonos* may have been overrepresented relative to their weight in the rural population.

External Allies and Leadership

In the South, as in much of Brazil, the key actor in mobilizing the landless during the early 1980s was the CPT. Although Catholics clearly predominated, the CPT was officially ecumenical and in some areas Lutherans were also prominent.[19] The CPT brought together members of the clergy, seminarians, and laypeople. Most, but not all, CPT "pastoral agents" (as CPT activists were often called) appear to have been college or seminary educated and of middle-class origin; others were children of local small- and medium-holder families.[20] Other church-linked organizations also played a significant role in organizing the landless. These included the Youth Pastoral Service, a community outreach program connected to the CNBB, and a progressive Catholic nongovernmental organization (NGO) in southwestern Par-

19. The Lutheran Church has a strong presence in some areas of the southern countryside, a result of the substantial number of people of German descent in the *colônias.*

20. Interview with Friar Wilson Tallagnol, longtime CPT activist, March 4, 1998, Porto Alegre, RS.

aná called ASSESSOAR (Association for Rural Studies, Consultation, and Technical Assistance), founded by Belgian priests in the 1960s.

In some areas of the South, rural union leaders and leaders of union opposition movements also played an important role in organizing the movement.[21] These were rural workers themselves, usually smallholders. Union activism was itself often a consequence of earlier organizing work by the progressive church (Schmitt 1996). Activists from the CPT and other church groups were quite active in some areas during the late 1970s and early 1980s, organizing rural workers to try to take over conservative STRs.[22] Political parties as such did not play much of a direct role in the movement's emergence in the South. PMDB politicians contributed occasionally, making monetary contributions or granting access to public infrastructure. The PT, the party embraced by most Catholic activists, was still a relatively weak force, particularly in rural areas. Its expansion in the southern countryside accompanied that of the landless movement and the combative rural union movement, and involved many of the same activists.[23]

These organizations and the individuals linked to them played numerous roles in the movement. They mapped out strategies for organizing workers and dealing with authorities, the media, and other external actors. They identified potential leaders among the landless and invited them to participate in activist training workshops. They helped to recruit and organize landless families in local villages and municipalities. To facilitate recruitment and consciousness-raising, they published easy-to-read booklets justifying, often in religious terms, the need for land reform and other social changes. Clergy linked to the CPT and ASSESSOAR gave religious services in the movement's camps and during marches and demonstrations. Finally, these entities helped provide a variety of material resources, such as transportation; meeting infrastructure; and food, clothing, and medicine for campers.

Although these "advisors," as the religious and rural union activists were called, usually sought to help the landless take control of their own strug-

---

21. Interview with Adão Pretto, former leader of the STR in Miraguaí, RS, September 2, 1999, Porto Alegre, RS. Pretto played an important role in the formation of the landless movement in Rio Grande do Sul. He later became a federal deputy for the PT.

22. Schmitt finds that some 90 percent of *cutista* rural union activists in northwestern Rio Grande do Sul had been involved in progressive church organizations, such as the Youth Pastoral Service (Schmitt 1996, 195).

23. Interview with Angela Schwengber, a former MST militant from the Alto Uruguai, November 1997, São Paulo, SP.

gle, during the early going, by virtue of their experience, authority, and access to resources, they largely directed the movement.[24] As their numbers and experience increased, however, the landless began to take greater control. Despite the movement's heterogeneous social base, these were usually young men and women of *colono* stock. Some got involved in activism only after joining the movement for economic reasons, but many entered largely or wholly out of political conviction. For the latter, Catholic groups such as the Youth and Rural Pastorals usually served as bridges to activism within the landless movement.

Organization

The process of organizing the landless movement took one form in Rio Grande do Sul and Santa Catarina and another in Paraná. In the first two states, the movement emerged from an activist network concentrated in a particular region. A significant activist group was built up in each state in 1981 and 1982, resulting in the formation of a state landless commission in 1983 (Torrens 1991; Lisboa 1988). The mobilization of landless families was already proceeding in a number of *municípios* in each state, and this process accelerated after the formation of a state leadership structure. Activists traveled to rural villages and town centers, attempting to organize small groups, or "nuclei," of families, numbering no more than twenty. Where there were various groups in a *município*, each was represented on a *município*-wide landless commission. These, in turn, were represented on the state commission, composed of both landless workers and their advisors.

In Paraná, by contrast, a number of groups developed relatively independently in different regions of the state. The first arose in the western end of the state in the second half of 1981 and was called the Movement of Landless Rural Workers of Western Paraná (MASTRO). Others sprang up in 1982 and 1983, until there were four such organizations, with the strongest being the MASTRO and its counterpart in southwestern Paraná, the MASTER. As with the state landless commissions in Rio Grande do Sul and Santa Catarina, these entities sought to form local family groups and *município*-level landless commissions. The four regional groupings finally came together in mid-1984 to form a state organization.

24. Interview with David Stival, former CPT activist, March 16, 1998, Porto Alegre, RS.

Grassroots organizing efforts proceeded more rapidly in Paraná than in the other states. By the end of 1984, the movement was organized in several dozen *municípios,* compared with about thirty in Rio Grande do Sul and about eighteen in Santa Catarina (Lisboa 1988; Torrens 1991, 1992). In each state, a landless movement secretariat was eventually set up, staffed by advisors, landless individuals, and student volunteers. The secretariats served as nerve centers for the movement and as a link to external actors, such as the media and authorities. The earliest was in Rio Grande do Sul, where it was established in mid-1981 by the committee created to support the campers at Encruzilhada Natalino.

In addition to these local and state organizational structures, the southern movement had an emerging regional structure, fruit of the CPT's efforts to create a broader organization. In 1982 the CPT's southern regional division (composed of the three states of the South, plus neighboring Mato Grosso do Sul and São Paulo) began bringing together pastoral agents and workers in the states under its jurisdiction. During these meetings, agents and landless activists discussed the challenges and opportunities they faced and possible responses to them. In February 1983, they founded an entity called the Movement of Landless Workers of the Southern Region and formed a commission to lead it. Rio Grande do Sul's state secretariat in Porto Alegre became the regional secretariat and its newsletter the regional newsletter. Because it provided a forum for discussion between activists in different areas, this regional coordination encouraged a homogenization of organizational structures, such as family groups and *município* commissions (Görgen 1987).

Grassroots Recruitment

Grassroots recruitment of landless families all over the South took place mainly through small-group meetings in rural villages and town centers, in a process known by activists as "base work." The meetings were often organized with the help of a local clergy member, union leader, or sympathetic politician. They were held in a church, union hall, or community center. If local groups and authorities were uncooperative, they could be held in a private home. In some cases, activists drew on existing grassroots groups organized by local clergy, such as youth groups or "reflection groups," the usual southern term for CEB. Landless activists worked by themselves or with the help of an advisor and used pamphlets published by the CPT to support their arguments. Meetings were held regularly, once every few weeks or couple of months.

Since it was often organized by clergy or religious laypeople and took place in the context of a church or CEB, base work tended to have a strong religious flavor. Group discussions might begin with a Bible reading or prayer, and the need to struggle for land was often justified on the basis of scripture. After discussing the problems of local rural workers and identifying their structural roots, activists would ask, "Does God want it to be this way? If not, what can we do about it?"[25] The struggle for land was compared to Moses's trek across the desert in search of the "promised land." Agrarian reform was portrayed as a necessary step in the creation of an egalitarian "new society" that would embody Christian values (Lisboa 1988). The role of religion helped defuse potential ideological objections to the movement, undercutting accusations of its opponents that movement militants were dangerous "communists."[26]

Activists sought to frame landlessness as a collective problem, with roots in both long-standing social structures and elitist state policies. Land scarcity and other problems *colonos* were experiencing, they emphasized, were a result of modernization policies that systematically favored large producers. Rural workers who lacked land were not simply unfortunate or incompetent individuals, but rather *sem terra,* a class of people discriminated against by elites and the authoritarian state. Movement activists also underscored the absence of alternatives for rural workers who lacked land. By the early 1980s, some of the *colonos* who had migrated to frontier regions had returned. Their problems, related to poor soils, faulty infrastructure, distant markets, and disease, became an argument for rejecting the federal government's colonization offers. They also stressed the lack of opportunities for gainful employment in the cities, given the economic crisis and the relatively low educational level of most rural workers.

In attempting to legitimate political organization and protest, activists pointed out that the authoritarian state itself, through the 1964 Land Statute, had declared that large, fallow properties should be distributed to the landless. The *sem terra* had a legal right to land. By pressuring the government, they were merely asserting this right. Finally, the activists argued

25. Interview with Friar Wilson Tallagnol, longtime CPT activist, March 4, 1998, Porto Alegre, RS.

26. Interview with Darci Maschio, MST activist and member of the first Rio Grande do Sul state landless commission, March 10, 1998, Ronda Alta, RS.

that, politically speaking, the time was ripe to press for change. They pointed out that recent attempts to push for land reform in the South had resulted in concessions and a warm public reception. The regime was losing support and, at least in Rio Grande do Sul and Paraná, the new state authorities had made promises of distributing land.

Movement Tactics

Although there was some variation in the tactical approaches employed by the landless movement across the South, there was also a certain basic similarity. This resulted in large measure from the common origins of the movement in the progressive church and the fact that the CPT southern region and, later, the Movement of Landless Workers of the Southern Region provided a broader forum for pastoral agents and landless workers to discuss their experiences and exchange ideas.

In most cases, demands for land reform were initially presented to authorities in a "civilized" fashion, through letters, meetings, or petitions. Municipal and regional assemblies of landless workers were also used to demonstrate the movement's force and the extent of demand for land. Marches and demonstrations also occurred on a number of occasions. If these more pacific tactics did not yield results within a reasonable period, more confrontational tactics were often considered. With regard to the latter, by the end of 1984 a certain consensus was beginning to emerge around a tactical approach referred to as *acampar*, or "to camp," which involved a combination of land occupations and roadside encampments. This approach would be consolidated in the second half of the 1980s and become the core of the landless movement's tactical repertoire.

Camping generally began with a land occupation.[27] Weeks or months before the actual occupation, landless activists would begin conducting research on rural properties in a particular region. They generally sought properties that belonged to the state government, were vulnerable to expropriation, or were in the process of being expropriated.[28] Under the Bra-

27. What landless activists and sympathizers termed "occupations" were called "invasions" by critics of this tactic, including landowners, conservative politicians, and much of the press.

28. The rationale for occupying a property in the process of expropriation was twofold. First, it helped to ensure that the process of expropriation would go forward, rather than being blocked by landowner pressure or bureaucratic obstruction. Second, it allowed the families involved to stake a personal claim to the property, which might otherwise be distributed to the clients of a local politician.

zilian Constitution, only federal authorities could expropriate private land. However, state governments sometimes owned significant quantities of rural land, and in some cases they could also be pressured into purchasing land to supply to the landless. Well before the day of the occupation, the family groups participating in base work were advised by militants to begin preparing. They would need to gather materials for creating a simple shanty; obtain food and other provisions for several weeks; and secure some form of transportation, often a rented truck. For security reasons, they were not told where the occupation would take place, and they often did not know precisely when it would happen until a day or two before.

Occupations generally occurred late at night to avoid detection. They involved anywhere from twenty to a few hundred families. Occupations were truly a family affair: men, women, and children were expected to participate. This made repression more difficult and was useful for propaganda purposes, demonstrating to the public that the men were "family men" and not criminals or vagrants. Once the families had cut the fence and entered the property, they would set up their shanties, generally made of a wooden or bamboo frame draped with black plastic sheeting.[29] They would be clustered together in a single camp. Crude lavatories would be constructed and, time allowing, perhaps a dispensary and a large tent for meetings.

In many cases, the families were expelled from the occupied property. An expulsion usually resulted when the landowner petitioned a local judge for an expulsion order. When granted, such an order would be carried out by the Military Police, which (its name notwithstanding) is controlled by the government of each state. Depending on the perceived disposition of authorities, the landless sometimes used this moment to bargain. If authorities would offer certain concessions, the landless might agree to leave the occupation without delay and without offering resistance. Such concessions usually included a written commitment to settle the families within a specified time frame or to provide them with food while they remained camped, or both.

Authorities often wanted families to return to their homes. It became customary to refuse this demand; the families stayed camped until they gained land or gave up trying. Once expelled, they would set up their camp

---

29. The sheeting was common in rural areas of the South, where it was used to shield crops from harsh weather conditions.

elsewhere, typically on the side of a public road. There, they would await settlement or an opportunity to mount a new occupation, of either the same property or a different one. The camp served as a living symbol of the land problem, visible to the public and media. It also functioned as a constant threat of a land occupation, which troubled authorities and local elites. The tactic thus served to exert continuous, if low-intensity, political pressure.

The internal structure of the camps followed the same basic model used at Encruzilhada Natalino. Leadership was exercised collectively, through commissions, and other commissions were organized to take care of specific issues. Rotation in leadership positions was encouraged to foment broad participation. Personalistic leadership was to be avoided; the camp had no president or chief, but rather a set of elected representatives. Advised by movement activists, the campers settled on a disciplinary code, which usually prohibited quarreling, drinking, beating children, and failing to participate in camp activities. At least one member of a family had to remain in the camp at all times. Campers were expected to adhere to the code rather rigidly, and they could be expelled if they did not.

While the camping process was first and foremost a political pressure tactic, it could also have a transformative impact on the people participating in it. Case studies of landless camps suggest that shared hardship and exposure to repression and public prejudice tended to engender, at least for a time, feelings of group solidarity and a stronger sense of class consciousness (Stival 1987; Franco 1992; Schmitt 1992). Although the camps were certainly not free of internal conflict, participants often established ties of trust and affection. They also began to see themselves as *sem terra*, a class of people excluded and maligned by society. Activists sought to encourage this process and to give it religious significance. Again, the story of the Exodus was frequently used as a metaphor. The personal transformations wrought in the camping stage encouraged continued involvement in the movement, even after the land was won. Participants in a number of settlements established in the South during the emergence period "liberated" one or more of their number to function as full-time activists in the movement. Other settlers would work a liberated activist's land and provide him or her with a share of the revenues.

Camping is best understood as a creative synthesis of existing movement tactics. There is, of course, hardly an older movement tactic than that of land occupation. The tactic of camping had been popularized by the MASTER in the 1960s and was probably familiar to rural activists throughout the South. However, the MASTER had generally refrained from land occupations, preferring to camp next to properties it wanted authorities to expropriate (Eckert 1984). MASTER families, moreover, usually returned to their homes as soon as authorities had taken their names and promised them land. In fact, landless activists were generally critical of the MASTER, on the grounds that it was subservient to Governor Brizola and lacked a radical political consciousness.

The frequency with which occupations and camps were used during this period varied from state to state. In Rio Grande do Sul, after the early flurry of activity in the 1978–81 period, there were few occurrences until 1984, when the newly formed MST launched its first offensive in the state. In Santa Catarina, after the Burro Branco occupation, the emphasis was also placed mainly on mobilization and organization. In Paraná, by contrast, there were numerous occupations in the early 1980s (Torrens 1992). Some were tied to the emerging church-centered activist network, but others were more isolated efforts.

Why the South?

That the landless movement emerged with greatest intensity in southern Brazil is ironic, given that this region boasted the most equitable landowning structure. Probably the most common explanation is that the stronger tradition of popular landownership in the South made the deterioration of land access a greater threat to established social and cultural traditions in this region than in others (Stedile and Fernandes 1999; Wolford 2003). In other words, though often better off economically, the southern landless experienced greater relative deprivation than their counterparts in other regions because of the unusual strength of ties to the land in the South.

This argument probably holds considerable truth: the southern expression *sem terra* embodied the idea that rural workers should have land of their own. Nevertheless, the importance of this factor can easily be exaggerated. As I noted, a substantial proportion of the movement's social base in the South was made up of people from a nonsmallholder tradition. In fact, *caboclos* may well have been overrepresented in landless camps relative to their weight in the rural population. Just as important as ties to the land in shaping the movement's southern roots were other factors, especially rapid agricultural change, a favorable political opportunity structure, and strong grassroots organizational capacity.

As discussed earlier in the chapter, the social changes wrought by agricultural modernization during the 1970s were particularly deep in southern Brazil. Paraná was clearly the extreme case. In a few short years, tens of thousands of former sharecroppers, tenant farmers, and squatters in this state were left without access to land. Their plight made them available for recruitment into the landless movement. It is largely for this reason that the movement grew more rapidly in Paraná than in any other state. Rio Grande do Sul also experienced substantial declines in sharecroppers and tenant farmers, reflecting the rapid process of mechanization and the rise of soybeans.

The South also provided a relatively propitious political opportunity context for the movement. It is no coincidence that Rio Grande do Sul, the state with the best claim to being the cradle of the movement, has long been one of Brazil's most progressive. The strength of reform-oriented forces contributed in an important way to the movement's growth in this state, as was evident during the conflict at Encruzilhada Natalino, when unions, churches, and other allies of the landless put pressure on authorities to back down from their confrontational stance. In Paraná and Santa Catarina, progressive forces were not as strong. Nonetheless, both states were a far cry from most of northern and northeastern Brazil, where the dominance of conservative elites linked to agriculture went largely unchallenged. In these regions attempts to organize rural workers were often met with deadly violence, which almost always went unpunished.[30]

With regard to their organizational capacity, the southern landless benefited from the unusual strength of preexisting social networks in the southern colônias. These communities were (and to some extent still are) well known for their rich associative life. In much of Brazil, rural towns and villages were often dominated by landowners and allied elites, and civil society was weak. In contrast, the more equitable smallholder-dominated communities of southern Brazil were characterized by strong associative tendencies and participatory institutions, especially churches (Navarro 1996a, 1996b). Youths in smallholder villages were expected to "participate in the community," by joining church groups, unions, sports teams, and so

30. It is telling that, despite being the center of the movement for land reform, the South had easily the lowest number of murders related to rural conflict of any region during the 1979–84 period (Umbelino de Oliveira 1999, 31).

on (Franco 1992). This associative life was an organizational resource for the movement. Landless workers could be recruited through existing institutions, and many rural villages were already characterized by strong ties of group solidarity and a wealth of community leaders.

In addition, the movement's organizational strength in the South probably reflected the impact of another indigenous resource: the somewhat higher level of literacy among rural workers in this region, especially those of *colono* stock (Navarro 1995). A higher level of literacy facilitated pastoral agents' attempts to politicize landless workers and, especially, to form a solid indigenous leadership base with the ability to cope effectively with the myriad practical tasks involved in organizing a major social movement.

The importance of these resources is evidenced in the different roles assumed by *colonos* and *brasileiros* within the southern movement. Although the latter frequently joined the movement, they appear to have been largely absent from its leadership. In my research in Rio Grande do Sul I found that virtually the entire leadership of the landless movement was of *colono* origin. *Caboclos* were also widely seen as trying to avoid engagement in collective activities when possible and were therefore labeled "individualistic" or derided as "lumpen" (Benincá 1987; Franco 1992; Zimmerman 1994). These patterns may reflect ethnic discrimination on the part of *colonos*. However, they probably also have to do with the peculiar strength of horizontal social ties in *colono* communities and the relatively high level of education, both of which encouraged community involvement and favored the development of leadership skills.

The Landless Movement in Other Regions

While the mobilization of rural workers to press for agrarian reform was most intense and well organized in the South, it was by no means limited to that region. What I have defined as the landless movement appeared in diverse social settings, but it tended to be more sustained and organized in the more developed regions, particularly the Southeast. It was also in these regions that, in terms of tactics, it most resembled the southern movement, employing not only occupations, but also other protest tactics, such as roadside camps and, occasionally, marches and demonstrations. In other regions, it was often limited to land occupations. However, even where the pressure tactics involved resembled those of the South, the movement

generally lacked the cohesion and extensive organization that characterized the southern movement.

Land occupations also arose in some more backward areas, located
mainly in the Amazon basin, that had recently constituted the agricultural
frontier, but were now coming under the control of large landowners. In
these areas, landless rural families had traditionally established themselves
on unclaimed land, practicing a largely slash-and-burn-type agriculture.
Church activists had been heavily involved in trying to help these families
avoid eviction by the increasingly numerous landowners and land grabbers,
or *grileiros*. During the late 1970s and early 1980s, workers in these regions
sometimes moved toward more organized occupations, aimed at pushing
federal authorities to expropriate the land. These struggles generally took
place in remote areas and did not involve other, more public protest tactics.
Rather than appealing to public opinion, occupiers often sought to resist
landowners and police through brute force. More often than not, authorities responded only when deadly violence had occurred or was threatening
to happen.

Southeast

One of the earliest significant episodes of landless mobilization arose in the
Baixada Fluminense area of Rio de Janeiro state, not far from the city of
Rio de Janeiro, Brazil's second largest. There, in late 1978, former rural
union activists who had been involved in an intense land struggle before
1964 resumed their efforts, this time with the help of Catholic activists.
This group mounted several occupations of fallow properties in the region.
The largest, in 1984, brought together close to six hundred families. Many
of the families involved in these actions were urban shantytown dwellers,
although even these tended to be of rural origin. They scored a number of
substantial victories, but the movement failed to spread beyond the local
area (Novicki 1994).

São Paulo also experienced substantial landless activism (Fernandes
1996). Land occupations and camps began to appear with some frequency
after 1983, when a PMDB governor came to office and promised to use public
land for agrarian reform. Movement activity emerged independently in various parts of the state. In the urban region of Campinas, mobilization for
land reform arose from a CEB-based activist network. Many of the families
involved had moved relatively recently from rural areas, but now found

themselves unemployed. In southeastern São Paulo, tenant farmers and sons of smallholders began organizing occupations of a huge property that belonged to the state but was leased to commercial producers. The families were aided by rural unionists and sympathetic Catholic clergy. Finally, in the Pontal do Paranapanema, a cattle ranching region in the southwestern corner of the state, PMDB activists organized a land occupation with some three hundred families, which drew mainly on construction workers unemployed after the completion of a hydroelectric dam in the region. These movements engaged in occupations, roadside camps, and (in the case of Campinas) demonstrations.

CPT activists in São Paulo worked to bring together local landless groups in various parts of the state and to link these efforts to the broader organizing campaign of the CPT in the southern region. Such efforts notwithstanding, the landless movement in this state was not as heavily influenced by the progressive church movement as it was in the South, where the strong role of the Catholic Church in smallholder communities helped give the CPT (and the landless movement) unusual force.

In the northeastern corner of the small state of Espirito Santo, unemployed agricultural wage laborers began to organize in 1983. Influenced by the CPT and combative unions, they began to shift the demands they made on the newly elected PMDB state government from unemployment benefits and jobs to land. They began to see themselves as *sem terra* (Bussinger 1994). The progressive church was very active in Espirito Santo and its efforts to organize rural workers helped to create a solidly organized local movement, with a substantial group of activists and strong links to combative rural unions. In this sense, the organizational process was reminiscent of that in the South, but there was a difference in that the movement's leadership maintained the hope that state authorities would make good on their agrarian reform promises and did not occupy land during this period.

Center-West

Landless mobilization was substantial in two states of the Center-West: Mato Grosso do Sul and Goiás. Both were dominated by extensive cattle ranching, although commercial farming was beginning to make major inroads, especially in Mato Grosso do Sul.

Mato Grosso do Sul, like São Paulo, was part of the CPT's southern region and the landless movement's development was influenced by events in the adjacent southern states. Like Paraná, Mato Grosso do Sul experienced rather frequent land-related conflicts during the late 1970s and early 1980s, some involving occupations. In the early 1980s, tenant farmers in the southern part of the state began organizing with the help of the CPT to avoid expulsion from large properties. At least one major land occupation grew out of this conflict. In about 1982 the CPT and rural union activists associated with it began trying to create a broader and more organized movement for land reform (Farias 1997). CPT activists based in the southern municipality of Glória de Dourados began to recruit landless families, most of them underemployed wage laborers or would-be tenant farmers with no land. They organized them into *município*-level landless commissions, as in the South.

With eleven such commissions formed, the CPT organized a broader meeting in late 1982, at which a state landless commission was elected. After attempting for more than a year to pressure authorities through pacific means they decided to occupy land. Settlers from the former *fazenda* Burro Branco in Santa Catarina arrived to help in the effort (Fernandes 1999, 61). In April 1984, several hundred families occupied a large private farm. Although they were quickly expelled, the families stayed together and mounted a camp on a property owned by the local Catholic diocese. A few months later, the state government purchased a farm to serve as a provisional settlement for the families. By the end of 1984, there were two other camps in the state (Farias 1997).

Catholic clergy in Goiás had played an important role in the creation of the CPT, and CPT activism was strong in the state. Goiás still had a large frontier area during this period and much of this activism was focused on helping *posseiros* resist expulsion and building up the local rural union structure to help them. Nonetheless, in some regions of the state, CPT activists and combative rural union leaders helped landless workers organize land occupations to pressure authorities for land reform (Fernandes 2000, 125–30).

Northeast

Most land-related conflicts in the Northeast during the late 1970s and early 1980s involved squatters, resident farm workers, or tenant farmers trying to resist eviction. Isolated land occupations occurred in several states, but there was little in the way of more sustained and organized landless activity in the region (Fernandes 2000). Probably the main exception to this general rule was in the western area of the state of Maranhão, which constitutes part of the eastern border of the Amazon basin. This had been a frontier area until the late 1960s and still had many squatter conflicts. There, a local movement organization called CENTRU (Center for Rural Worker Education and Culture) was involved in both defending squatters and organizing land occupations. Like the movement in Rio's Baixada Fluminense, CENTRU was led by rural union activists who had been involved in struggles for land before the 1964 coup. Catholic activists were also involved in organizing land occupations in this region (Adriance 1995).

North

During the early 1980s, rural land conflicts in the North, the quintessential frontier region, usually involved long-term squatters. These struggles were particularly intense in the southeastern quadrant of the state of Pará, which had seen a massive influx of both rich and poor people seeking land during the previous fifteen years. The CPT was deeply involved in this struggle, and in the associated movement to foment rural union activism. It was sometimes aided by activists from the Communist Party of Brazil (PC do B). A substantial group of activists emerged from this movement, although many fell victim to landholder violence. Although resistance struggles predominated, in some regions of the North, notably southeastern Pará, organized occupations of private (often illegitimately held) land began to occur in significant numbers during this period (Branford and Glock 1985; Adriance 1995). However, these appear to have been relatively isolated, local efforts.

State Responses to Pressure

For the most part, the targets of landless movement pressure tactics were the state governments. In many cases, opposition candidates in the gubernatorial elections of 1982 had promised to settle landless rural families, using either state-owned lands or private properties purchased on the market. Even some pro-regime candidates had made such promises. Few governors advanced very far in this direction, but some managed to settle a few hundred families, as well as to raise the expectations of landless rural workers. Although data are lacking, state-level land reform action appears to have been most extensive where there was substantial movement pressure and progressive political forces were relatively strong, such as in Rio Grande do Sul, Rio de Janeiro, and São Paulo.

In most regions, the federal government was not very active in land reform under Figueiredo. The major exception was the Amazon, where land-related violence was increasing rapidly. The mounting violence in this region was embarrassing to the government, and authorities were worried about a possible radicalization of rural workers, egged on by an increasingly militant Catholic Church (Branford and Glock 1985). In addition, the CNBB was making increasingly strong public statements condemning the regime for neglecting agrarian reform and for either repressing workers directly or allowing them to be massacred by landowners. A number of Catholic clergy and lay activists had also been killed defending *posseiros*, further angering church authorities.

Thus, beginning in 1980, the government set up a number of special agencies in the Amazon to speed up colonization, land titling, and, in rare cases, expropriation of private holdings.[31] The local activities of the federal land reform agency, INCRA, were subordinated to these new agencies. In 1982, President Figueiredo created the Extraordinary Ministry for Land Affairs (MEAF), to extend this policy to the national level. However, reform activity remained concentrated in the Amazon basin, including the North and parts of the Center-West and Maranhão. Authorities focused on granting legal titles to people already occupying public land in order to resolve situations of conflict, but also granted new land, virtually all of it public, to more than thirty-seven thousand families during 1979–84 (Gomes da Silva 1997, 111).

If federal authorities expected to reduce the level of violent conflict in the countryside, the results must have been disappointing. A data set compiled by Umbelino de Oliveira suggests a fairly steady increase in murders related to rural social conflict since 1970. From 103 in the 1970–74 period, the number of murders increased to 237 in 1975–79, and to 499 in 1980–84.

---

31. The most important of these agencies was the Executive Group for the Lands of the Araguaia-Tocantins (GETAT), which was responsible for an area that included parts of Pará, Goiás, and Maranhão. This was considered a particularly sensitive area. It had been the site of a communist-led guerilla movement in the early 1970s. In addition, the federal government was in the process of establishing a massive mining operation, the Greater Carajás Project, in the region.

As a rule, about half the murders each year occurred in the Amazon basin, reflecting both the intensity of conflict and the weakness of the rule of law in this largely frontier region (Umbelino de Oliveira 1999, 31).

Constructing the MST

In the wake of Encruzilhada Natalino, CPT activists resolved that the time was ripe to begin constructing a broader organizational structure to lead the struggle for land reform. For the poor, strength lay in numbers. Only an entity representing the landless all over Brazil could muster the political force to "break the spinal column of the *latifúndio*," as one *gaúcho* CPT activist put it.[32] Although CPT leaders from many states were involved, the effort was spearheaded by the southern regional division and, in particular, by the states of the South. In early 1982, the CPT began organizing regional meetings of rural workers and pastoral agents to pave the way for a national meeting later that year (Fernandes 1999). The first was that of the southern states, held in July. This meeting was the starting point for the process of regional organization discussed earlier, which created the Movement of Landless Workers of the Southern Region. I have not found any record of the other meetings, and there do not appear to have been any other regional organizations formed.

The national meeting was held in September 1982 and was attended by rural workers, union leaders, and pastoral agents from sixteen states, with all the major regions represented. It took place in Goiânia, capital of the state of Goiás. The participants represented not only landless rural workers, but also squatters, tenant farmers, and resident farm workers threatened with eviction. Participants debated about what kind of national organizational structure might be created. Some pastoral agents felt that the structure should be limited to a *sem terra* commission within the CPT (Stedile and Fernandes 1999, 46). Others felt that the landless needed an organization of their own, formally autonomous from the church. This appears to have been the predominant view within the CPT southern region leadership. This perspective also seemed to gain majority support at the meeting, and a decision was taken to form a Provisional National Commission of Landless

32. Interview with Friar Sergio Görgen, longtime CPT activist, March 18, 1998, Porto Alegre, RS.

Rural Workers, which was charged with preparing a second national land-less meeting, to be held in late 1983 or early 1984.

This effort quickly bogged down, however, as part of the commission opposed the initiative, alleging that local struggles for land needed more time to mature and gain strength before a national movement organization could be created.[33] At this point, the recently created Landless Movement of the Southern Region, which was determined to push forward with the campaign to create a national entity, took matters into its own hands. It organized a meeting in January 1984 at a Catholic Church facility in the city of Cascavel, in Paraná. The leadership invited rural activists from all over Brazil, as well as a variety of progressive organizations. Workers and pastoral agents from seven other states were present at the meeting, which was attended by about ninety people.

Although the participants came ready to discuss the idea of a national organization, there were disagreements. Some pastoral agents, albeit a mi-nority, still felt that such an organization should be formally linked to the CPT.[34] Resistance also came from rural union leaders, particularly those from the North. They felt that an autonomous entity might undermine the cam-paign to turn the unions into tools of class struggle. This concern was rooted in regional differences in how the struggle for land had evolved. In the South, although union activists participated, the movement had formed outside the unions. The southerners were leery of the restrictions that the union structure, with its ties to the state, would impose on their autonomy (Torrens 1992). In frontier regions, activists were organizing the struggle through the unions, forming opposition groups to contest STR elec-tions. Those who favored this approach feared that creating an entity inde-pendent of the STRs would divert people and resources away from union organizing.[35] Although they did not frontally oppose this initiative, they were not enthusiastic about joining it and they warned against the effects of "union parallelism" (Leroy 1991, 167).

Nevertheless, the meeting had been the Landless Movement of the Southern Region's initiative and the views that dominated that organiza-tion prevailed. The meeting thus resulted in the founding of the Movement of Landless Rural Workers (MST). The MST would struggle for both agrarian

33. *Boletim Sem Terra,* October 1982.
34. Interview with Darci Maschio, MST activist and member of the first Rio Grande do Sul state landless commission, March 10, 1998, Ronda Alta, RS.
35. Interview with former CPT activist Emmanuel Wambergue, July 14, 2005, Marabá, PA.

reform and a more just, fraternal society (Fernandes 1999). It would be an autonomous, worker-led national organization, independent of the church, political parties, and unions. In a rather precarious balancing act, the leadership of the Southern Region claimed that the new organization would actually be part of the rural union movement, participating in the struggle to transform conservative unions, but it would not be subject to the authority of union leaders.[36] The choice of name reflected the fact that in the South those who struggled for land reform were known as *sem terra*. Although members of the southern movement were often referred to as the landless *colonos*, the new entity adopted the term *rural workers* to avoid a regional bias and emphasize that the entity represented all categories of poor cultivators interested in agrarian reform (Stedile and Fernandes 1999).

Plans were also made to hold a national congress in January 1985 that would unveil a truly national organization and define its leadership. For now, the MST existed only on paper. During the rest of 1984, members of the Landless Movement of the Southern Region worked to enlist activists from other states to participate in the congress and the MST. With the help of the CPT and other progressive organizations, they fanned out across the country. João Pedro Stedile, the *gaúcho* activist who had become coordinator of the CPT's southern region in the early 1980s, moved to São Paulo to set up a national secretariat and strengthen the organization's alliances with national political actors.[37] The newsletter of the Landless Movement of the Southern Region now became the official newspaper of the MST, the *Jornal Sem Terra*.

Explaining Movement Emergence

Between 1978 and 1984 previously scattered signs of a popular demand for agrarian reform gave way to a significant social movement concentrated in southern Brazil but present at some level in every region of the country. Why did the landless movement emerge as a substantial force during this period?

Existing accounts of the movement's emergence usually offer a multifaceted explanation, but particular emphasis is placed on grievances. These

36. *Jornal Sem Terra*, March 1984.
37. Interview with Flademir Araújo, former editor of the *Boletim Sem Terra*, March 5, 1998, Porto Alegre, RS.

analyses stress, in particular, the role of rising absolute deprivation in the rural sector, related to the military regime's "conservative modernization" policies and their negative impact on land availability and popular welfare. They point to the spread of low-labor-intensity commercial crops and the increasing adoption of labor-saving technologies, the declining demand for tenant farmers and sharecroppers, the rising price of farmland, and the increasing problems with indebtedness and consequent land loss. These changes, analysts argue, helped provoke the movement's formation by expelling families from their holdings and making it harder for new generations to "socially reproduce" themselves as small farmers. Virtually every examination of the movement's emergence includes some version of this argument.

I agree that the rapid pace of modernization during the late 1960s and the 1970s helped lay the groundwork for the emergence of the movement through its negative impact on land access in the countryside, particularly in the South and Southeast. The agricultural census data presented in Table 1 document this impact. This standard grievance-based account, however, is insufficient because it ignores other forces operating in Brazilian society that also had an important influence on the intensity of potential demand for rural land redistribution. In particular, a more complete account must also consider trends in the urban sector, agricultural wage labor, and the availability of land on the frontier.

Despite rising inequality in income and land tenure, social indicators in agriculture improved markedly during the 1970s. This, as I argued above, was in large measure a result of the rapid growth of the predominantly urban economy. The expanding industrial and urban service sectors helped to absorb the labor expelled or marginalized from agriculture. Changes in agriculture itself also contributed. Opportunities for wage labor increased and the opening up of new frontier areas, mainly in the Amazon, provided many landless and land-poor families with free or inexpensive access to farmland.

Had these trends continued into the 1980s, they would have made it harder to create a mass movement struggling for land reform. They would have given poor people of rural origin a broader array of alternatives, including ones that were more socially acceptable than engaging in land occupations and other forms of protest. They also would have taken more poor families out of rural villages and small towns in the South and other established agricultural regions where the movement mainly emerged.

However, these trends did not continue. The crisis of the Brazilian economy brought sharp increases in unemployment and poverty in the cities. Many people of rural origin sought shelter in the agricultural sector, but the impact of modernization on land access during the previous decades could not be wholly reverted. The amount of land in small farms increased, but not as quickly as the number of farmers. As a result, the average size of establishments declined, exacerbating the land shortage. The growth of agricultural wage labor, meanwhile, stagnated. The ability of the agriculture frontier to serve as an escape valve for the social pressures generated by modernization in older regions was declining as well, as most of the accessible farm land had already been claimed.

It may be argued that landless rural workers, especially in the South, where the smallholder tradition is strong, would have preferred to struggle for land reform regardless of the other options available to them. In fact, the discourse of the landless movement as it developed in the early 1980s emphatically rejected the alternatives to agrarian reform as almost inherently undesirable (Stival 1987; Schmitt 1992; Franco 1992). Campers and movement leaders emphasized poor soils and health conditions and the lack of infrastructure on the frontier. With regard to the cities, they cited unfamiliar customs, rigid workplace rules and schedules, discrimination against people with rural accents, and lack of opportunities for workers with low levels of education. Agricultural wage work was often described as a loss of liberty, particularly by people of *colono* origin.

It is important to contextualize these assessments, however. By this period, the alternatives to camping had been substantially foreclosed and former urban and frontier migrants who found themselves in landless camps were, almost by definition, people for whom the migratory experience had been a failure. Just as important, the decision to join a movement that frontally challenges the status quo almost requires of the participant a justification that portrays other options as fundamentally flawed. Schmitt makes this point with regard to urban migration: "The 'landless' as a collectivity in struggle does not accept leaving the countryside. That does not impede that, in some moments, the individuals engaged in that process may see in the move to the city a possibility, but as *acampados* and, therefore, as protagonists of a social conflict, they reject migration to the urban context as an alternative" (Schmitt 1992, 196). In other words, many of the same people who expressed a sweeping rejection of the alternatives to struggling for land after joining the landless movement might well have accepted these options had the relatively favorable conditions associated with them during the late 1960s and 1970s continued to prevail.

A balanced grievance-based account of the landless movement's emergence must thus refer not only to the impact of agricultural modernization on land access, the overwhelming emphasis of previous studies, but also to other changes in Brazilian society that rendered economic strategies used in earlier years less viable and, consequently, increased the relative attractiveness of struggling for land in one's own state.

Changes in the capacity of the landless to mobilize for agrarian reform also played an important role in the movement's emergence as a significant force. The increase in organizational capacity was mainly a reflection of the growth of a powerful progressive movement within the historically conservative Brazilian Catholic Church. Echoing existing analyses, I would argue that the grassroots organization and consciousness-raising work of activists associated with the progressive church were of critical importance in the movement's emergence. They helped turn what would otherwise have been isolated outbursts of local protest activity into a large and sustained social movement, especially in the South.

Church activists, particularly those linked to the CPT, provided organizational resources of both an objective and a subjective character. With regard to the former, they provided knowledge of the larger political context and how to deal with government officials, the press, and other elite actors and supplied material resources such as food, transportation, and meeting facilities. The subjective resources were at least as important. In particular, the agents provided an ideological framework, rooted in religious faith, which served to legitimate popular organization and political pressure for land reform. This ideology was diffused through CEBS, youth groups, sermons, leadership training courses, and the numerous pamphlets published by the CPT and other church entities. Case studies suggest that the belief that what they were doing was morally just and religiously sanctioned encouraged the landless not only to enter the movement but also to stay in the struggle during hard times (Adriance 1995; Benincá 1987; Gaiger 1987; Marcon 1997).

For a relatively poor and uneducated population such as the landless the contributions of the popular church were arguably essential for mounting anything more than local, short-term protest actions in favor of land redistribution. In all probability, no lasting national or even regional organizational structure would have emerged to push forward the struggle for agrarian reform without this external assistance.

Although they were clearly the critical force, the Catholic Church and its associated organizations were not the only actors that contributed to the movement's organizational resources during this period. Lutheran activists also played a significant role in the South, often working through the CPT. Rural labor activists, particularly those associated with the combative, or *cutista*, current, also helped the landless organize in many municipalities. However, as I mentioned above, rural union activism was itself often at least partially the product of prior church activism.

Whether we see the movement's emergence as a result of activist strategy is a question of definition more than of empirical analysis. Clearly, the development of liberation theology was a major cultural innovation that produced a powerful collective action frame used by many social movements. The rise of the popular church also brought organizational innovations that, as I argued above, played a critical role in the rise of the landless movement, including the creation of the CEBS and the CPT. These were undoubtedly important changes. The question, however, is whether they were innovations by landless movement activists or by activists of a prior movement within the Catholic Church. I believe that the second view is more useful, since it reflects the fact that the landless benefited from a process of change within the church over which they had no real control.

The aggravation of grassroots social grievances in the early 1980s and the organizational resources contributed to the agrarian reform cause by the popular church help us to understand why the landless movement emerged when it did. At least as critical to the movement's emergence, however, was a change in the political opportunity structure created by the decay of the military dictatorship, in terms of both institutions and societal support. It was largely because of this shift that not only the landless movement but also a multitude of other social movements emerged during this period.

As noted in Chapter 1, political opportunity theorists cite the decay of authoritarian regimes as an example of the kind of political change that gives rise to broad waves of protest. The relationship between democratic transitions and protest has also been explored in empirical studies (O'Donnell and Schmitter 1986; Oberschall 1996; Hipsher 1998). The causal dynamics scholars sketch out are fairly similar. As the old regime's support base erodes, particularly among key elites, the leadership may make selective concessions to the desire for greater openness. These, however, often serve only to advertise their weakness, promoting more open dissent. Members of the authoritarian coalition start to prepare for the future by seeking new allies, including previously excluded groups. Regime stalwarts may also try to co-opt such groups in order to preserve their power. The sense that the threat of repression is declining and that the possibility of concessions, including full democratization, is increasing makes both diehard activists and "normal" people willing to invest time and effort in pressuring for change.

In broad strokes this is what occurred during the Brazilian transition (Hipsher 1998; Hochstetler 2000). The initial, elite-led liberalization process helped to give rise to stronger shows of dissent. These, in turn, pushed the ruling elite to continue the opening. Eventually, the manifestations of discontent came to include open social protest, initially in the form of the São Paulo–based strike waves of 1978–79. The regime's failure to decisively crack down on these actions signaled its weakness to other groups, helping to prompt an expanding wave of protest nationwide. The new unionism thus played the role of what Tarrow (1994) has called an "initiator movement," helping to trigger the onset of a mass protest cycle by demonstrating the existence of a relatively favorable political opportunity structure. The expansion of electoral competition in the early 1980s provided further impetus for mobilization by encouraging even erstwhile supporters of military rule to distance themselves from the regime and compete for popular support.

Land occupations had existed even prior to the late 1970s, but the sense of opportunity created by the industrial strikes, the reforms announced by Geisel at the end of his term, and Figueiredo's pledge to continue the transition energized church activists and rural workers alike. João Pedro Stedile, one of key leaders in the landless movement's emergence in the South, has emphasized this idea: "We cannot disconnect the rise of the MST from the political situation of Brazil in that era. That is, the MST didn't arise just from the will of the peasant. It could only become an important social movement because it coincided with a broader struggle for the democratization of the country. The struggle for agrarian reform added to the resurgence of the workers' strikes, in 1978 and 1979, and the struggle for the democratization of the country" (Stedile and Fernandes 1999, 22). Although Encruzilhada Natalino was in part a response to the existing climate of political opening, it also had an "initiator" impact of its own in the

South, similar to that of the ABC strikes, but at a regional level and largely specific to the question of land reform. By demonstrating the intensity of public support for the landless, the camp at Ronda Alta underscored the regime's vulnerability. It thus encouraged activists to intensify their organizational efforts across the South.

The competitive state-level elections of 1982 reinforced the sense of opportunity by allowing and motivating political elites to compete for popular support. In numerous states, including Rio Grande do Sul, Paraná, and São Paulo, land redistribution was one of the promises that victorious candidates, even relatively conservative ones, made to the electorate (Torrens 1992; Fernandes 1996; Carter 2002). These pledges helped facilitate the movement's recruitment efforts, as landless and land-poor workers tried to ensure their place on the list of beneficiaries by joining an established movement.

The emergence of the progressive church influenced the movement's growth not only by increasing the organizational capacity of the landless, but also by pressuring authorities for land reform at the national and local level. In particular, the CNBB's growing criticism of the regime's neglect of agrarian reform and its brutal treatment of rural workers helped push authorities to accelerate land distribution, particularly in frontier areas. Arguably, the federal government's modest land reform efforts during this period helped to spur, rather than quell, land conflicts in the countryside (Schmink and Wood 1992).

Conclusion

By the end of 1984, the landless movement had become a significant social movement of national scope. Without question, the movement was most cohesive and broadly organized in southern Brazil. However, landless rural workers were going on the offensive to pressure authorities for agrarian reform in many other areas of the country. In addition, a movement organization was taking shape with pretensions of leading the struggle for agrarian reform at the national level. Although rooted mainly in the South, the MST also had ties to activists in other regions. In southern Brazil, at least, the press was beginning to talk about the *sem terra* as a significant actor. Grassroots protest, combined with the mounting violence of squatter conflicts in frontier areas and the advocacy of the Catholic Church, was helping to revive land reform as a political issue.

In this chapter I have sketched a broad-based explanation of the landless movement's formation, involving three basic factors that coincide with the theoretical arguments made by the grievance/discontent, organizational capacity, and political opportunity perspectives. Rapid agricultural modernization and the demise of trends that had helped to offset its negative welfare consequences generated rising social grievances in the Brazilian countryside in the early 1980s, creating a social environment propitious for activists to recruit landless workers to pressure the state for land redistribution. Meanwhile, the grassroots organizing work of the popular church movement increased the organizational capacity of the landless population, helping turn what might otherwise have been isolated incidents of protest into a broader movement. Finally, an expanding political opportunity structure, rooted in the national political context of regime opening, encouraged mobilization and protest for land reform by diminishing the threat of harsh repression and improving the prospects for gaining concessions from authorities.

THREE   Growth Amid Decline, 1985–1994

Social protest activity, which had been so intense in Brazil during the early 1980s, lost much of its vigor during the second half of the decade. The demise of the protest cycle in both the cities and the countryside was sealed by the victory of conservative Fernando Collor de Mello in the presidential election of late 1989. A corruption scandal that exploded in 1992 triggered a new outbreak of major demonstrations, eventually leading to the president's removal from office. However, the protest wave that helped oust Collor did not bring a more lasting revival of social movement activity.

The landless movement was a notable exception—probably *the most* notable exception—to the general rule of movement decline in the late 1980s and early 1990s. Although its expansion stagnated somewhat under Collor, overall the landless movement grew substantially during this period. Land occupations, the movement's main tactic, increased in number and spread to new regions. Its expansion was largely driven by the development of the MST, which transformed itself from a loose coalition of local groups based mainly in the South into a centralized organization of national scope.

In this chapter I address a somewhat different question from those discussed in Chapter 2 and the other empirical chapters. Rather than explaining longitudinal variation in protest intensity within a particular movement, here I try to account for differences in the growth trajectory of different movements that emerge within the same cycle of protest. Specifically, I seek to explain why the landless movement persisted and even grew despite the general decline of social movement activity in Brazil following the transition to democracy. In Chapter 1, I spelled out the general strategies the major theoretical perspectives on social movements would seem to offer for explaining this type of variation. In the present chapter I evaluate those strategies in light of this empirical case.

A secondary, but nonetheless important, objective of the chapter is to analyze the internal development of the MST. I do this here because it was during this period that many of the fundamental characteristics of the MST took shape, in its organizational structure, tactics, and relationship to its social base of campers and settlers. Although the MST would experience major changes in the intensity of mobilization and protest in subsequent periods, these basic features of the organization would remain largely unchanged. I also discuss, to a lesser extent, some of the other actors within the movement.

Existing research has not addressed the question of why individual movements that emerge within the same cycle of protest subsequently experience different growth trajectories, but as I discussed in Chapter 1, each theoretical perspective offers potential answers. From a grievance/discontent perspective, variation in growth trajectories may result from differences in how the sources of discontent evolve. Over time, socioeconomic changes or state actions may attenuate the grievances of some groups, while failing to attenuate, or aggravating, those of others. From the standpoint of organizational capacity theory, this type of variation may be a function of differences in the solidity of the organizational structures from which movements arise or of differential access to external assistance. Some movements may retain access to the resources of elite groups, while others lose them. The activist strategy perspective suggests that variation in movement trajectories be explained in terms of the effectiveness with which activists respond to the challenges they face; specifically, it focuses on the decisions they make about organizational forms, tactics, goals and rhetorical appeals. Finally, political opportunity would point to differences in the vulnerability or receptivity of authorities to particular movements within a protest cycle, rooted in such factors as elite allies, institutional structures, or the policy preferences of the governing party.

Existing empirical research on the landless movement has essentially ignored the question of why the movement continued to grow despite the general decline of social protest in Brazil. The analysis I develop in this chapter rejects explanations based on both grievances and organizational capacity. There is little reason to believe, I argue, that the landless movement was privileged with regard to either of these two variables. Activist

strategy, by contrast, does help us to understand the movement's exceptionalism. I make the case that the decision to employ the land occupation
as the movement's core tactic was central to the landless movement's survival and growth. However, I emphasize tactical choice for somewhat different reasons from those that movement scholars typically have advanced.

The central virtue of this tactic, I argue, was that it made the movement
into one that, for the most part, did not involve the pursuit of a public
good, in Olson's (1965) sense of a policy that must be supplied to everyone
in a group if it is supplied to anyone at all. Consequently, it was not as
vulnerable as other movements to the free-rider problem and not as reliant
on the normative or idealistic incentives that, according to movement
scholars, social movements usually use to overcome this problem. Thus,
when the end of Brazil's military dictatorship brought a decline in such
incentives for involvement in social protest, most social movements faded,
but the landless movement was able to continue its expansion.

The MST played a critical role in exploiting this advantage of land occupations because it employed this tactic aggressively and helped to diffuse
it across the country. In addition, the MST built on the occupation strategy
in creative ways. Perhaps most important, it used the resulting encampments as spaces for political indoctrination, collective identity building,
and leadership formation. This approach generated a steady stream of new
activists and helped to ensure that many people who obtained a plot of
land through the MST would continue to contribute to this organization's
struggle even after becoming settlers.

Nonetheless, the movement's ability to resist the trend toward decline
cannot be reduced to purely a question of strategy. The tactic of occupying
the target of their demands was simply not available to other social movements to the same extent. Some of these movements pursued goods, such
as higher wages or women's rights, that physically cannot be occupied.
Others pursued goods that could potentially have been occupied and (in
the case of urban land) sometimes were. What set the landless movement
apart from these movements was its political opportunity structure. In particular, the special constitutional status of rural land, as the only form of
private property whose ownership is clearly conditioned on its being put to
productive use, made Brazilian authorities politically vulnerable to pressure
to redistribute unproductive land occupied by the landless.

The chapter begins with an overview of the major political and socioeconomic trends of the 1985–94 period. It includes a discussion of the ambi-

tious land reform program announced at the outset of civilian rule, the conflicts it provoked, and its eventual demise. This section is followed by a brief account of the decline of the social protest cycle set in motion during the late 1970s. The focus then shifts to the landless movement itself. I first outline the overall trajectory of landless protest activity, using data collected by the CPT. Then I discuss the development of the groups directly involved in organizing the landless, focusing mainly on the MST, easily the most important actor in the movement. Finally, I come back to the question of the movement's exceptional trajectory during this period, fleshing out the arguments outlined above.

Democracy and Disappointment

Democratization had generated expectations of improved governance and greater popular welfare, but the first decade of civilian rule proved to be a period of crisis and disillusionment in Brazil. The individual chosen to lead the new civilian regime died unexpectedly before he could assume office and his replacement, José Sarney, presided over a government plagued by clientelism and unable to lift Brazil decisively from its economic slump. Collor, his successor, promised to sweep out corrupt officials and reinvigo-rate the economy through market-oriented reforms. His government, how-ever, proved to be even more venal than Sarney's and failed to overcome the twin curses of high inflation and sluggish growth. Economic relief would come only at the tail end of this period under interim president Itamar Franco. For leftists, these problems were compounded by the failure of democracy to bring significant redistribution of Brazil's economic re-sources. Land reform was no exception to this rule. The agrarian question returned to the political agenda in 1985 with the announcement of a major program of land redistribution. In the end, however, little was done to implement it and the new constitution approved in 1988 made it more difficult for federal authorities to expropriate private farmland.

In 1984, the last full year under military rule, Brazil had experienced a mass movement for direct popular election of the first civilian president. Although the "Direct Elections Now!" movement failed to achieve its goal— the president was ultimately chosen by a special electoral college—it helped generate public support for PMDB candidate Tancredo Neves. Pro-regime forces had hoped to impose their own candidate, but the Democratic

Social Party (PDS; the post-1979 version of ARENA) was divided over the nomination. A dissident faction broke off and created a new party, the Party of the Liberal Front (PFL), which allied itself with the PMDB. The PFL's Sarney, ex-governor of the conservative northeastern state of Maranhão, became Neves's running mate.

Neves prevailed in the January 1985 electoral college vote, but died (of natural causes) before he could take office. Sarney, a supporter of the military dictatorship, became the first president of the new civilian regime; seeking to attenuate this irony, he switched his affiliation to the PMDB. Inaugurated in March, the new president led a broad and unwieldy coalition. The heterogeneous PMDB included everything from rural oligarchs to communists. Its partner, the PFL, was an alliance of conservative local bosses, mainly from the Northeast.

Sarney's presidency was undoubtedly a letdown for most Brazilians. Probably the biggest disappointment was the failure to revive Brazil's economy, troubled by the foreign debt burden and steadily rising prices. A stabilization plan adopted in 1986 slowed inflation and brought strong growth, just in time to help the PMDB triumph in the legislative elections of that year. The elections were particularly important, since the new Congress, acting as a constituent assembly, would also draft a new constitution. Following the elections, however, prices resumed their climb, despite a number of new stabilization plans. By the late 1980s, the economy was once again in serious problems. Sarney came under pressure to cut spending and trade protection and sell off Brazil's many state enterprises, but the government's adherence to the emerging neoliberal consensus was half-hearted and failed to address the country's macroeconomic imbalances. Various corruption scandals also undercut Sarney's popularity.

Public disgust with Sarney helped opposition candidates of all stripes in the 1989 presidential election campaign. In the second-round runoff, Collor, the previously obscure governor of the small, backward northeastern state of Alagoas, faced Lula, the former São Paulo union activist and leader of the growing PT. Young, charismatic, and conservative, Collor promised to fight government corruption and implement "modernizing" neoliberal reforms. He ran as an outsider, representing a virtually unknown party. Lula promised fundamental social reforms, including land reform, which would move Brazil closer to socialism. Collor won a narrow victory.

Once in office, Collor formed a loose coalition with the two major conservative parties, the PFL and PDS. True to his outsider approach, however, he tried to govern largely alone, using his decree powers to sidestep Congress. To tackle Brazil's economic problems, he implemented a draconian stabilization package and market-oriented structural reforms, especially trade liberalization. These measures were not enough to overcome inflationary pressures, however, and the crisis deepened. In late 1991 a rising tide of corruption charges added to Collor's problem. He responded by forging a stronger partisan alliance, anchored by the PFL, but this initiative was too little and too late to save his government. In mid-1992, corruption charges blossomed into a major scandal, setting in motion impeachment proceedings. A substantial grassroots movement for the president's ouster soon emerged. In September, Collor was impeached and provisionally replaced by his vice president, Itamar Franco, a little-known politician with no party affiliation. In late December, he was removed from office altogether.

Public rejection of Collor's corruption fed a more general condemnation of the conservative political elites and parties associated with him. President Franco responded to this climate by putting together a broader and more progressive alliance and implementing emergency social policies. In terms of the economy, growth had returned, but inflation was still out of control. Franco downgraded neoliberal reform and focused on reviving the economy. Runaway inflation continued to bedevil Brazil until the second half of 1994, when an innovative stabilization plan designed by finance minister Fernando Henrique Cardoso slowed the price surge and boosted economic growth.

Hoping to capitalize on the anticipated success of this plan, known as the Real Plan, because of the new currency it introduced, Cardoso launched his candidacy for president in May. A prominent intellectual and one of the founders of dependency theory, Cardoso had entered politics during the dictatorship as a member of the MDB. In 1988, as a senator for São Paulo, he had joined a group of center-left PMDB leaders who abandoned the party, protesting against its growing clientelism. They formed a new party, the Party of Brazilian Social Democracy (PSDB), which promised clean government and moderate social reform. The centrist PSDB allied itself with two conservative parties: the PFL and the (inappropriately named) Brazilian Labor Party (PTB). Propelled mainly by the successes of the Real Plan, Cardoso captured an easy first-round victory in the October election. The losing candidate was, once again, the PT's Lula.

Bogged down by debt and inflation, the Brazilian economy produced little net growth during the 1985–94 period. Agriculture was something of a bright spot, easily outperforming manufacturing and construction, for example (Baer 1995, 193). Social indicators improved in the mid-1980s, as a result of Sarney's temporary success in stabilizing the economy, but declined thereafter. Poverty and unemployment did not reach the peaks experienced during the recession of the early 1980s, but the average real income in 1993 was actually somewhat lower than a decade earlier, presumably because of the effects of inflation, which exceeded 1,000 percent a year in the late 1980s and early 1990s (Giambiagi et al. 2005). Although growth was stagnant, neoliberal reforms undertaken during this period set in motion important structural changes in the economy. Spending cuts and trade liberalization, particularly under Collor, affected both industry and agriculture. The trade opening hit domestic industry hard, leading to layoffs and the growth of informal employment (Neri, Camargo, and Reis 2000). Farmers struggled to deal with the loss of subsidized credit, price supports, and trade protection, forcing a process of rationalization (Coelho 2001).

The agricultural census conducted in 1995–96 is not directly comparable with the 1985 version, making it somewhat difficult to assess changes in this sector.[1] Data from the federal government's quasi-annual household survey, known as the PNAD, provide some useful evidence, although the PNAD did not include the North until 2004. The number of farm establishments and the number of people active in agriculture declined sharply in the mid-1980s with the revival of the urban economy, but increased again as a new recession took hold toward the end of the decade (Helfand and Brunstein, 2001). The overall trend during the 1985–94 decade was one of moderate decline on both variables, probably reflecting the impact of cuts in agricultural support programs and trade liberalization. The South was the region most affected, partly because a free trade agreement (known in Brazil as MERCOSUL) involving the Southern Cone countries exposed southern dairy and wheat farmers to greater competition from their Argentine and Uruguayan counterparts.

The decade following the return to civilian rule was particularly disappointing for Brazilian leftists, since many had hoped that democratization would allow previously repressed popular sectors to pressure successfully for the redistribution of wealth and income. Although some advances were

---

1. No agricultural census was conducted in 1990 and none has been conducted since 1995–96.

made, in general this period brought few major redistributive initiatives (Weyland 1996). The trajectory of agrarian reform policy was one of the biggest sources of disillusionment.

During his campaign in 1984 Tancredo Neves had made vague promises of implementing the Land Statute. Given his conservative background, Sarney seemed unlikely to make good on these promises. Nevertheless, shortly after coming to office in March 1985 he announced an ambitious plan to settle 1.4 million landless families during his five-year term. The unveiling of the National Agrarian Reform Plan (PNRA), caused an uproar. Landowners and other conservatives attacked it viciously, arguing that it would provoke conflict, disrupt production, and possibly bring military intervention (Gomes da Silva 1987). Organized groups, including the powerful National Confederation of Agriculture (CNA), lobbied hard against it. Rural land conflicts multiplied, as large landowners accelerated their efforts to "cleanse" their properties of squatters, tenant farmers, and other potential claimants, and the landless occupied farms deemed vulnerable to expropriation.

Sarney ended up yielding to conservative pressures. Implementation of the PNRA was delayed, and when it was finally decreed into law in October 1985, it had been changed in ways that were bound to frustrate its progress (Gomes da Silva 1987). Large landowners were not satisfied with this outcome, however. They wanted to make sure that the constituent assembly that would be convened in January 1987 would be the definitive burial ground of agrarian reform. Thus, at the end of 1985 a group of prominent landowners founded the Democratic Rural Union (UDR). By the end of 1986, the UDR claimed to have more than a hundred local chapters and tens of thousand of members. The UDR engaged in both institutional tactics, particularly campaign fund-raising, and mass protest. At the local level, its chapters were involved in organizing security arrangements for rural properties, which sometimes amounted to virtual militias. Despite its frequent association with violence against rural workers, the UDR sought to project an image of itself as the representative of a class of modern rural businesspeople, or "agricultural producers" (Bruno 1997).

Realizing the importance of the constituent assembly, pro–land reform groups also worked hard to push for a new constitution that would at least preserve the relatively favorable legal framework established by the Land Statute. The CONTAG, CPT, MST, and other groups sponsored two "popular amendments" that together garnered more than 1.2 million signatures

(Michiles et al. 1989, annex 1).[2] They also organized a mass demonstration that brought some ten thousand people to Brasília in October 1987.

These efforts were ultimately unsuccessful. An informal center-right coalition known as the Centrão delivered a partial, but important, victory to large landowners (Gomes da Silva 1989). Although it reaffirmed the "social function" of rural land, the new constitution, ratified in October 1988, stated flatly that "productive" properties could not be expropriated. This was a step back from the Land Statute, which had potentially allowed expropriation based on both low productivity and sheer size. To make matters worse, the document was silent on important issues. It failed to specify the criteria for determining whether a property would be considered large or unproductive and did not discuss the process by which ownership of expropriated land would pass to the federal government. The gaps would have to be filled by regular legislation. The absence of explicit provisions on these issues did not prevent altogether the federal government from expropriating private land, but it did make expropriations more difficult by facilitating legal challenges.

Even before the new constitution was ratified, it was clear that Sarney's agrarian reform would be only a shadow of the program announced in 1985. By the end of his government, the INCRA had settled some ninety thousand families, more than any previous government, but less than 7 percent of his stated objective (INCRA 1999, 23). Agrarian reform continued to proceed slowly in the early 1990s. During his campaign Collor had pledged to settle five hundred thousand families. Few believed these promises, and in office he did nothing of the sort. Between 1990 and 1992, the INCRA (the federal land reform agency) settled about thirty-eight thousand families (INCRA, n.d.).[3] Repression against landless activists intensified, reflecting the conservative political climate.[4] Franco promised to accelerate agrarian reform. Although his settlement results were quite modest, repression faded and, perhaps more important, two pieces of legislation needed to fill the gaps

2. The *popular amendment* was an institution that allowed citizens' groups to make proposals to the constituent assembly via petition. Reflecting the activist ferment of the era, 122 such amendments were submitted (Michiles 1989, part 4). The assembly adopted parts of many of these proposals but they were not bound to follow them.

3. Most of these were settled on land expropriated earlier under Sarney.

4. Repression of landless protest was generally undertaken by the Military Police forces, which are controlled by the state governments. However, under Collor, the Federal Police, which is mainly an investigative force, also played a significant role in monitoring and arresting landless activists.

in the 1988 Constitution with regard to rural land expropriation were signed into law.[5] These legislative victories reflected the crisis of conservative forces following the Collor debacle (Oliveira 1996).

The new agrarian reform laws were a significant defeat for large landowners, but they probably helped to spur a new kind of landowner organizational drive. The UDR was officially disbanded as a national entity in late 1993. This decision reflected the organization's success in defeating the PNRA and rolling back aspects of the Land Statute. At the same time, it probably also reflected a recognition that the UDR had suffered in the court of public opinion as a result of its association with violence against rural workers.[6] Instead, landowners were seeking to build a more constant and disciplined base of support in Congress. Their legislative caucus was referred to as the *bancada ruralista* and, by the end 1994, it was already becoming known as a potent force, more disciplined than most of Brazil's parties.[7] The caucus was made up mainly of legislators from frankly conservative parties, but also included some from the PMDB and even the "social democratic" PSDB.

Decline of the Protest Cycle

Social protest activities faded in frequency and intensity during the second half of the 1980s in both urban and rural areas (Cardoso 1994; Doimo 1995; Hochstetler 2000). Many movement activists abandoned high-commitment political activities or channeled their efforts into party politics or nongovernmental organizations (NGOs) (Gohn 1997). A hard core of activists often continued the struggle, but movements tended to lose their ability to organize mass protest events. Although analysts differ about the precise peak of the cycle, virtually all agree that by the time Sarney took office in 1985

5. One of these, the Agrarian Law, defined what properties, in terms of size and productive characteristics, would be eligible for expropriation. The second, the Law of the Summary Rite, defined the process by which the INCRA became the owner of an expropriated property. The existence of this law diminished the potential for landowners to block expropriations in the courts.

6. The most notable case was that of Chico Mendes, the internationally known leader of the rubber tappers' movement in the state of Acre, who was gunned down in 1988. The UDR was alleged to have played a role.

7. *Bancada* means "legislative caucus." The word *ruralista*, which has no direct translation in English, is used in Brazil to refer to any large agricultural producer. The *bancada ruralista* was officially called the Parliamentary Front for the Support of Agriculture, but that name was rarely used.

it had entered a phase of decline. By then, as Hipsher notes, "overall, the popular movement appeared to be in crisis. The movements were no longer able to mobilize large numbers of people and they began to move from a politics of protest to a politics of making proposals" (1998, 167).

Individual movements had somewhat different trajectories. Doimo (1995), who studied five urban social movements, found that, though all had reached their peak level of activity by the mid-1980s, there was substantial variance in trajectory (chap. 4). For example, the "cost of living" movement, which protested the effects of inflation on real wages, emerged in the mid-to-late 1970s and had virtually disappeared by 1980. In contrast, the housing movement entered the 1990s with significant strength. Rodrigues (1995) and M. Oliveira (1998) view the decline of the urban new unionism, the most influential movement of the protest cycle, as beginning in the late 1980s, following the end of the constituent assembly. By the 1990s strikes were, in comparison, few and far between. Hipsher notes that the number of strikes and strikers actually peaked in 1979, only a year after the movement was born in São Paulo's ABC (Hipsher 1998). Students of the combative rural unionism also place the beginning of its decline, in terms of mass mobilization and protest, in the late 1980s (Schmitt 1996; Houtzager 1997).

The end of the regime transition also led to a reflux in the activist role of the Catholic Church (Doimo 1995). With the transition to democracy, many within the church hierarchy felt that the progressive church's essential reason for being, to provide "a voice for the voiceless," had lost relevance. The church, they argued, needed to return to its spiritual mission. This shift was backed by the Vatican, which took a number of measures intended to undercut leftist forces within the Brazilian Catholic Church. Although many church authorities continued to defend progressive causes, support for grassroots mobilization and consciousness-raising declined noticeably. CEBs decayed or shifted to purely spiritual work, and activist organizations such as the CPT found support for their mission among the church's top brass increasingly scarce (Goes 1997).

The quiescence of Brazilian civil society was interrupted in 1992 with the eruption of large demonstrations demanding Collor's impeachment in a number of cities. However, the movement dissolved after Collor's fall, failing to produce a lasting revival of protest activity. Under Franco, there emerged a nationwide grassroots campaign against hunger, but this was largely a charitable drive, rather than a protest movement.

Growth of the Landless Movement

Contradicting the general trend toward movement decline, the landless movement grew substantially during the 1985–94 period. Even during the Collor years, which were the most difficult period for the movement, landless protest did not suffer a sustained decline. The CPT has collected and published data on land occupations annually since 1987, in a report titled *Conflitos no Campo-Brasil.* Only national totals are available for 1987, but more detailed data are available from 1988 on. The data are compiled from a combination of published sources, such as newspaper articles, and firsthand accounts. Unfortunately, there are no data available regarding other forms of protest for agrarian reform, but since the land occupation is the movement's core tactic, the number of such actions and the number of people involved in them constitute good measures of the intensity of protest.

At the national level, both the number of land occupations and the number of landless families involved in them in 1994 were almost double the 1987 totals (Figs. 1 and 2).[8] Occupation activity declined in 1990, the year Collor took office, but rebounded in the later years of his government. Under Itamar Franco, there was a slight acceleration. The sharp falloff in activity in 1990 was probably related to Fernando Collor's electoral victory, which was deeply discouraging to popular movements.

Perhaps the most striking aspect of the geographic distribution of land

Fig. 1   Land occupations in Brazil, 1987–1994

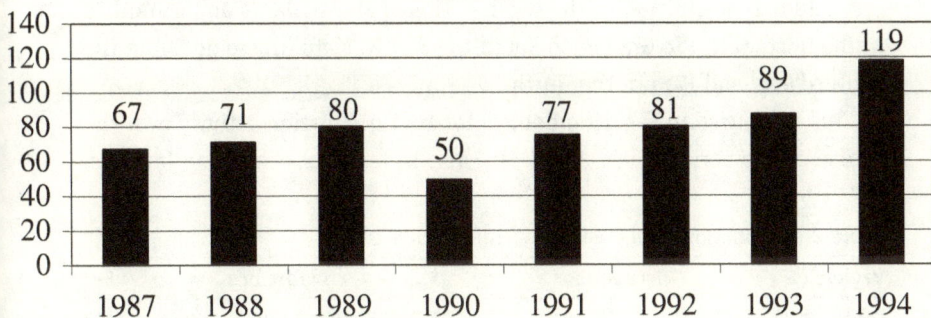

Source: CPT 1990, 1991, 1992, 1993a, 1994, 1995.

8. Each head of household is counted by the CPT as one "family," even if that person has no spouse or children. The MST and other groups involved in the struggle for land use the same method of counting the people participating in their protest actions.

Fig. 2   Occupying families in Brazil, 1987–1994

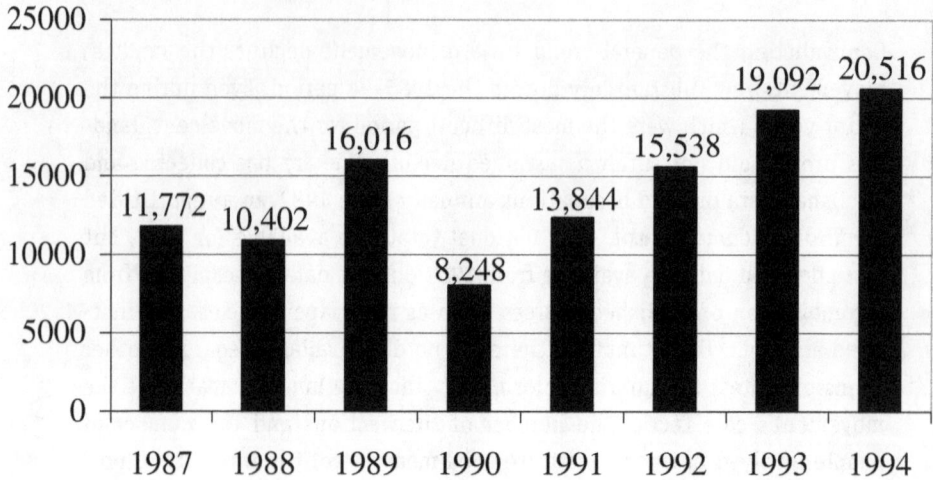

Source: CPT 1990, 1991, 1992, 1993a, 1994, 1995.

occupations during the 1988–94 period was its dispersion. Nine different states had at least 30 occupations, with the leader, Paraná, registering 58. Eight states had more than 5,000 families involved in occupations, with São Paulo, at 14,546, being the leader. Although the Northeast, with about half of Brazil's rural population, clearly led the other major regions, it was by no means dominant, accounting for about a third of the total occupations and families (Table 2). In every major region there was at least one state where occupation activity was particularly intense. The top performers included, in addition to the two mentioned above, Bahia and Maranhão in the Northeast, Rio Grande do Sul in the South, Mato Grosso do Sul in the Center-West, and Pará in the North.

Shifts occurred in the geographical focus of occupation activity over the course of the period (Figs. 3 and 4). First, in terms of occupying families,

Table 2   Occupations and families by region, 1988–1994

Region	Occupations	%	Families	%
Center-West	85	15.0	15,765	15.2
North	95	16.8	8,853	8.5
Northeast	183	32.3	33,494	32.3
South	133	23.5	27,162	26.2
Southeast	71	12.5	18,382	17.7

Source: CPT 1989a, 1990, 1991, 1992, 1993a, 1994, 1995.

Fig. 3   Land occupations by region (% of total)

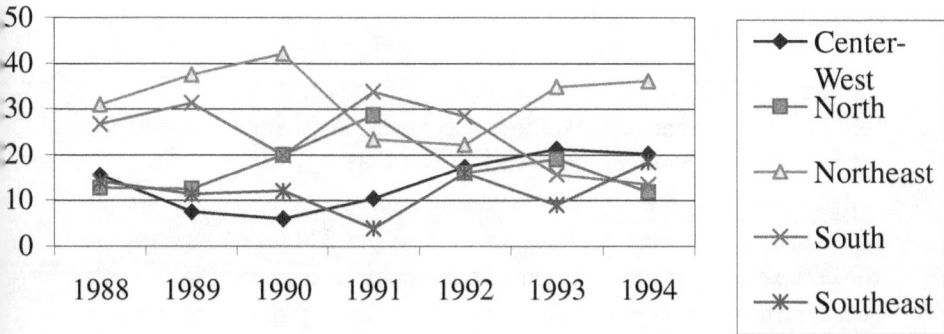

Source: CPT 1989a, 1990, 1991, 1992, 1993a, 1994, 1995.

Fig. 4   Occupying families by region (% of Total)

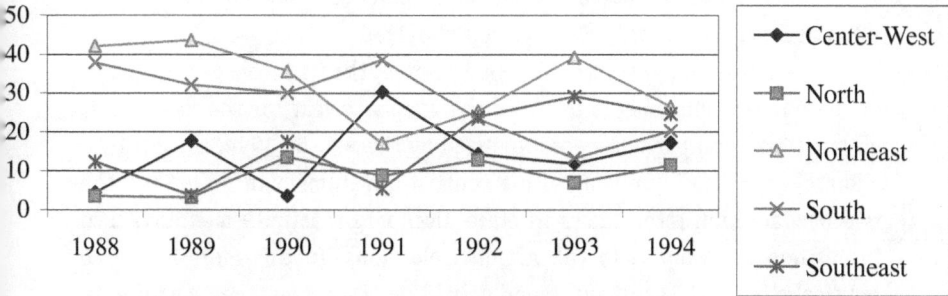

Source: CPT 1989a, 1990, 1991, 1992, 1993a, 1994, 1995.

there was a general deconcentration, as the MST's typically massive occupations spread beyond the South and certain northeastern states. A connected trend was the decreasing relative weight of the South, especially
during the Itamar Franco years. Occupation activity in the South maintained its intensity, but other regions grew. Although it is not visible in
these figures, there also occurred a deconcentration of occupations within
certain regions, especially the Northeast, where activity had initially been
focused largely in the state of Bahia.

The third and perhaps most striking shift was the growing importance
of the Southeast in the 1990s, especially in number of occupying families.
This shift was driven mainly by the MST's offensive in the Pontal do Paranapanema region of southwestern São Paulo (Fernandes 1996). In this region,
many of the rural "properties" were illegitimately held, fruit of a long process of land grabbing, or *grilagem*. In the early 1990s, the MST began sending

experienced activists from various parts of Brazil to the Pontal to organize occupations. The goal was to pressure the state government, the legitimate owner of most of the landholdings, to recoup the larger ones and redistribute them to landless families. Although it had only gained one provisional settlement by the end of 1994, the MST succeeded in generating high expectations and was able to organize vast occupations.

With regard to the organizational affiliation of the occupying groups, the 1989 CPT data show that the MST was responsible for 61.2 percent of the occupations and 78.2 percent of the families occupying. The disparity between these two figures reflects the larger average size of MST actions. For the years 1990–94, we can compare the MST's account of its own occupations with the more general CPT figures. For the number of occupying families, the MST and CPT data are not comparable. As Table 3 suggests, the MST was responsible for an average of about 65 percent of all the land occupations in Brazil during the 1989–94 period overall.

The two outlying years would seem to reflect the MST's role as the anchor of the landless movement. In 1990, the toughest year for the movement, all but seven occupations were organized by the MST. By 1994, the political climate was much improved, with a centrist government in power and the two new agrarian reform laws in place. Occupation activity may have also intensified in response to the national elections. In this more favorable political climate, less organized and politicized groups were more willing to try their luck at pressuring authorities. As a result, the relative weight of the MST decreased.

Development of the MST

As these data suggest, the MST played a critical role in the landless movement's survival and modest growth during the late 1980s and early 1990s.

Table 3   MST occupations as percentage of total

Year	Total Occupations	MST Occupations	% of Total
1989	80	49	61.2
1990	50	43	86.0
1991	77	51	66.2
1992	81	49	60.5
1993	89	54	60.7
1994	119	52	43.7

Source: CPT 1990, 1991, 1992, 1993a, 1994, 1995; Petras 1998.

The sustained level of protest activity, even during the difficult Collor years, was largely a reflection of this organization's geographical expansion and organizational consolidation. When the MST held its first national congress in January 1985 in Curitíba, the capital of Paraná, it was little more than a loose alliance of local activist groups, concentrated mainly in the South and strongly dependent on the Catholic Church. Over the next several years, this alliance would gradually develop into a relatively autonomous and impressively cohesive organization with a substantial presence in twenty-one of Brazil's twenty-three states and in all its major regions. Although the MST would continue to evolve in later years, this was a critical period in its history, when many of its most basic characteristics were established. It is therefore worthwhile to examine the MST's internal development during the 1985-94 period in some depth.

Goals and Tactics

From its earliest moments, the MST sought a radical restructuring of Brazil's landholding system, based on the expropriation of all private farms that were either unproductive or beyond a maximum size limit (MST 1986b). The MST's objectives were never limited to agrarian reform, however. It also desired socialism, not only because the leadership endorsed socialist principles, but also because they believed that a truly fundamental land reform could not be achieved under capitalism.[9] The MST was aware that the concrete material benefits that individual landless workers and families gained by struggling for land were "the motor force" that allowed it to "massify" its actions and gain political influence (MST 1989b, 10), but the leadership felt that the struggle should not remain a merely "economic" or "corporative" one. This force must be turned into a political struggle for a broad agrarian reform, from which all Brazilian landless workers would benefit.

Early on, the land occupation consolidated itself as the MST's core tactic, around which the rest of its tactical repertoire was built. As stated in Chapter 3, during the early 1980s, while the movement was still under church tutelage, occupations were sometimes considered a tactic to be used only when less aggressive means, such as demonstrations and petitions, were

9. The MST rejected armed struggle. However, this decision was apparently not absolute. A manifesto and leadership handbook published in 1986 stated, "The use of arms should be understood as an instrument to be used in certain phases of the struggle for social transformations, if necessary" (MST 1986b, 150).

exhausted. The activists who formed the core of the MST leadership considered this stance excessively timid, and once the MST struck out on its own, occupations became the rule rather than the exception. During its inaugural congress, the MST adopted the phrase "Occupation is the solution" as one of its mottos.

Occupations continued to be coupled with encampments at roadsides or in other public areas. Although these were usually formed following the expulsion of a group of campers from an occupied estate, they could also be created prior to occupying land. Under the MST, camp discipline became even more rigorous. Campers were expected to be present in the camps and contribute to routine tasks, such as digging latrines, mounting security patrols, and attending organizational meetings. In addition, they were supposed to participate in nonoccupation protest tactics, such as marches and demonstrations in urban areas; road blockages; and occupations of public agencies, such as state branches of the INCRA or the state agricultural secretariat. Campers who were undisciplined or refused to comply with these demands would be expelled from the camp.

To an even greater extent than they did during the movement's emergence phase, the encampments functioned as spaces for political indoctrination and collective identity building. An important task of MST activists was to "work the consciousness" of campers, cultivating a leftist political perspective and loyalty to the goals, methods, and symbols of the MST. The idea was to strengthen the commitment and resolve of the campers. If they could be made to understand the deeper, radical purpose of the MST, they would be more likely to resist cooptation and repression and to remain committed to the MST's struggle once they gained land. Some of them, furthermore, might decide to dedicate their lives to the MST, becoming full-time activists. Political indoctrination also took place in the land reform settlements established through MST pressure, but the camps were a privileged space for it. The hardship and direct conflict with the state that they involved tended to promote class consciousness. Furthermore, campers were essentially a captive audience, since at least part of each family was obliged to stay in the encampment at all times and to follow the directives of MST activists.

The MST was frequently willing to physically confront police, landowners, and private security guards or gunmen who sought to expel it from occupied farms or other locations where it was engaged in protest. This disposition, combined with the willingness of the MST's opponents to use violence, led to sharp conflicts, some of them deadly. Deaths grew more common as the MST expanded outside the South to regions, such as the North and Northeast, where the rule of law was weak. However, in general, MST protestors did not carry firearms. When they participated in occupations and other actions, campers and settlers were encouraged to bring farm implements: machetes, sickles, and hoes. These symbolized their agricultural vocation and could be used for self-defense without inviting the kind of repression that would come from carrying guns.

The MST's tactics were influenced by the evolving political context. As the prospects for land redistribution darkened in the late 1980s, the MST's initial reaction was to dig in its heels and intensify its pressure on authorities. If the government was not going to implement land reform, the MST would do so itself by occupying land and simply refusing to leave it. This attitude was expressed in the motto adopted by the MST at its 1989 national meeting: "Occupy, resist, produce." The leadership also sought to increase pressure on federal authorities by organizing coordinated national protest campaigns. During a particular day or week, each state MST organization would mount some kind of protest event or, better yet, several of them. These "days of struggle" began in 1989 and were consolidated as a tactic in the early 1990s, occurring two or three times a year.[10]

During the Collor years victories became even scarcer and repression increased. In this context, the MST began to shift its strategic focus from stubbornly resisting authorities to trying to appeal more directly to the urban public, by then close to 80 percent of the national population.[11] This change responded to a growing sense that, if waged exclusively in the countryside, the struggle for land would be "suffocated" by landowner power and state neglect. The movement needed to take its struggle to the cities and convince the urban majority of the virtues of land redistribution, including a slowdown in rural-urban migration and cheaper food prices (MST 1996). With this idea in mind, in late 1994 the MST leadership formulated a

10. "Days of struggle" seemed to drop out of the MST's repertoire after Collor's fall, perhaps because the national political context made them seem less necessary. They would reappear in the late 1990s.

11. The Brazilian census bureau defines as urban that portion of any *município*'s population that lives in the administrative center, which is almost always the most densely populated area of the *município*. Some analysts argue that this definition artificially inflates the size of the urban population, since it classifies as urban many small towns of the interior with only a few thousand people. Nevertheless, no one questions the fact that by 1990, Brazil's population was predominantly urban.

new motto to be officially adopted at the organization's third congress the following year: "Agrarian reform: everyone's struggle."

Organizational Structure

By the late 1980s, the MST had settled on a national leadership structure featuring two main institutions. Broad policy decisions would be made by the National Coordination, composed of two representatives from each state. A smaller body, the National Directorate, was charged with the day-to-day management, as well as with strategic thinking and long-range planning. Its members were chosen by the National Coordination on the basis of competence alone. In practice, the directorate was the key decision-making body. One of its tasks was to oversee the National Secretariat in São Paulo, which served as an administrative center, coordinating collective activities and fund-raising. At the state level, the MST was organized in a similar fashion. In each state there existed at least a State Directorate. Where the MST was more developed, there was a State Coordination as well. Some states also had regional leadership structures.

In addition to these core decision-making institutions, the MST gradually developed "sectors" to deal with specific issues, such as grassroots recruitment, education, finance, women, settlement production, and international relations. They were organized through leadership structures at the national level and, depending on the number of activists available to staff them, in the individual states and substate regions. Leadership at all levels was collective, a legacy of the popular church's participatory *basista* philosophy. Rhetorically, and generally in practice as well, personalist leadership styles were strongly discouraged.

The MST professed to adhere to Lenin's principle of "democratic centralism." Issues were to be debated openly and collectively; once a majority had decided to back a particular view, that decision was binding on all. Decisions about leadership selection and other key issues were, in fact, discussed by collective bodies. Some were even voted on in mass assemblies, often in the context of state and national meetings, but decisions were generally taken by consensus rather than through real electoral processes, involving secret ballots and meticulous vote counts.[12] This gave respected senior leaders a determining role in shaping key decisions.

12. Interview with Angela Schwengber, a former MST militant from the Alto Uruguai, November 1997, São Paulo, SP.

The distribution of power within the MST became progressively more cen-tralized during the course of the late 1980s. In his study of the MST's devel-opment in Paraná, Torrens (1992) noted an upward shift of decision-making authority. Decisions were increasingly made by the State or National Direc-torate and largely imposed on campers, settlers, and local activists. In my own research in various states during the late 1990s, I also found evidence that important decisions were made by the State Directorates, sometimes acting on directives from the national leadership. Leaders often claimed that individual camps had autonomy, but in practice, key decisions were usually made at the state level and merely rubber-stamped by camp leader-ships. States had substantial autonomy in deploying resources and plan-ning protests, but when the national leadership made a decision, it was obeyed.

The increasing centralization of power at the national level is reflected in internal documents. In its 1986 handbook, the MST had said that the national leadership institutions were a forum for discussing broad strategic issues and coordinating joint projects. Local and state groups maintained "total autonomy and power of decision" (MST 1986b, 57). In contrast, a 1989 booklet laying out the "general norms" of the MST made no mention of local and state autonomy (MST 1989a). In fact, it warned that landless groups that did not obey the MST's rules would not be recognized as part of the organization.

Like the emphasis on resistance to expulsion from occupied properties, the drive to centralize decision making during the late 1980s was in part a response to the increasingly difficult political context. Centralization was seen as a way of intensifying the pressure on federal authorities by coordi-nating demands and protest initiatives at a national level. As articulated in an editorial in the MST's internal newspaper, "We need to break with this federalism that makes each movement take care of its state alone. We need to increase our force, guarantee pressures and organization in all of the states."[13]

Leadership

A central goal of the MST was to become less dependent on the Catholic Church. Although the struggle for land had emerged in part as a result of

13. *Jornal Sem Terra,* April 1989.

church activism, the top leadership was wary of the limits that continued dependence on this institution could place on their ability to aggressively pressure the state for agrarian reform.[14] These concerns mounted as leftists within the church grew increasingly isolated in the late 1980s. A critical aspect of the MST's drive for autonomy was an attempt to build its own corps of activists and leaders. It achieved considerable success in this area. By the early 1990s the MST had dozens, if not hundreds, of well-trained activists dedicated exclusively to this organization.

Who were these people?[15] The "activists" I refer to are people who were involved in organizing MST activities on a frequent or full-time basis, and whose participation was not limited to their own camp or settlement. These were only a small minority of the organization's mass base of campers and settlers. Using the MST's own terminology, I distinguish, within this category, between "leaders," a group that consists basically of those who belonged to state or national leadership bodies, and "militants," who did not.

From its inception, the MST had stressed that rural workers themselves should lead the organization (MST 1986a, 1989b). In reality, however, activists were of diverse social origins. Militants were usually members of camper or settler families and were generally of very modest backgrounds. Those who came to occupy leadership positions were not, on average, from much more prosperous families. However, those who constituted the national leadership arguably were. In fact, a substantial part of the national leadership was made up of offspring of relatively prosperous southern smallholder families. Typically, these were individuals who had entered the movement in the early or mid-1980s largely or exclusively out of political conviction, rather than economic need.

In terms of educational level, militants in the South tended to have at least four years of formal education and the ability to read and write. However, in the Northeast and other underdeveloped regions, militants often had little or no formal education. Literacy was close to being a requirement for leadership, so those who could not read or write generally did not go beyond the militant level. Individuals who reached the national leadership often had at least a high school education, and a number of prominent leaders had attended a college or seminary. More educated leaders were

14. Interview with Darci Maschio, MST activist and member of the first Rio Grande do Sul state landless commission, March 10, 1998, Ronda Alta, RS.

15. My discussion of this question is based mainly on interviews with more than fifty people who were MST campers, settlers, or activists during 1985–94.

generally either from solid smallholder families or had been raised mainly in a town or city.[16]

Among the leadership, there were many people who had pre-MST activist experience. This was particularly true of the national leaders, who had often entered the movement in the early and mid-1980s after participating in the popular church. In fact, several top leaders had actually been progressive church activists before dedicating themselves exclusively to the MST. The most prominent of these was João Pedro Stedile. The former *gaúcho* CPT leader ran the MST's National Secretariat and, at some point during the late 1980s or early 1990s, became an official member of the National Directorate. By the end of the 1980s, with the decline of church activism and the MST's growing autonomy, fewer MST activists had a pre-MST political background. Rather, most of the new militants were MST campers and settlers who had joined the movement initially out of economic necessity.

Southerners played a central role in the MST's leadership, even outside the South. In other regions, local activism was often more limited and a low level of literacy impeded leadership formation. Moreover, even where the CPT and combative rural unions were strong, local activists were not necessarily interested in joining or even supporting the MST, which was often seen as an outside organization.[17] Thus, where it expanded, the MST could not always count on tapping into existing activist networks. To compensate, the MST often sent southern activists to lead its struggle in other regions.[18]

Campers and settlers sometimes contributed on a part-time basis, but activism in the MST often involved a full-time commitment. As I mentioned in Chapter 2, collective groups in southern settlements often "liberated" settlers to work in the MST, taking care of their plot and providing them with a share of the revenue. The dearth of such groups made this less common outside the South. Instead, most activists depended exclusively on the modest stipends provided by the State or National Secretariat. Even

16. Even if they had grown up in an urban area, militants and leaders tended to have at least a childhood background in agriculture. Few MST activists were purely urban people.

17. Interviews with former MST activists Nilza Pessoa de Souza (February 2000, João Pessoa, PB) and Advonsil Cândido Siqueira (November 5, 1999, Belém, PA). Each worked to establish the MST in their respective state during the late 1980s and early 1990s but encountered resistance from local activists.

18. For example, almost all the *gaúcho* MST leaders I interviewed had spent some time organizing the struggle in another state. One *gaúcho* MST leader told me that at least thirty activists from his state were helping to lead the struggle in other states. Interview with Augusto Olsson, March 24, 1998, Porto Alegre, RS.

the top leadership did not enjoy more than a lower-middle-class lifestyle. Although they did not receive much in the way of material compensation, rural youths who joined the MST often gained a new feeling of belonging, as well as the social prestige associated with being part of an influential, if controversial, organization.[19]

Political indoctrination and training of potential activists began informally in the MST's camps and settlements, but promising individuals were generally invited to participate in formal training programs at the state, regional, and national levels. The most advanced program was held at the MST's permanent National School in Santa Catarina and obligated most students to leave their home states for several months at a time. The National School brought in activists from all over Brazil and graduating from it became a source of considerable prestige and upward mobility within the MST.

These courses involved a combination of ideological instruction, personal improvement, and practical leadership skills. The aim, first and foremost, was to cultivate a radical political perspective. Participants were taught elementary Marxist sociology, in classrooms adorned with images of Marx, Lenin, and Mao. A great deal of emphasis was placed on the need for activists to read and study, based on the idea that this would make them less vulnerable to manipulation and cooptation by elites and the state. They were also pushed to change their personal behavior, becoming more disciplined and less individualistic. Students in these courses were even advised to cultivate an orderly personal appearance.[20] Finally, they were taught how to deal with concrete organizational challenges, such as running a meeting and rewarding exemplary conduct.

This strategy seems to have been rather successful in fomenting ideological homogeneity, personal discipline, and commitment to the MST. There were few signs of ideological cleavages or factionalism. The MST's success in this area has not always been seen in a positive light, however. Critics of the MST have frequently commented that its training courses turned naive rural youths into "robots" whose political "consciousness" was limited to their skill in parroting the revolutionary slogans formulated by top leaders and ideologues (Torrens 1992; Navarro 2000).

19. A number of activists told me that the MST had become their life, or a surrogate family.
20. One training manual, for example, advised activists to take good care of their teeth (MST 1991, 43).

Material Resources

When it held its first congress in January 1985 the MST was strongly dependent on the CPT and other church entities not only for leadership, but for material resources as well. The drive for autonomy thus also involved a quest for new sources of material support. Priority was placed on deriving as many of the MST's resources as possible from its own campers and settlers. In practice, however, virtually all of the MST's financial resources came, either directly or indirectly, from external actors, particularly foreign NGOs, the federal government, and various progressive domestic groups.

Campers were not in a position to contribute much, so within the MST's own social base, the onus fell on settlers. By the late 1980s, most of the settlers' financial contribution to the MST probably came from their subsidized government credits. In 1986, responding to pressure from rural activist groups, the federal government established a special subsidized agricultural credit program for agrarian reform settlers, called PROCERA (Special Credit Program for Agrarian Reform). MST policy in 1989 was that settlers should contribute 1 percent of each credit. By 1994 the guideline was set at 1–5 percent, to be determined by each state (MST 1994c, item 56). In addition, the MST called on settlers and their associations and cooperatives to contribute 5 percent of any grant received from a state agency or NGO.

In practice, the percentages were flexible and depended on the loyalty of local settlers. However, individuals and groups who did not contribute could be subject to strong sanctions; if possible, they would be excluded from future distributions of credit.[21] Settler families and groups that did not comply with the regional or state MST resolutions regarding financial contributions could be excluded from the organization. Exclusion could mean social isolation, as well as lack of access to some of the resources the MST obtained through political pressure and links to funding agencies.

Another, probably equally important source of funding were foreign NGOs, mainly European religious foundations.[22] Torrens (1992), for example,

21. The MST wanted authorities to establish this as a national policy (MST 1989a, item 89). Although this does not seem to have occurred, the MST was probably successful in imposing this policy in some areas.

22. Two people who worked in the MST National Secretariat during the second half of the 1980s said that the MST was heavily dependent on foreign NGO funding during this period. Interviews with Angela Schwengber, a former MST militant from the Alto Uruguai, November 1997, São Paulo, SP, and Flademir Araújo, former editor of the *Boletim Sem Terra* and, later, the *Jornal Sem Terra*, March 5, 1998, Porto Alegre, RS.

argues that such support was critical in making the MST in Paraná more independent from domestic church groups. The MST also continued to receive assistance from Catholic dioceses, domestic Catholic NGOs, and other domestic groups, such as urban labor unions. This included use of infrastructure, such as buses, office space, and printing presses; donations of food for MST camps; and occasionally loans and cash. Sympathetic public officials, generally linked to the PT, also helped with funding and infrastructure.

Crafting Solidarity

From early on, the MST leadership was conscious of the need to build not only human and material resources, but also a strong collective identity that would cement the organization's membership through affective bonds. In the early years of the movement, religious faith had fulfilled this function. Activists and the rank and file had come together around powerful religious symbols, such as the large wooden cross at Encruzilhada Natalino, and such biblical metaphors as the story of the Exodus. Religious symbolism, however, was less readily available to nonclergy, and the activists who eventually took control of the MST were not necessarily deeply religious. Thus, it became necessary to create a new, more secular set of cultural symbols and practices.

Over the years, the MST developed a methodology for promoting what it called *mística*, or "mystique," among its activists and mass membership base. This somewhat diffuse concept referred, in essence, to feelings of friendship and solidarity and the sense of holding common values and being part of a common struggle, embodied institutionally by the MST. According to an activist manual: "*Mística* is the internal motivation that we feel when we are in contact with the collectivity, which animates us and increases our will to participate more and more. . . . It is everything that makes us feel good, satisfied, and that makes us vibrate, leaving us with a feeling of longing and wanting to participate again" (MST 1991, 34–35).

Activities meant to promote *mística* occurred mainly in the context of leadership meetings and mass assemblies. These, the MST underscored, could not be cold bureaucratic affairs. They had to be festive events involving singing, skits, poetry, chants, or homage paid to past heroes or fallen companions. Meeting facilities had to be decorated with posters, flowers, and visual symbols of the struggle. In anticipation of any important gathering, a committee was formed to develop a creative cultural program, including an opening and closing ceremony. To some extent, these practices were an updated version of popular organizing methods developed earlier by the popular church, but with the MST, they took on a more secular and overtly politicized tone.

Two important tools of *mística* activities were the MST's official flag and hymn. Both expressed the MST's determination to struggle. The flag, adopted in 1988, featured a young couple, the man holding aloft a machete, superimposed on a map of Brazil. A bright red background surrounded this central symbol. Meant to be sung with a clenched fist raised to the sky, the hymn was a call to arms for Brazilian workers, making only passing reference to land: "With our arm raised we will dictate our history / Suffocating with force our oppressors / Let's raise the red flag / Let's wake up this sleeping fatherland / Tomorrow belongs to us, the workers." The flag and hymn were of obligatory use at all MST activities.[23] They were to be treated with honor and respect. The hymn was authored by Ademar Bogo, a former Catholic seminarian from Santa Catarina who was probably the MST's most important ideologue.

Grassroots Recruitment

The social characteristics of the people recruited into the MST shifted over time. Although they had never completely dominated MST camps, offspring of smallholders and smallholders who had lost their land were a major component of the organization's mass base during the early years. As the MST expanded geographically into regions with a weaker independent farming tradition, the smallholder influence faded and people accustomed to wage labor or more precarious forms of access to farmland took on a larger role. MST campers also tended to become more urban. They included agricultural wage laborers living in towns and small cities, as well as individuals who worked in low-wage urban professions, such as street vendors, truck drivers, or construction workers. The INCRA and some state land agencies technically required that settlers be "rural workers." However, in practice this rule was not rigorously enforced. Although increasingly recruited in urban areas, the vast majority of campers continued to be of rural upbringing and to have at least some experience working in agriculture.

23. One MST activist manual even suggested that the bodies of colleagues killed during the struggle be wrapped in the flag for burial (MST 1991, 34).

The shift toward urban recruitment seems to have reflected a number of different factors. First, in many areas, the agricultural labor force was increasingly concentrated in town centers, rather than on farms or in villages. By the early 1990s, even some more backward states were becoming predominantly urban. Those who had left the countryside, moreover, were often the poorest of the poor, the landless wage laborers. Their desperate economic situation made them more disposed to join the struggle for land. In addition, urban areas offered important strategic advantages. Landless families were less dispersed, progressive actors were closer at hand, and landowners had more trouble interfering in the recruiting process.

The character of grassroots recruitment also changed in another way. Earlier, landless families had often been recruited through existing grassroots organizations, such as church groups and unions. Over the years, bloc recruitment through such networks became less prominent. They were often weaker outside the South, and where they existed, they did not always favor the MST. In addition, the decline of church and union activism tended to undermine progressive grassroots groups all over the country. Increasingly, MST militants arrived in a town or village and simply recruited families door to door.

Settlements and Collectivism

The settlements "conquered" by pressuring the state were always regarded as a crucial part of the MST (MST 1986b). As was discussed above, the MST strove to harness the human and material resources of its settlers by urging them to participate in protest actions, "liberate" individuals for full-time activism, and make monetary contributions. Settlements also played a crucial role as models of what agrarian reform could accomplish when it came to settler welfare and farm production. Because of the importance of settlements to its ongoing struggle, the MST devoted a great deal of attention to the question of how to best organize them. Probably the single biggest and most controversial issue was how and to what extent to prioritize collectivism.

As far back as the early 1980s, the landless movement's leadership in the South had favored collective production. For pastoral agents, this was seen as a way both of improving settler welfare and promoting a fraternal ethos consistent with liberation theology's critique of capitalist individualism. The MST reinforced this emphasis and gave it a more explicitly political overtone. Collective production would increase efficiency, allowing settlers to cultivate more land, buy more machines and modern inputs, and diversify their production (MST 1986b). From a political standpoint, collective production had two advantages. First, it meant that former campers would not lapse into anomic individualism once they gained land. They would remain organized and develop ties of solidarity, rather than engaging in divisive competition. Second, collective production groups would facilitate the "liberation" of individual settlers for full-time activism.[24]

The MST leadership was particularly interested in promoting fully collective production, in which there was almost no private farmland and each family received wages based on the number of hours they worked. The MST stressed in its documents that the decision of how to organize production belonged to each family; nevertheless, in at least some regions, MST activists exerted a good deal of pressure on member families, beginning in the camping phase, where they were encouraged to form groups that would later become settlement cooperatives.

By the end of the 1980s fully collective production groups existed in a number of settlements, almost all of them in the South. In 1989, the MST decided to intensify its efforts to collectivize production and to make that drive part of a broader campaign to create a network of cooperatives. The entire structure would be known as the Settlers' Cooperative System, or SCA (CONCRAB 1999). The key to the SCA would be settlement-level collective groups, now termed Agricultural Production Cooperatives (CPAS). These would be prioritized, in order to become public showcases for the MST's economic success. Regional cooperatives would coordinate marketing and collective purchases among various settlements. State-level Central Agricultural Cooperatives (CCAS), bringing together all the CPAS and settlement associations in a state, would be set up to provide advice and services and coordinate collective marketing, transport, and purchasing of inputs and machinery. Finally, the CCAS would be linked to a national entity called the National Confederation of Agrarian Reform Cooperatives of Brazil (CONCRAB).

The MST's long-term vision was to leave behind subsistence production and push toward a model of large-scale, highly capitalized cooperative farms. Settlers would eventually be essentially wage laborers instead of individual farmers, exchanging their "peasant" identity for a "worker con-

24. Interview with Isaias Vendovatto, former member of the MST National Directorate, March 10, 1998, Ronda Alta, RS.

sciousness" (CONCRAB 1999, 11). Labor liberated by the mechanization of production would be absorbed in local agroindustrial ventures, so that the children of settlers would not feel compelled to migrate to the cities. The MST's leadership felt that, with the increasing industrialization of agriculture, settlers who did not modernize would not be economically viable.

By the end of 1994, the MST had more than forty CPAS, seven CCAS, and six regional cooperatives, but the aggressive campaign in favor of collective production had generated problems. Many settlers had abandoned their CPAS, and those who had not joined—the vast majority—often felt marginalized from the MST. The push for collectivism had often divided settlements and in some cases led settlers to distance themselves from the MST. As a result, the MST decided to soften its advocacy of fully collective production somewhat and put more emphasis on promoting less "advanced" forms of cooperation, such as collective purchases of inputs and machines (CONCRAB 1997).

Relations with Other Progressive Actors

The MST's growing influence and its fierce defense of its autonomy and methods made it controversial, even among leftists. Relations with the popular church were sometimes strained. This was particularly true outside the South, where the MST's presence was not always welcomed. CPT activists complained that the MST insisted on imposing its own rules and methods on local workers without respecting local traditions of struggle.[25] Aggressive tactics designed in the South, they argued, were not fit for regions with more conservative politics, where rebellious workers were often murdered. Complaints also arose about the MST's occasionally heavy-handed promotion of collectivism. The fact that many MST activists were from out of state served to intensify resentment.

During the 1980s, the MST had close relations with the top leadership of the *cutista* rural union movement.[26] At the state and local level, however, even CUT activists did not always get along with the MST. They had many of the same criticisms as pastoral agents, and the fading of the combative union movement brought new tensions. In the early 1990s, the CUT began talking about extending membership to the CONTAG. This was a turn away

25. Interview with Father Hermínio Canova, CPT coordinator for the Northeast, May 24, 1998, Recife, PE.
26. In contrast, the MST's relations with the CONTAG were distant, if not antagonistic.

from its original, more radical strategy of creating a parallel union structure, or taking over the STRS one by one. The MST was highly critical of this idea, which it saw as surrendering to conservative forces, and its criticism made collaboration with the CUT harder.[27]

The MST tended to have less problematic relations with the urban Left. The leadership maintained good relations with many *cutista* urban unions, as well as with the largely urban-based PT. Agrarian reform was one of the party's key planks and in the 1989 and 1994 presidential election campaigns, Lula had promised a major agrarian reform. The MST as an organization supported the PT and campaigned in favor of its candidates. Some of the landless movement's founders in the South had become successful PT politicians by the early 1990s, and some of the MST's own activists (although generally not the most important ones) ran for local office on PT slates.

Other Landless Groups

As the data presented earlier in the chapter suggest, there were many land occupations not linked to the MST, especially when the political climate was relatively promising. Many non-MST occupations were organized by rural workers themselves, with little or no help from political activists. This was particularly true in regions that had recently made up the agricultural frontier. In such areas, as described in the preceding chapter, organized land occupations were really an extension of traditional squatting practices, in which migratory farming families settled on unused public land. Nevertheless, even in these cases, union or church activists were often sought out for legal and political support after the fact. In other instances, activists were involved from the very beginning, often initiating the effort themselves.

Like those affiliated with the MST, non-MST landless groups sometimes established camps after being expelled from an occupied property. This, though, was probably more the exception than the rule. Especially in frontier regions, where there was little in the way of a public opinion or media presence to appeal to, such groups were more likely to return to where they came from, rather than camp at the roadside. Partly as a result, landless

27. Interview with Altemir Tortelli, vice president of the CUT, April 15, 2000, São Paulo, SP. In 1995 the CONTAG did become part of the CUT.

workers engaged in non-MST actions were also less likely to engage in other types of protest actions for land reform, such as marches, demonstrations, or occupations of the INCRA.

As a rule, non-MST activist groups had a different relationship to their social base than the MST had with its own base. Although the non-MST groups undoubtedly expected some degree of loyalty from campers and settlers, they were less controlling than the MST. They did not try to enforce as rigid a brand of discipline in their occupations and camps, and did not subordinate them to a broader organizational logic defined at the state and national level. Nor did they try to push settlers to adopt certain types of production. At the same time, in many states, non-MST groups did not have the financial and human resources the MST had at its disposal to devote to the struggle. Moreover, they did not fight as aggressively for credit and other types of assistance for "their" settlers. Hence, although the MST expected a greater commitment from its base, it also tended to offer more in return. Below, I briefly discuss some of the main non-MST actors in the struggle for land.

Rural Unions

In many areas of Brazil, local rural unions were the key organizational actors behind land occupations. In some cases, union involvement occurred mainly after an occupation had already taken place. The occupiers sought out union leaders in order to benefit from their expertise, access to legal assistance, and contacts with local officials and progressive organizations. Although union leaders were not involved in the actual preparation of the land occupation, the prospects of gaining their assistance after the occupation had taken place undoubtedly emboldened landless families to take actions they would otherwise not have engaged in. In other cases, union leaders played an important role even before the occupation, informing landless families about a vulnerable property, or actually recruiting them in local communities.[28]

Most rural union leaders were of rural worker origin and had probably grown up in the *municipio* where they were engaged in activism. Since land occupations were relatively bold actions, union leaders involved in them

---

28. Interview with Francisco de Assis Soledade da Costa, Southeast region coordinator, Federation of Workers in Agriculture of the State of Pará (FETAGRI-PA), October 9, 1999, Marabá, PA.

were often leftists. They were usually affiliated with the CUT and often had a background in the progressive church. Union leaders frequently acted in alliance with other local progressive actors, including party and church activists. In many areas, combative STRs were closely linked to the CPT, FASE (a Catholic NGO), or individual clergy, forming a network of activism (Maybury-Lewis 1994).

In a small number of states, the state rural union federation had a policy of supporting the struggle for land through occupations and other forms of protest. Nevertheless, STR-led occupations were usually local affairs. They were organized by individual STRs and did not involve much coordination at higher levels. Moreover, unlike the MST, union leaders did not generally recruit families from outside the *município* where the occupation was taking place. Doing so could cause political problems with other STRs, since it involved subtracting actual or potential members and leaders from one STR and adding them to another. Families settled with the help of a local STR often were or became members of the union and depended on union leaders in dealing with elected officials and government agencies.

In the South, after the mid-1980s, the rural unions were generally not involved in the landless movement. This was the role of the MST. In other regions, the extent of STR involvement in the movement varied by state and local area. In states with particularly combative unions, such as Pará and Bahia, STRs organized or supported occupations in several *municípios*. In other states, union involvement in the movement was spottier.

Other Actors

CPT activism in the landless movement during this period usually took the form of supporting the efforts of other actors, such as the STRs and the MST. The CPT provided legal assistance, political support, contacts to church authorities, and access to funding from foreign NGOs. In some cases, CPT activists were more directly involved in organizing land occupations. Perhaps the clearest case of this type of involvement was in the state of Mato Grosso do Sul. There, the CPT had initially supported the implantation of the MST; then, in about 1987, there was a falling out between the two organizations. The CPT continued to organize land occupations on its own, sometimes in collaboration with more combative STRs. Its relationship to the MST was one of competition.

A few organizations not directly linked to the church, unions, or MST

organized land occupations during this period. One, the CENTRU, was mentioned in the preceding chapter. The CENTRU was active in resistance struggles and land occupations in the northeastern state of Maranhão. In
addition, in a few areas, new activist groups began to appear during the
Franco years devoted more or less exclusively to organizing land occupations. At least two such groups sprung up in 1994, the Struggle for Land
Movement (MLT), active in Bahia and Pará, and the Landless Movement of
Southern Mato Grosso (MST-SMT) (Fernandes 1999, 254). They would become
much more numerous during the second half of the 1990s.

Explaining the Landless Movement's Exceptionalism

As the preceding discussion shows, the landless movement was a clear exception to the general rule of movement decline after the early 1980s. It
not only survived, but managed to grow significantly and spread to new
areas of the country. How can we explain its unusual trajectory relative to
other democratic transition–era movements?

One possible explanation lies in the evolution of grievances. A griev-
ance/discontent-based account might be centered on the idea that the
grievances of the rural landless increased or remained constant after 1985,
while those of other groups tended to decline. This is a plausible argument
when comparing the landless movement to movements whose central purpose was either achieved or rendered irrelevant through the regime transition process, such as the movement for political amnesty in the late 1970s
and the 1984 movement for direct presidential elections. After amnesty
was granted and the presidential election passed, these movements lost
their reason for being.

However, there were many social movements that did not fall into this
category that nevertheless declined. Many movements that arose during
the transition era had as their main goal the pursuit of social reforms or
better wages and working conditions. The transition to democracy did not
in itself address their demands. Nor is there much reason to believe that
Sarney's social policies did, since these were not particularly generous.
Moreover, the economic decline after 1987 only served to aggravate social
indicators. Although the landless movement's members were among the
poorest of the poor, there is little reason to believe that the landless as a
group experienced a steeper decline than others. In fact, as the preceding

discussion suggests, the movement's social base was heterogeneous and not really distinct from that of many other popular movements, such as the rural union movement and, to a lesser extent, movements that sought to represent the needs of the urban poor.

If absolute necessity does not explain the movement's exceptionalism, perhaps relative deprivation can do a better job. Sarney's aborted land reform proposal might have generated feelings of deprivation by raising the hopes of landless workers very high in 1985, only to dash them in subsequent years. Was it a strong feeling of being robbed that motivated the landless to continue struggling after other movements had given up? This seems rather implausible. The struggle to obtain a plot of land was a protracted process (sometimes lasting a number of years) that involved substantial hardship and sacrifice for men, women, and children. It is hard to believe that resentment over the abandonment of the PNRA would have led people who would otherwise not have subjected themselves to the rigors of camping to do so. Moreover, even if such an effect existed, it certainly would have faded by 1990, under a new government.

From an organizational capacity perspective, one possible answer to this puzzle is that the preexisting organizations and networks from which the landless movement emerged were unusually strong, giving it exceptional staying power. My discussion of the MST's development in this chapter should cast some doubt on this idea. Although the social networks from which the MST arose in the southern *colônias* were indeed quite robust, as was emphasized in Chapter 2, during 1985–94 the movement increasingly expanded into communities with weaker social ties. Bloc recruitment, as I mentioned, was replaced by door-to-door recruitment. Yet this shift did not affect the movement's ability to recruit new members. On the contrary, MST activists often came to view church- and union-based associative networks as an obstacle.[29]

Another possibility is that the landless movement continued to benefit from external resources to a greater extent than did other movements. External resources are, in fact, central to some accounts of the decline of social movements in Brazil. In particular, most analysts argue that the partial withdrawal of the Catholic Church from its activist role played a critical part in the decline of popular protest, because it deprived movements of

---

29. Top MST leader José Rainha made this point to me in an informal conversation in Teodoro Sampaio, São Paulo, in November 1997. He said the church *atrapalha,* or "gets in the way," of the MST's struggle.

many of the resources that the progressive church had provided (Doimo 1995; Houtzager 1997). Church activism had helped both to legitimize the use of protest tactics and to facilitate organization through such entities as the CEBS, the CPT, and youth groups. After the mid-1980s these spaces declined or took on a more spiritual orientation, and church authorities no longer backed movements as vigorously.

Unfortunately, this argument does not provide a firm basis on which to differentiate the landless movement from other movements of the 1980s. Few movements were as closely identified with the popular church as was the landless movement. Throughout the early 1980s, the movement was highly dependent on Catholic Church resources. The MST did make concerted efforts to diversify its sources of funding and build its own corps of activists, but it seems unlikely that it was the only SMO that was aware of the need to do so. Because of its rejection of postwar populism, the Brazilian Left in general tended to be wary of relying heavily on non-working-class allies. All else being equal, the church's backpedaling should have affected the landless movement as much as the many other movements that had emerged with its assistance. And yet it did not. The landless movement was able to advance in spite of its growing independence from the CPT and other church groups.

I should also address another capacity-based argument used to explain movement decline in Brazil. A number of authors have noted that the consolidation of party competition during the 1980s had negative effects on social movement cohesion, undermining the ability to organize protest events. Some argue that party competition divided movement activists, as some sided with the PT and others with the PMDB, undercutting movement unity (Mainwaring 1989). Others assert that the establishment of electoral competition and the opportunity for holding public office lured some activists out of grassroots organizing and into campaigning and government (Doimo 1995).

At the mass level, the landless movement was probably more divided in party preference than the urban movements these authors focus on. Many campers, especially outside the South, were even clients of local PFL and PTB bosses. At the leadership level, the MST was solidly pro-PT, but this was also true of the rural and urban new unionism, which declined noticeably in the late 1980s; therefore, the extent of party divisions is not a compelling explanation of the movement's exceptionalism. It is possible, though by no means clear, that proportionately fewer leaders left the landless movement for electoral politics than left some other movements. The loss of leaders to party politics was not a common complaint of the MST leadership. However, this difference hardly seems enough to explain the movement's exceptional trajectory.

Thus, neither the grievance/discontent nor the organizational capacity perspective provides much leverage on the question of why the landless movement continued to grow while other movements declined following Brazil's transition to democracy. The activist strategy perspective, by contrast, does shed substantial light on this issue.

Specifically, I would underscore the importance of the decision to prioritize land occupations. While doing so, I focus on tactical choice for reasons that are somewhat different from those typically cited by social movement researchers, who have mainly looked at the effectiveness of certain tactical approaches in causing problems for elites or drawing the attention of potential supporters and bystander publics. The use of land occupations was important mainly because it created a distinctive set of incentives for movement participation. Unlike most other movement tactics, the land occupation allowed participants to stake a personal, or family, claim to the fruits of their efforts. When Brazilian authorities responded to the pressures exerted by landless campers, they generally did so by settling only the families involved in the camp, rather than others who did not participate. In contrast, when movements relied exclusively on other types of tactics, such as demonstrations, marches, or strikes, the participants were generally no more likely to benefit from resulting concessions than were other people with similar needs who did not participate. The activists did the work, but everyone shared in the benefits.

In other words, through the use of land occupations and the resulting encampments to pressure the state, the movement largely sidestepped the problem of free riding articulated by Olson (1965). As was outlined in Chapter 1, Olson argued that people with a common interest in some good usually fail to act collectively to obtain it because they lack an individual incentive to do so. To a large extent, the problem lies in the fact that the goods that groups seek are, according to Olson, public goods. This means that those who do not contribute to obtaining the good cannot feasibly be denied its benefits if the good is provided. Because of this problem, collective action that stands to benefit a large group will occur only if potential beneficiaries are provided an additional, "selective" incentive, such as an economic reward for participating or punishment for nonparticipation.

Of course, as movement scholars have emphasized, collective protest often occurs in the absence of significant selective incentives. This is mainly because participation is motivated by nonmaterial incentives, such as political principle and a sense of moral responsibility (Fireman and Gamson 1979; Hirschman 1982). Hence, the free-rider problem is certainly not an insuperable obstacle. Nevertheless, its existence means that movement organizations that pursue collective goods usually rely strongly on the more normative motivations of potential recruits. While such motivations can, to some extent, be created by the framing strategies of activists and movement organizations, their existence is also a function of the broader environment in which movements function. In some times and places, nonmaterial incentives for activism are stronger than in others.

In Brazil during the 1970s and early 1980s such incentives were strong, largely because of the existence of an unelected, repressive, and deeply conservative military government that had resulted from the forceful overthrow of a relatively democratic regime. Particularly once the economic expansion that had helped to legitimate military rule began to falter, this situation functioned as a potent source of political grievances, motivating protest activity. Even social movements that were organized to pursue essentially economic goals were also driven by a principled rejection of dictatorial rule. The strikes mounted by urban workers, for example, were "much more than an instrument of pressure circumscribed to the arena of workers relations." Rather, they were "confounded with the social mobilization effort for the re-democratization of the country" (M. Oliveira 1998, 24).

The return to civilian, democratic rule, however, undermined this source of incentives for movement activity. It thus helped bring about the end of the protest cycle. In this context, the land occupation offered key advantages as a tactic. Unlike participants in most other social movements, those who participated in these actions were not, primarily, pursuing a public good. When the state responded positively to land occupations, it was by providing land only to those involved in the initiative. There was little opportunity to free ride and, as a consequence, the movement was less dependent on the existence in the larger society of strong normative motivations capable of overcoming this problem. It could rely, rather, on the narrow desire of each camper or family of campers to obtain an individual plot of land from the government.

This does not mean, of course, that the movement did not depend on idealistic incentives at all. As I have made clear, MST activists displayed high ideological commitment and a deep loyalty to their cause. cpt and union leaders were often also motivated by strong beliefs and moral values. However, the fact that the recruitment of the landless into the camping process did not rely heavily on nonmaterial motivations for participation was a huge advantage in generating mass mobilization. It is telling in this sense that, when one of the founders of the mst in Rio Grande do Sul tried to organize a movement of smallholders to push for a more subsidized line of agricultural credit in the late 1990s, one of the demands he and other leaders put forward was that authorities award the new credit only to those who had participated in protest actions (Görgen 1998, 17). Clearly, these activists were conscious of the obstacle that free riding can pose to social movement growth.

As this discussion suggests, Olson's assumption (implicitly accepted by virtually all social movement researchers who have commented on his theory) that collective action necessarily involves the pursuit of a public or collective good is flawed. At least under some conditions, social movements can seek goods that do not fit Olson's definition of a public good. In such instances, the free-rider problem is less relevant as an obstacle to achieving collective action, although other obstacles remain. The landless movement is an especially impressive example of this phenomenon, but as I discuss further in this book's Conclusion, it is not an isolated case.

If the emphasis on land occupations was critical to the landless movement's ability to escape the trend toward movement decline, as I have argued here, then the mst must receive much of the credit, since it employed this tactic especially aggressively and was responsible for diffusing it to areas of the country where it was relatively rare. In addition, the mst's creative use of occupations and the resulting encampments contributed in important ways to the movement's growth. One of the key aspects of its strategy was how it exploited the social contexts created by land occupations and camps to recruit activists and foment commitment to its cause among its mass base.

As I have discussed, the landless movement's camps provided a particularly favorable setting for political indoctrination and the creation of a strong collective identity that would bind landless families to the mst and its cause. Part of the genius of the mst's approach to the struggle was how it took advantage of this setting. The mst used the camps as privileged spaces for political indoctrination and worked hard to foment a strong collective identity, tying families together into a cohesive body. It also sought to identify and cultivate those campers who showed the most promise of becoming committed and effective activists and, eventually, leaders. Largely as a result of these efforts, the MST was able to benefit from a steady stream of new activists, which helped to make it largely self-sustaining, or even self-expanding, in terms of activist personnel.

This aspect of the MST's strategy also helps us to understand why, even after gaining their plot of land, many settlers continued to make donations to the MST and to participate occasionally in protest initiatives for agrarian reform, subsidized credit, and other goods sought by the movement. This is an important issue to address because, with regard to settler participation in the MST, there was, in fact, a substantial free-rider problem. Settlers who did not contribute to the MST's struggle could not have their land taken from them, and they could not, for the most part, be excluded from other benefits, such as subsidized agricultural credit, resulting from MST protest actions.

To some extent, settler contributions can be explained in terms of what Olson calls "selective incentives," including the threat of social sanctions by other settlers, or the loss of certain material benefits (for example, access to NGO grants) resulting from a close association with the MST. However, selective incentives were by no means the only reason settlers continued to be part of the MST. As Fireman and Gamson (1979) point out, a movement cannot rely on social sanctions to spur participation unless there already exists a core group of activists large and dedicated enough to deliver them. At least as important were the affective ties and principled beliefs that arose from settlers' past participation in the MST camping process. This process, as I have discussed, tended to promote a leftist political consciousness; a sense of loyalty to the MST; and feelings of solidarity, both with other settlers and with rural workers still struggling for a piece of farmland. Thus, while a person's initial involvement in the MST was usually motivated largely by individual economic incentives, the process of struggle itself generated other kinds of incentives that kept many people engaged in the organization's efforts even after gaining land.

Activist strategy was thus a key aspect of the landless movement's exceptional trajectory. Nevertheless, it would be far too simplistic to argue that the decision to rely on occupations as the movement's core tactic was, in and of itself, what set the landless movement apart from the others. This tactic was simply not available to other social movements to the same extent. Certain special characteristics of farmland made the use of occupations by the landless feasible. One of these was simply the fact that farmland is a good that physically exists, even prior to the decision by authorities to distribute it. Transition era movements that sought goods that do not have a physical presence, such as gay rights, or were essentially the product of state action, such as child-care centers for working mothers, could not readily employ this tactic.

However, even movements that sought physically existing resources could generally not use this tactic. A movement organization that decided to seize cars, homes, refrigerators, or department stores in the hope that authorities would cede or expropriate them from their private owners would almost certainly have been sternly repressed. In Brazil, as in most societies, property rights to these types of goods are not open to question. This was largely true of urban land, as well. At least in Brazil, when movements have occupied privately owned urban lots or buildings, in the hope of pressuring authorities to seize and redistribute them, they have rarely been successful (Gohn 1991). Consequently, those seeking land in cities have usually occupied abandoned public land. In most (although certainly not all) cases, the sites targeted are located in marginal areas, far from the city center, and are of little economic value. The families who enter these areas often encounter little resistance. Since these actions are not generally intended to pressure authorities, they cannot readily be characterized as constituting a social movement.

What set the struggle for farmland apart from the movements for these other goods was the political opportunity structure. The political coalitions or elite groups supporting land reform were probably no stronger than those supporting the demands of some other transition era popular movements. However, the legal, institutional structure confronting the landless was unusually favorable. As I discussed earlier, the Brazilian Constitution states that farmland has an inherent social function, based primarily on the intensity of its use. Consequently, a large parcel of private farmland that is underutilized can be expropriated by the federal government and distributed to those who have little or no land of their own, provided that the original owner is compensated at fair market value. Although social function conditions are also placed on some other types of property (including urban land), only in the case of rural land is the requirement of effective use so strong and explicit.

Because of these constitutional provisions, Brazilian authorities were vulnerable to the political pressure exerted by landless protestors in a way that they would not have been to groups that occupied other goods. Although progressive forces have not been strong enough to force the universal implementation of the social function requirements placed on private farmland, the existence of these requirements has provided a loophole large enough to make the occupation of large rural estates a relatively effective tactic. Postdictatorship governments were never able to stonewall occupations altogether. The idea that farmland has an inherent social function has probably also affected the use of publicly owned farmland. State governments have often felt politically obliged to cede un- or underused public land to the landless, especially to groups bold enough to occupy them.

Conclusion

While other democratic transition era movements tended to decline after the establishment of democratic rule, the landless movement continued to grow, albeit gradually. Although it stagnated under the Collor government, landless protest began to rebound during the Franco years. By 1994, land occupation activity in Brazil had reached unprecedented levels. The movement's survival was in large measure a reflection of the expansion of the MST, which transformed itself from a loose network linked to the Catholic Church and largely restricted to the South into an autonomous, centralized, national organization with a large corps of activists and a strong collective identity.

I have argued that the landless movement's exceptionalism has much to do with activist strategy and, in particular, tactical choice. The adoption of the tactic of land occupations had the effect of creating an unusually favorable set of incentives for movement participation. This incentive structure made the landless movement less vulnerable to the deterioration of normative incentives for movement activism in Brazil following the end of the military dictatorship. The MST's distinctive approach to the struggle built on this advantage in a number of ways. In particular, it used the social contexts created by the occupations and resulting encampments as spaces for political indoctrination and the generation of group solidarity and organizational loyalty.

It would be incorrect, however, to reduce the movement's exceptional trajectory during this period to a product of strategic choice. Occupation as a tactic was simply not as available to other social movements. The fact that the landless movement could use this tactic relatively successfully has to do, as I have argued, with the peculiar characteristics of farmland. First, it is a tangible good that exists prior to the state's decision to distribute it. Second, it has an exceptional constitutional status, as the only type of private property whose ownership is clearly conditional on its production use. Since the latter trait was important because it affected the vulnerability of the state to pressure for concessions, my argument provides further support for the political opportunity perspective.

FOUR Takeoff, 1995–1999

The growth of land occupations in Brazil during the early 1990s had been steady but relatively gradual. In the mid-1990s, this situation changed dramatically, as occupation activity accelerated abruptly all over the country. Its rapid expansion during this period transformed the landless movement into probably the largest rural movement in Brazilian history. After the abrupt leap of the mid-1990s, occupation activity continued to increase at a more gradual pace, leveling off in 1999. Although land occupations continued to grow in number, other forms of protest became a more prominent element of the movement's tactical repertoire in the late 1990s. This shift was driven mainly by the MST, which sought to come up with more effective ways to pressure federal authorities.

The takeoff of landless protest occurred at approximately the same time as two other important changes related to the agrarian question in Brazil. First, this issue abruptly reemerged as a key topic of public discussion and media coverage, even attracting attention abroad. Second, President Fernando Henrique Cardoso, who took power in early 1995 and was reelected in late 1998, implemented the most significant agrarian reform program the country had ever experienced. The true extent of this program was debated, and the reform certainly did not constitute a major alteration of Brazil's land tenure structure. Undoubtedly, however, the pace of settlement accelerated markedly.

In this chapter I explain the intensification of landless protest during the 1995–99 period, as well as its relationship to the other two changes described above. As in Chapter 2, here I evaluate the various theoretical explanations of longitudinal variation in movement intensity in light of my empirical findings. In addition, I set the stage for my analysis of the movement's decline beginning in 2000. As I will argue in Chapter 5, the crisis of the landless movement had much to do with the MST's growing frustration with federal policies and its attempts to force a change through bolder tactics and a broader political strategy.

The theoretical framework outlined in Chapter 1 offers a number of strategies for explaining the upsurge of protest for land reform in Brazil in the second half of the 1990s. Grievance/discontent theory would suggest that we view it as a reflection of the aggravation of socioeconomic conditions among the movement's potential social base or of some change that made the landless feel relatively deprived. The organizational capacity perspective might point to the strengthening of indigenous organizations and social networks. Since these tend to change rather slowly, however, the most plausible account based on this perspective would focus on the external resources available to the landless. The activist strategy perspective would point to effective innovations in pressure tactics, framing strategies, organizational structure, or goals. Finally, the political opportunity perspective would explain the rapid increase in movement activity in terms of an increased disposition on the part of authorities to meet land occupations with concessions, rather than repression.

Somewhat surprisingly, existing studies of the landless movement do not offer an in-depth analysis of its expansion during this period.[1] More casual interpretations have emphasized factors that support either the grievance/discontent perspective or political opportunity. Taking the first position, Fernandes (1998) argues that the upsurge of protest resulted from the negative impact of neoliberal economic policies, begun by Collor and deepened by Cardoso, on employment in both agriculture and the urban sector (47). Supporting the second view, media commentators have often attributed the upsurge to Cardoso's settlement program, suggesting that land occupations multiplied because of the government's willingness to reward occupations with concessions.[2]

I agree with Fernandes that a growing employment deficit, at least in the agricultural sector, provided fairly fertile ground for the movement's growth; nevertheless, my analysis more strongly supports a political oppor-

---

1. The major exception is Ondetti 2006b, in which I offer a similar empirical account to this one, but take a somewhat different theoretical angle.

2. Posing the question of why protest for land had increased sharply, a writer in *Veja* affirmed, "One possible conclusion is: the growing distribution of lots itself stimulates the expansion and the aggressiveness of the MST." See "Caso de polícia," *Veja*, April 8, 1998, 28–29.

tunity interpretation. The timing and geographical distribution of the increase in protest activity suggest that the movement expanded mainly because landless workers and activists began to perceive that the Cardoso government would be more likely to respond positively to occupations than past governments. The movement's organizational capacity did grow during this period, but this change largely followed the major upsurge of protest in the mid-1990s and cannot, therefore, explain it. Similarly, the MST did implement some strategic innovations during 1995–99 in tactics and, arguably, goals, but these changes occurred relatively late in the decade.

Although I agree with the idea that protest grew under Cardoso because the government was more likely to respond positively, my interpretation adds an important dimension missing from existing analyses. The movement's takeoff was not, as some authors suggest, simply a response to the belief that the new "social democratic" president would be more vulnerable to pressure. Cardoso's victory had been a defeat for leftist, pro–land reform forces and his governing coalition was a blend of the conservative, pro-landowner forces dominant during the late Sarney and Collor years and more urban, centrist actors. Early on, his willingness to accelerate land reform was very much in doubt. The MST, at least, was pessimistic about the prospects for greater settlement activity.

What tipped the political scales clearly in favor of reform was the political impact of two especially large, brutal, and publicly visible police massacres of land occupiers in the Amazon region. Because these incidents drew the attention of the press, civil society, and the general public to the gravity of the land problem in the countryside, turning this issue into almost a cause cèlébre, they essentially forced Cardoso, from a political standpoint, to accelerate reform. The public impact of the massacres also contributed to a decline in police repression of land occupations. Both of these changes, the acceleration of land distribution and the decline of repression, had the effect of stimulating mobilization and protest for land. Although existing accounts have often acknowledged the influence of these incidents of violence on Cardoso's land reform policy, they have either not linked them to the intensification of protest or have at least implicitly seen the causal relationship as running in the opposite direction (Filho 1997; PT 1999).

While it generally supports the political opportunity perspective, this argument also validates some of the criticisms of how it has been conceptualized. It suggests, first, the need to pay more attention to the subjective side of political processes than opportunity theorists generally have. It demonstrates that important shifts in the political opportunity structure can be produced by transformations in the subjective priorities of public opinion and civil society, independent of the institutional changes, alliance shake-ups, and electoral changes stressed by the literature. In addition, my analysis of the role of the major landless massacres of the mid-1990s on the growth of protest underscores the relatively neglected notion that a social movement's political opportunity structure may be partially a product of its own actions. Although landless activists did not purposely provoke the massacres or control their subsequent political impact, these incidents were partly a product of the movement's own aggressive pressure for land redistribution, which posed a threat to the interests of local rural elites and their allies within the state.

The chapter is divided into three main sections. The first contains a discussion of some of the major political and socioeconomic developments during this period, including Cardoso's surprising land reform program. In the second section I turn to an examination of the growth of the landless movement. I begin by discussing broad patterns of protest activity, then I take a closer look at the increasingly diverse set of groups behind this activity. In the third section I examine the reactions of other important actors, including landowners, the media, public opinion, and federal authorities, to the movement's expansion. In the final section of the chapter I develop the arguments outlined above on the causes of the landless movement's takeoff and their theoretical implications.

Stability, Neoliberalism, and Agrarian Reform

The key challenge facing the Brazilian government between 1995 and 1999 was how to both maintain the price stability achieved in 1994 and give it deeper roots, in order to return to the pattern of sustained growth left behind in the 1980s. Although the Cardoso administration was by no means one dimensional, all other concerns were secondary. Price stability was preserved, but growth faltered after 1997, and some of the government's structural reforms proceeded slowly. As growth slowed, unemployment escalated. Agriculture continued to go through a difficult restructuring process and the volume of agricultural employment dropped substantially.

Somewhat surprisingly, since it had not been a major element of his campaign and had few supporters within the governing alliance, agrarian reform emerged as Cardoso's most visible social policy initiative. In the early going, this policy seemed in danger of being forgotten. By the end of 1996, however, a new agrarian reform ministry had been established, new expropriation legislation had been pushed through Congress, and officials were trumpeting land reform as one of their key programs. As I argue below, the most important factor in elevating agrarian reform on the government's list of priorities was the political impact of two brutal massacres of land occupiers in the Amazon region.

Cardoso and the Politics of Stability

Cardoso was inaugurated as president in January 1995 in a climate of strong public optimism, resulting mainly from the end of hyperinflation. By stopping inflation, the Real Plan had abruptly increased the purchasing power of wages, enhancing general welfare and reducing poverty. Economic growth had also accelerated in the second half of 1994, helping to bring down unemployment. Stabilization had restored Brazil's self-confidence. The president's impressive background and international prestige contributed to the feeling that Brazil was ready to become a "modern" country.

Unlike Collor, Cardoso had been careful to put together a broad partisan alliance. With the entrance of the PMDB following the election, his coalition came to include almost all of Brazil's major non-Left political parties. The PT had made significant gains in the congressional elections, but it was only the fourth-largest party in Congress, behind the PMDB, PFL, and PSDB, all members of Cardoso's coalition.[3]

Cardoso had campaigned on a broad platform, but his clear priority was to preserve the newfound economic stability, his most precious political resource. At least in the short term, this would involve relatively disciplined fiscal and monetary policy. However, the government's objective was to consolidate stability through a series of market-oriented structural reforms, including public service reform, pension reform, privatization, and trade liberalization, continuing the trend begun under Collor. The idea behind these initiatives was to make the Brazilian economy more efficient and to reassure investors that Brazil would not relapse into economic "populism."

3. In 1996, the Brazilian Progressive Party (PPB), Brazil's most conservative major party and the most direct descendant of ARENA, also joined the coalition, although its adherence was only partial.

These goals placed the government in a frontal confrontation with the traditional defenders of the interventionist state, particularly public sector workers. In a critical early demonstration of his resolve, in May 1995 Cardoso used army troops to repress a protest campaign by oil workers, who sought to block the privatization of the state oil company by occupying a number of refineries. This event was a major blow for the CUT and signaled the force of the government's argument that "privileged" groups would not be allowed to endanger its attempts to "defend stability."

Not all groups that demanded concessions received the same treatment. Facing high interest rates and low prices, agricultural producers began pressuring the government for debt relief in early 1995. Some of them owed the state-owned Banco do Brasil tens of millions of dollars. In June, they held a major demonstration in Brasília, clogging the streets of the capital with their farm trucks. The leaders of the powerful *bancada ruralista* took up the cause, reminding the president publicly that his reforms could not pass without their support. Cardoso ended up making important concessions, initiating the first phase of an extended process of agricultural debt restructuring.[4]

Although Cardoso had implied during his campaign that reducing social inequality would be an important concern of his government, during his first term he introduced no major redistributive programs, with the partial exception of land reform. The president's wife, anthropologist Ruth Cardoso, headed an agency that coordinated social initiatives; but the Solidary Community received meager funding from the technocrats who directed economic policy. Even the relatively conservative newsmagazine *Veja* commented on the stinginess of Cardoso's social programs.[5]

Criticism of his social policies undoubtedly troubled Cardoso, but the president faced even more daunting problems. Although certain neoliberal reforms, including privatization, advanced rapidly, other key measures, including ones designed to improve federal finances, were bogged down in Congress (Kingstone 2000). The breadth of Cardoso's legislative coalition was often not enough to overcome the indiscipline of the political parties that composed it, and the fact that many of the proposed reforms involved constitutional changes. The failure to advance in this area helped make Brazil one of the victims of the late 1997 "Asian flu" financial crisis. Specu-

4. "A turma do calote," *Veja*, April 17, 1995, 30–37.
5. "Procura-se um miseravel," *Veja*, April 17, 1996, 66–69.

lative pressures on the currency forced the government to adopt sterner belt-tightening measures, putting a damper on economic growth.

Nonetheless, the government was successful in keeping inflation low and defending the real's one-to-one peg to the dollar. As a result, in 1997 Cardoso was able to secure congressional support for a constitutional amendment allowing presidential reelection, and in October 1998, he won another first-round victory over the PT's Lula. Despite these successes, Cardoso's second term began poorly. In January 1999, unable to resist continued speculative pressure, the government devalued the real. To attract capital back into the country, Cardoso adopted a tough new stabilization package backed by the International Monetary Fund (IMF), including sizable budget cuts. Although high inflation did not return, the economy stagnated and Cardoso's popularity plummeted to unprecedented lows.

Socioeconomic Trends

Economic growth averaged a solid 3.5 percent per year between 1995 and 1997; by contrast, in 1998 and 1999, the economy was stagnant. While it lasted, growth helped offset mounting job losses in the industrial sector, caused by trade liberalization and privatization (Neri, Camargo, and Reis 2000). Open unemployment, which had declined in late 1994, grew gradually in 1995 and 1996. In mid-1997 unemployment began to accelerate. By the end of 1998 it had reached 8 percent, a rate not seen since the early 1980s. The poverty rate remained basically stable throughout the 1995–99 period at about 28 percent of the Brazilian population (Neri 2006, 3).

Agricultural producers faced serious difficulties after the introduction of the Real Plan, which increased agricultural imports, pushed down domestic agricultural prices, and increased the debt burdens of many producers, especially the largest. Although Cardoso, as noted above, acceded to a restructuring of agricultural debts, he generally continued the move toward reducing government intervention in agriculture, albeit at a slower pace than that of Collor (Coelho 2001). Price supports were weakened, trade was liberalized, and government credit continued to decline. Nevertheless, agricultural output grew quickly, outperforming industry, for example (Helfand and Rezende 2001).

Under Cardoso, productivity in agriculture also grew rapidly. Output growth occurred without an expansion in the area planted. Importables were particularly strongly affected by the increased competitive pressures.

Although yields generally increased, the area planted in such crops as beans, corn, rice, and wheat declined (Helfand and Rezende 2001). These changes affected the South, the major producer of import-competing agricultural products, disproportionately. For example, grain production in the South increased by almost 25 percent between the 1995–96 and 1999–2000 harvests, despite the fact that the area planted in grains remained virtually unchanged (Coelho 2001, 52).

Poverty among people employed in agriculture, which had dropped sharply with the Real Plan in 1994, remained essentially stable thereafter (Corrêa 2000, Table 7). Income in agriculture largely held its ground, but there was a tendency toward decline among some groups, especially family farmers (Del Grossi and Graziano da Silva 2000a, 85). Change in the size of the agricultural workforce during this period was substantial. Data from the PNAD household survey show that employment in agriculture declined by 8.4 percent between 1992 and 1997 (Laurenti and Del Grossi 2000, 20).[6] The decline affected both wage and family labor significantly. The bulk of this drop occurred in 1996, when about a million people left the farm sector. The 1996 decline was probably not primarily a response to improving urban job conditions, since the economy did not perform unusually well that year. Rather, it is often viewed as a product of the Real Plan's impact on interest rates and agricultural prices (Leite 1999). After 1996, the workforce stabilized, with the exception of a temporary upturn in 1999, a crisis year for the urban economy.

Unfortunately, the PNAD did not begin to include the North region until 2004. From the standpoint of evaluating national trends, this is not a major problem since the North has a small population, but it does impede our ability to examine trends across regions. For the four other regions for which data are available, the 1992–97 decline was quite heterogeneous, ranging from 3.7 percent of the workforce in the Northeast to 15.6 percent in the Southeast. In the South and Center-West the declines were 13.4 percent and 8.1 percent, respectively. The 1995–96 decline was also regionally varied, being greatest in the Northeast (10.2 percent) and smallest in the Southeast (2.4 percent).

---

6. As I mentioned in Chapter 3, an agricultural census was conducted in 1995–96, but a change in the timing of the data gathering makes direct comparison to previous censuses misleading. I use 1992 as a point of departure for examining changes in the agricultural workforce during this period because the PNAD methodology changed that year, making comparison to previous years more difficult.

The Rise of Agrarian Reform

During his 1994 election campaign, Cardoso had promised to settle 280,000 families, 40,000 in 1995, 60,000 in 1996, 80,000 in 1997, and 100,000 in 1998. According to official figures, Cardoso actually slightly exceeded this total, settling some 288,000 families. His settlement total was more than double the combined totals of the Sarney and Franco/Collor governments (Table 4). Officials claimed that Cardoso's settlements totals exceeded those of all the 1964–94 governments combined (INCRA 1998).

As in the past, settlement activity was concentrated in the Amazon. About 60 percent of the families were settled in states at least partially included in this largely frontier area, where land is relatively cheap and agriculture is backward (INCRA 2000c). The South and Southeast combined accounted for less than 10 percent of the total. Efforts to obtain land were aided by a drop in land prices following currency stabilization, which undercut the use of land ownership as protection against inflation (Carneiro 2000). Since compensation for expropriated land is supposed to reflect its market value, the going price of farmland affects the cost of undertaking agrarian reform.

In addition to underscoring the acceleration of settlements, officials trumpeted a number of other policies related to agrarian reform. They pointed to support programs for settlers that were introduced or expanded, including credit, technical assistance, infrastructure, and primary education. They boasted about legal measures to facilitate reform, among them an improved Summary Rite law, which made it harder for landowners to block expropriations. Finally, they pointed to a new World Bank–funded subsidized credit program for land purchases, called the Land Bank (INCRA 1998).

Not everyone was impressed by these claims. The MST and other progressive groups complained that too much of the reform was concentrated in the sparsely populated Amazon basin. In some cases, these settlements

Table 4   Families settled by the federal government, 1985–1998

President	Families	Annual Average
Sarney (1985–89)	89,950	17,990
Collor (1990–92)	38,425	12,808
Franco (1993–94)	21,763	10,881
Cardoso (1995–98)	287,994	71,999

Source: INCRA n.d., 2000c.

amounted to the legalization of longtime squatter holdings, some on public land. Activists complained that many families were placed in existing settlements, rather than on newly expropriated land, and that complementary projects, such as housing, infrastructure, and credit, often took years to be implemented. They argued that, with definitive establishment of the Land Bank in 1998, the government was trying to phase out expropriation, the key to a major land reform. But perhaps the most serious accusation was that the INCRA padded its settlement figures, by including, for example, families that had been settled under earlier governments. Data that has emerged in recent years lends some credence to this charge. In particular, the Institute for Applied Economic Research (IPEA), a federal research agency, has published settlement figures based on raw INCRA data showing that Cardoso effectively granted land to about forty thousand fewer families in his first term than official figures indicated (IPEA 2006, statistical annex, table 7.1). Nonetheless, even these numbers suggest that Cardoso probably settled more families in 1995–98 than had all previous presidents put together.

Although Cardoso did no more than implement the plan he had spelled out in 1994, the fact that land reform became a major program was somewhat surprising. This had not been a prominent aspect of the Cardoso campaign. When agrarian reform was mentioned in media coverage, it was usually in reference to the PT's bold proposal to settle eight hundred thousand families. Moreover, the character of Cardoso's coalition did not seem to bode well for this policy. Both the PFL and PTB were strongly tied to landowners, and the PMDB was not much better. Even the PSDB, the most progressive party in the alliance, had not one vocal defender of land reform among its leaders. The MST had warned that, if elected, Cardoso would surely "bury agrarian reform."[7]

In fact, the land reform effort seems to have been partly a product of new political pressures that emerged after Cardoso came to office. Until late 1995, the prospects for this policy seemed dim. The INCRA was under the control of the Ministry of Agriculture, run by José Eduardo Andrade Vieira, a banker, landowner, and president of the PTB. In May, another PTB leader, Brasílio Araújo Neto, was named president of the INCRA. Araújo Neto, a large landowner, had been a leader of the anti–land reform campaign in Paraná during the 1980s. His appointment was virulently opposed by progressive

7. *Jornal Sem Terra,* September 1994.

forces. Land reform went forward, but reports suggested that it was proceeding at a snail's pace.[8]

Although protest also played a direct role, the main factor in reverting
this situation were two particularly large and visible massacres of landless
protestors by the Military Police in the Amazon region. Because they caused
public outrage, and galvanized progressive groups at both the domestic and
international level these incidents forced Cardoso to give clear signs that
he was committed to speeding up land reform. The second massacre was
more influential, but its impact was partly a consequence of the fact that
it followed on the heels of the first, underscoring its significance.

The first massacre occurred on August 9, 1995 in Corumbiara, a back-
country *município* in the state of Rondônia. Before dawn, police descended
on a landless camp located on an occupied *fazenda*. In the conflict that
followed, nine occupiers, including a 7-year-old girl, and two police officers
were killed. Three of the landless were apparently executed and several
were subject to torture.[9] The occupation had been organized by activists
who had split off from the MST earlier.

The killings at Corumbiara provoked a great deal of media coverage, with
many expressions of outrage and dismay by columnists and editorial writers.[10] Commentators focused on the problem of police violence, as well as
the issues of land concentration and land-related violence. Many journalists and influential organizations, such as the National Conference of the
Bishops of Brazil (CNBB) and the Organization of Brazilian Attorneys (OAB),
called on Cardoso to take energetic steps to deal with these issues.[11] Leaders
of the PT organized protest events in Brasília to try to amplify the impact
of the massacre. Two major MST occupations in the Pontal do Paranapanema
in late August were probably even more effective in this sense, leading
columnists to ask whether land-related violence might now spread to São
Paulo, the heart of modern Brazil.[12] The sudden leap in attention to the
agrarian question was such that, as the MST's newspaper affirmed, "if some-
one were to arrive in Brazil during these days, he would certainly get the

8. *Folha de São Paulo*, September 6, 1995. By late July, the INCRA had spent only 3.2
percent of its annual budget.

9. See "Executados, torturados e humilhados," *Veja*, September 5, 1995, 38–41.

10. See "Barril de pólvora," *Folha de São Paulo*, August 16, 1995.

11. *Folha de São Paulo*, August 26, 1995.

12. See column by Marcela Beraba, "Ainda Corumbiara," *Folha de São Paulo*, August 26,
1995.

impression that the necessity of agrarian reform had just been discovered at this moment."[13]

In late September, Cardoso reacted to the tumult by replacing INCRA president Araújo Neto with Francisco Graziano, a close personal advisor. This move was interpreted as a sign that the president was taking more direct control over land reform. Cardoso vowed to make good on his plan of settling forty thousand families in 1995. Graziano did not disappoint. In short order, he expedited or set in motion numerous expropriation processes and began to root out local INCRA officials opposed to land reform. The MST was elated. In an editorial published in the *Jornal Sem Terra*, the National Directorate observed, "After the naming of the new INCRA president, one can perceive that the [the presidential palace] has begun to direct agrarian reform policy. . . . With these new initiatives, agrarian reform has become the only government program that is really of interest to the workers."[14]

Ironically, a scandal unrelated to his work at INCRA forced Graziano to step down several weeks later. The INCRA was without a permanent president for months, and settlement activity seemed to bog down once again.[15] Control over land reform reverted back to Andrade Vieira. Media attention to the land question seemed to decline, even though land occupations were mounting in the countryside. Then a second, even larger massacre served to shake the government out of its lethargy. On April 17, 1996, the Military Police confronted a group of some twelve hundred MST campers blocking a highway in southeastern Pará, a region notorious for its deadly land conflicts. The police opened fire, killing nineteen and injuring more than sixty. As with Corumbiara, evidence suggested that several victims had been executed, shot in the back of the head, or bludgeoned to death with their own farm implements.[16] This conflict in the small town of Eldorado do Carajás was probably the largest single incident of land-related violence in Brazil in several decades.

The massacre at Eldorado, partially captured on video by a local TV reporter, generated an avalanche of news coverage. Figure 5 shows the evolution of coverage of the agrarian question in the *Folha de São Paulo*, Brazil's

13. *Jornal Sem Terra*, October 1995.
14. *Jornal Sem Terra*, November 1995.
15. See column by Janio de Freitas, "A omissão confessada," *Folha de São Paulo*, April 21, 1996.
16. "Sangue em Eldorado," *Veja*, April 24,1996, 34–39.

Fig. 5   Coverage of the agrarian question in the *Folha de São Paulo,* 1994–1999

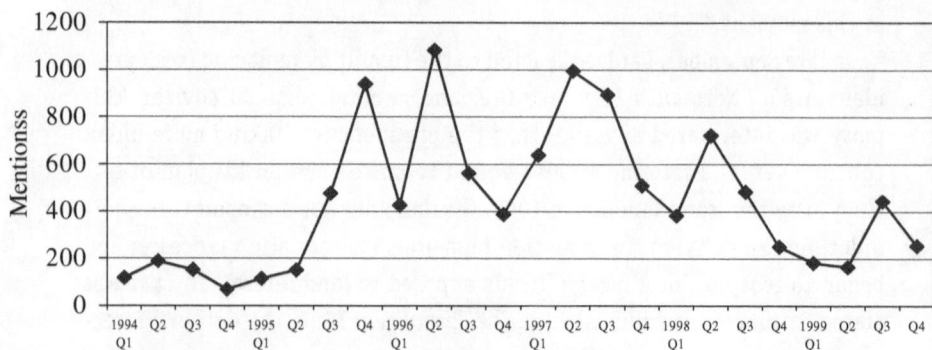

Source: Folha de São Paulo. CD rom archive.

largest-circulation newspaper.[17] Corumbiara had set off the first major spike in media attention to the agrarian question in the mid-1990s; Eldorado provoked an even sharper increase in coverage.[18] This upsurge helped to make 1996 a landmark year for news coverage of the agrarian question, as can be seen in Figure 6, which reflects the volume of articles and editorials on this issue in *Veja,* Brazil's major weekly newsmagazine. Eldorado's media impact is also suggested by the fact that a huge land occupation, perhaps the largest in MST history, occurred one day later, but received little coverage in the *Folha* and did not merit any mention in *Veja.*[19] The massacre was also covered by major foreign news outlets. The Parisian daily *Le Monde* put

Fig. 6   Coverage of the agrarian question in *Veja,* 1990–1999

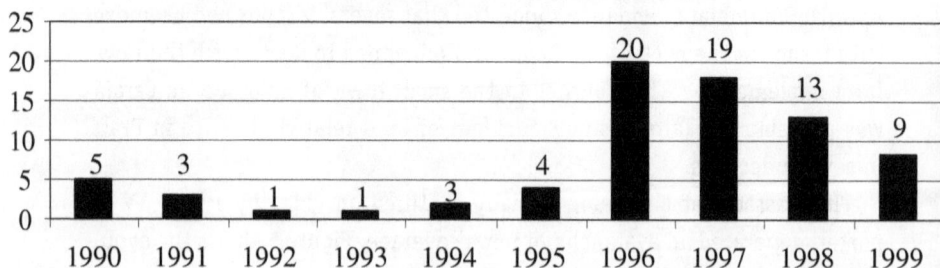

Source: Veja

17. The data were generated using a full-text CD-ROM archive of the newspaper. I used the search terms "agrarian reform or agrarian question or landless or MST or INCRA."

18. The third major spike in coverage during this period corresponds to the MST's national march to Brasília in early 1997, discussed below.

19. This occupation, involving thirty-five hundred families, occurred in Paraná. See *Folha de São Paulo,* April 19, 1996.

the story on page one and CNN broadcast it repeatedly, complete with images of the bodies.

Some news commentators placed part of the blame for the killings on the MST.[20] However, for the most part, commentators expressed moral outrage, concern about the situation in the countryside, and embarrassment that Brazil had not left such vestiges of its rural past behind. Some contrasted the bright image of a modernizing Brazil painted by the government with the "archaic" reality graphically illustrated by the killings at Eldorado, and others asked why Cardoso, the "social democrat," had money to bail out irresponsible banks and indebted landowners, but not for land reform.[21] The calls for an acceleration of land reform were more insistent than after Corumbiara, coming from both journalists and organized groups. Even the Vatican issued a letter in the name of Pope John Paul II condemning the killings and urging more attention to the land issue.[22]

A week after the incident, President Cardoso responded to an old demand of progressives by removing the INCRA from the Ministry of Agriculture and creating a new ministry, the Extraordinary Ministry for Land Policy, to house it. Raul Jungmann, a rising bureaucratic star with a history of leftist activism, was appointed minister. Cardoso also pledged to push forward legislative initiatives that had been introduced after Corumbiara but bogged down in Congress. These included a reform of the rural land tax, a measure limiting the right of judges to order expulsions of land occupiers, and a new Summary Rite, which would give the INCRA possession of a property forty-eight hours after the president's signing of an expropriation decree. Special measures were adopted to ensure peace and speed up reform in Pará. In its lead editorial the MST's newspaper affirmed, "With Eldorado, things change. . . . Brazilian society, indignant with what occurred in Pará, has come to demand agrarian reform with greater force."[23]

Landowners and their allies sought to block or water down Cardoso's agrarian reform initiatives in Congress. They gained some important concessions. The reform of the land tax, intended to increase taxation on un-

20. See column by Luis Nassif, "O sertão vai virar mar," *Folha de São Paulo*, April 21, 1996.

21. See column by Carlos Heitor Cony, "O grande culpado," *Folha de São Paulo*, April 21, 1996.

22. *Folha de São Paulo*, April 26, 1996, and *Folha de São Paulo*, February 15, 1997. In early 1998, the Vatican also released a document advocating the reform of unjust agrarian structures. Although it did not refer to any country specifically, it was widely understood as having been motivated by the Brazilian situation.

23. *Jornal Sem Terra*, May 1996.

productive land, was passed in late 1996. However, Cardoso had made so many concessions that the new law was innocuous. Revenues from the tax did not increase significantly. Antiviolence bills, including the measure limiting expulsion orders, were blocked. The major legislative victory for land reform was the new Summary Rite, approved in December.

The apparent acceleration of land reform did not promote the kind of massive landowner mobilization that Sarney's PNRA had, for a number of reasons. First, the program was far less ambitious than Sarney's original proposal. Second, in the mid-1990s Brazil was not about to draft a new constitution. The 1988 Constitution had protected the most modern and politically powerful agricultural producers. Landowners menaced by Cardoso's reform efforts were generally poorer and less influential. These sometimes claimed that their wealthier colleagues had abandoned them.[24] Finally, the UDR had shown that aggressive mobilization could backfire in the court of public opinion. It was better to rely on lobbying organizations and the influence of the *bancada ruralista*.[25]

In the immediate aftermath of Eldorado do Carajás indicators of public concern about the agrarian question remained strong. Media coverage of this issue continued to be heavy, and public interest was also reflected in various cultural phenomena, including the tremendous success of a *telenovela* (a kind of prime-time soap opera extremely popular among Brazilians) that appeared in late 1996 and early 1997. The struggle for land reform was a key theme of *The King of Cattle* and the program portrayed the struggle for land in a sympathetic light. Public interest in and concern about the rural land issue, combined with the mounting pressure of landless protest (discussed below), undoubtedly helped to keep the government's land distribution efforts going forward after 1996, but it was the massacre at Eldorado that seems to have consolidated the place of agrarian reform on Cardoso's agenda.[26]

24. Interview with Roosevelt Roque dos Santos, former national president of the UDR, May 17, 2000, Presidente Venceslau, SP. Sugarcane planters in the northeastern state of Alagoas also complained that the state's powerful sugar mill owners, most of them also planters, had not come to their defense against expropriations and land occupations. Interview with Reinaldo Marinho, vice president, Association of Sugarcane Planters of Alagoas (ASPLANA), February 20, 2000, Maceió, AL.

25. Interview with Gedeão Pereira, president of the Commission on Land Affairs of the state landowner federation in Rio Grande do Sul (FARSUL), September 8, 1999, Bagé, RS.

26. The police officers involved in the Eldorado incident were tried in late 1998 and, in proceedings marked by irregularities, declared not guilty. The verdict was subsequently annulled by a higher court. Another trial was conducted in 2002. The two commanding officers were convicted and sentenced to several life sentences. The rest of the officers involved were acquitted.

It is important to note that political commentators have generally agreed that Cardoso's agrarian reform program was not principally aimed at obtaining the political support of the rural workers who directly benefited from it (Sorj 1998); these workers constituted, in national electoral terms, a relatively small group. Rather, this policy was a response to the demands for action by the general public, particularly the well-informed urban middle class, which was the key support base for the São Paulo–centered PSDB.[27] Public opinion polls taken since the mid-1990s have consistently indicated that about 80 percent of Brazilians favor land reform. Although the massacres were pivotal in making agrarian reform a priority issue, sympathy for this policy was nothing new: since the 1960s, public opinion polls had shown that an ample majority of the Brazilian public supports land reform (CESOP 1996).

Federal spending on land reform peaked in 1997, at slightly over R$2 billion. In 1999, as part of his belt-tightening, Cardoso cut spending sharply, bringing it down to R$1.3 billion (INCRA 2000c).[28] In addition, Jungmann announced a restructuring of the program, with the grandiose title of "New Rural World." Ironically, much of it involved reductions in state support for settlers. The PROCERA credit program was abolished. Settlers were placed within an existing, less subsidized program for smallholders called PRONAF (National Program for Strengthening Family Agriculture). In addition, the government would now move to "emancipate" settlers from all government aid more quickly.[29] Dependence on the state, officials argued, was a disincentive to entrepreneurial activity. Despite the budget cuts, at the end of the year Jungmann claimed to have settled 85,226 families.[30] This was only a 15 percent decline relative to 1998, but IPEA settlement data suggest that the drop was actually almost double that (IPEA 2006).

Takeoff of the Landless Movement

The landless movement expanded tremendously during the 1995–99 period. Land occupation activity increased sharply in late 1995 and especially

27. Marcos Lins, president of the INCRA in late 1994 and early 1995, also underscored this point to me in an interview in Brasília, on April 28, 2000.

28. The decline was even greater in real terms, since the 1999 currency devaluation provoked inflation.

29. This meant that settlers would receive legal title to their plot of land and, in theory, begin making payments on it to the government. In practice, few settlers ever paid for their lots.

30. In 1999, Jungmann's agency also became a permanent ministry, the Ministry of Agrarian Development.

1996, then settled into a pattern of more gradual growth. Since campers were often settled more quickly than in past years, the increase in occupation activity mainly reflected a major acceleration in the pace at which new families entered into the movement. Although the multiplication of land occupations and camps was the most striking aspect of the movement's growth during this period, beginning in about 1997 other tactics came to play an increasingly large and prominent role in the movement's tactical repertoire. This shift was driven mainly by the MST, which, frustrated with federal government policies, sought to find new ways to intensify its pressure on authorities.

Land Occupations

Land occupation activity began to accelerate under Cardoso in late 1995, especially in the number of families taking part in occupations (see Figs. 7 and 8). This resulted mainly from the intensification of the MST's offensive in São Paulo's Pontal do Paranapanema. Led by José Rainha, the MST's char-

Fig. 7 Land occupations by month in Brazil, 1995–1996

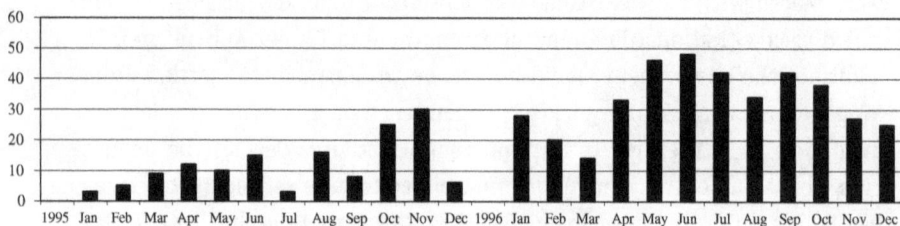

Source: CPT 1996a; 1997.

Fig. 8 Occupying families by month in Brazil, 1995–1996

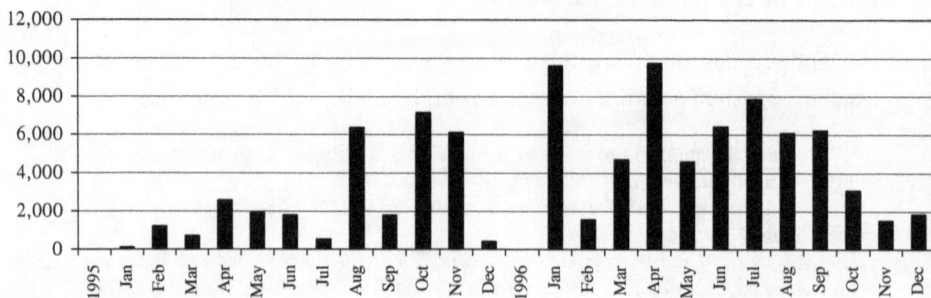

Source: CPT 1996a; 1997.

ismatic chief in the Pontal, activists organized thirteen occupations there in 1995, involving more than ten thousand families.[31] Nine of these actions occurred after Corumbiara, mainly in late August and October. This surge put pressure on new PSDB governor Mario Covas, who responded by promising to settle three thousand families in the region by the end of 1996. The surge in activity spread to other regions in November and January. After a lag in February and March, land occupations intensified again beginning in the second half of April, reaching unprecedented levels in the months that followed.[32]

Although occupation activity had begun to intensify visibly in late 1995, the sustained burst beginning in April helped make 1996 a landmark year, as Figures 9 and 10 clearly suggest. Relative to 1995, occupations in 1996 grew by 1726 percent and the number of occupying families by 107.0 percent. Never had land occupations grown so rapidly.

The leap in occupation activity in 1996 was geographically dispersed. At least with regard to the number of occupations, every region experienced rapid growth (see Tables 5 and 6). The region that experienced the largest percentage jump in occupations was the North, driven mainly by the state of Pará, where they increased almost five-fold. In terms of families, the South led the way. The Southeast was a partial exception to the rule of

Fig. 9 Land occupations in Brazil, 1990–1999

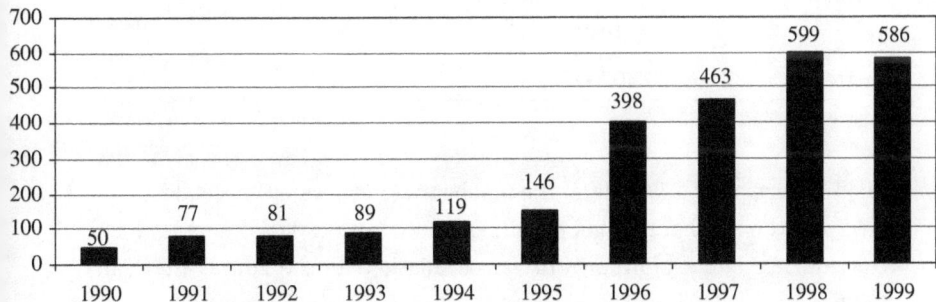

Source: CPT 1991, 1992, 1993a, 1994, 1995, 1996a, 1997, 1998, 1999, 2000.

31. Rainha was the biggest exception to the rule of nonpersonalistic leadership within the MST. Although the regional MST leadership was formally organized collectively, he was quite clearly the central figure, by virtue of his intelligence and personal charisma. Rainha's independence and pragmatic willingness to negotiate with conservative forces would lead the national MST leadership to limit his influence toward the end of the 1990s.

32. Only nine of the thirty-three land occupations listed by the CPT for April 1996 occurred before the Eldorado massacre. Unfortunately, six have no specific date (CPT 1997, 34–42).

Fig. 10   Occupying families in Brazil, 1990–1999

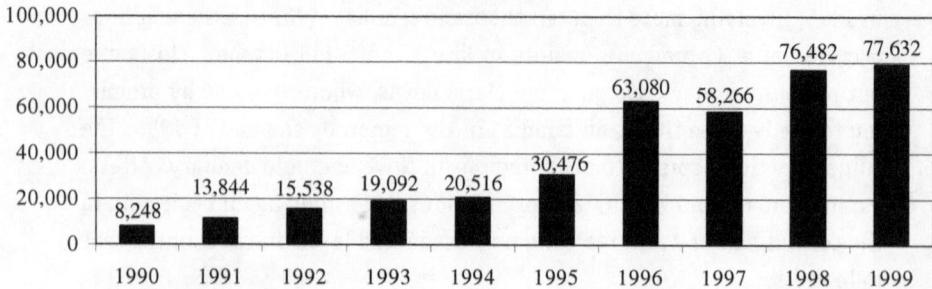

Source: CPT 1991; 1992; 1993a; 1994; 1995; 1996a; 1997; 1998; 1999; 2000.

Table 5   Increase in land occupations by region, 1995–1996

Region	Occupations 1995	Occupations 1996	% Increase
Center-West	26	68	161.5
North	11	53	381.8
Northeast	57	157	175.4
South	15	52	246.7
Southeast	37	68	83.8

Source: CPT 1996a, 1997.

Table 6   Increase in occupying families by region, 1995–1996

Region	Families 1995	Families 1996	% Increase
Center-West	3,771	10,321	173.7
North	2,002	6,898	244.6
Northeast	11,057	23,091	108.8
South	3,134	13,823	341.1
Southeast	10,512	8,947	− 14.9

Source: CPT 1996a, 1997.

rapid expansion in 1996. Here, the number of land occupations almost doubled, but the number of families fell. The decline in terms of families was a consequence of the slowdown in MST occupations in the Pontal after January.

After the abrupt leap in 1995–96, occupations and families continued to grow in number, but at a more gradual pace (see Figs. 9 and 10). In 1999, occupation activity showed some signs of reaching a plateau, as the number of families increased only slightly and the number of occupations suffered a small decline.

All told, 2,192 land occupations, involving 305,936 families, occurred in Brazil during 1995–99. The Northeast accounted for close to 40 percent of both occupations and families (see Table 7). The somewhat greater concentration of activity in this region relative to earlier years mainly reflected the growth of occupations in coastal sugarcane areas. Areas dominated by sugarcane become important sites of landless activity in a number of northeastern states, especially Pernambuco and Alagoas. Pernambuco, which had experienced relatively little landless activism prior to 1995, became the clear national leader. This state accounted for 348 occupations and 43,669 occupying families. Only three other states, Paraná, Mato Grosso do Sul, and São Paulo, had more than 200 occupations. Only five, São Paulo, Mato Grosso do Sul, Paraná, Bahia and Pará, had more than 20,000 occupying families.

The MST led the occupation charge in 1995, accounting for 63.7 percent of total land occupations in Brazil (see Table 8). This represented a substantial increase over its 1994 share, of 44.0 percent. Its actions were concentrated particularly in two states, São Paulo (in the Southeast) and Pernambuco (in the Northeast). This share dropped back to 44.2 percent in 1996, even though MST occupations increased by 90 percent relative to 1995 in absolute terms. In other words, 1996 saw a major increase in non-MST occupations. The proportion of land occupations linked to the MST fluctuated in the late 1990s, but generally tended to decline. Unfortunately, data on MST occupations are not available for 1999.

Relative to the previous five-year period, the total volume of occupation activity in Brazil during 1995–99 represented a 426.9 percent increase in

Table 7   Occupations and families by region, 1995–1999

Region	Occupations	%	Families	%
Center-West	416	19.0	57,892	18.9
North	189	8.6	28,283	9.2
Northeast	846	38.6	113,368	37.1
South	346	15.8	51,507	16.8
Southeast	395	18.0	54,886	17.9

Source: CPT 1996a, 1997, 1998, 1999, 2000.

Table 8   MST occupations as percentage of total

Year	Total Occupations	MST Occupations	% of Total
1995	146	93	63.7
1996	398	176	44.2
1997	463	173	37.4
1998	599	132	22.0

Source: CPT 1996a, 1997, 1998, 1999; Petras 1998; Fernandes 1999.

occupations and a 296.1 percent increase in families occupying. As Tables 9 and 10 demonstrate, every region experienced a major intensification of both occupations and families. The Southeast was the biggest gainer in occupations and the Northeast in occupying families. In all probability, not even the early 1960s exceeded the 1995–99 period in the intensity of mobilization and collective protest for land reform in the Brazilian countryside.

Other Tactics

Protest tactics other than land occupations had always been part of the landless movement's tool kit for pressuring authorities. As it grew in size during the second half of the 1990s, these actions also increased in number, although they continued to be associated primarily with the MST. Beginning in 1997, alternative tactics seemed to become a more visible element of the MST's repertoire. This was arguably a function of both their increasing number and size and their creativity and boldness.

In early 1997, the MST galvanized Brazil with a variation on an old tactic: the extended march to an urban area. Three "columns" of about one thousand MST campers, settlers, and full-time activists departed from different points of the country. They proceeded gradually, holding demonstrations and public meetings in towns and cities along the way. Two months later,

Table 9 Increase in land occupations by region, 1990–1994 to 1995–1999

Region	1990–1994	1995–1999	% Increase
Center-West	68	416	511.8
North	76	189	148.6
Northeast	131	846	545.8
South	89	346	288.8
Southeast	52	395	659.6

Source: CPT 1991, 1992, 1993a, 1994, 1995, 1996a, 1997, 1998, 1999, 2000.

Table 10 Increase in occupying families by region, 1990–1994 to 1995–1999

Region	1990–1994	1995–1999	% Increase
Center-West	12,490	57,892	363.5
North	7,974	28,283	254.7
Northeast	22,149	113,368	411.8
South	18,098	51,507	184.6
Southeast	16,527	54,886	232.1

Source: CPT 1991, 1992, 1993a, 1994, 1995, 1996a, 1997, 1998, 1999, 2000.

the columns converged on Brasília. On April 17, the first anniversary of Eldorado, they were joined in a major demonstration by about fifty thousand other, mainly non-MST protestors. The march and final demonstration received intense and generally sympathetic media coverage, confirming the MST as a force to be reckoned with. Nevertheless, they failed to significantly affect Cardoso's land reform program.

The following year brought new innovations, generally involving more disruptive and confrontational tactics. The coordinated national protest campaigns known as "days of struggle," which appeared to have largely dropped out of the MST's tactical repertoire after 1992, returned in 1998. Even more than before, they focused on occupations of government office buildings. In addition, they increasingly targeted federal agencies in charge of economic policy, rather than the INCRA. The powerful Ministry of Finance was a major target. In one day in March 1998 the MST occupied the ministry's offices in ten state capitals. Another, smaller day of struggle, involving occupations of the Ministry of Finance and other federal office buildings, occurred in March 1999.

In May 1998, MST activists in Pernambuco adopted another tactical innovation, looting supermarkets and trucks laden with food. The purpose of these initiatives, they said, was to draw attention to social problems caused by the drought in the Northeast and the government's failure to act on them. Although looting has long been a common practice during the Northeast's punishing droughts, the MST's leadership of these initiatives drew a great deal of attention. The MST also seemed to use the old tactic of land occupations in new ways, occupying farmland known to be productive. The media suggested that this tactic was commonplace, but it seemed to be limited to a few states.[33] Finally, in late 1998 the MST began occupying highway toll plazas in some states and preventing attendants from charging drivers. In one case, activists allegedly set toll booths on fire.[34] The tactic was an attempt to tap popular resentment over the privatization of public highways.

These more aggressive tactics were controversial, in part because they

---

33. By occupying productive *fazendas*, the MST usually sought to underscore that the constitutional clause concerning the "social function" of rural land allows the expropriation of private farms that are in violation of labor or environmental codes. These provisions have been ignored by federal authorities, who have based expropriation decisions exclusively on how intensively a piece of land is farmed.

34. *Folha de São Paulo*, November 12, 1999.

seemed to take the MST beyond the narrow mission of redistributing unproductive land to the landless, an objective that had broad support from the public. The MST, however, viewed them as a question of necessity. After observing society's reaction to the massacres at Corumbiara and Eldorado, the MST leadership had initially believed that Cardoso would be forced to make important advances in agrarian reform. But the MST soon perceived that Cardoso's reform would fall far short of their expectations. The decline of the agrarian reform budget after 1997, along with the New Rural World initiatives announced in 1999, deepened this impression. Cardoso's failure to implement a truly major reform was made more egregious for the MST by the fact that it was occurring during a moment of unprecedented public concern about the land problem. A historic opportunity to restructure Brazil's rural landholding system was being wasted.

The MST's opposition to Cardoso went well beyond the issue of land reform. For the MST leadership, the major obstacle to land redistribution—more important than the *bancada ruralista*—was Cardoso's adherence to neoliberalism.[35] Agrarian reform simply did not make sense in a liberal economy: small farmers could not survive without subsidies and trade protection. It was for this reason, in the MST's analysis, that Cardoso was interested only in doing just enough reform to satisfy public opinion, and no more. The government would not give settlers enough resources to prosper. On the contrary, it was interested in seeing them fail, so it would have an excuse to abandon land reform altogether.

Consequently, the defeat of neoliberalism and its political expression, the Cardoso government, became a paramount concern. The MST leadership felt that the PT and CUT were not doing an adequate job of this, having been cowed into submission by Cardoso's electoral successes. Thus, the MST increasingly focused its own criticism of Cardoso on his privatization program, his continued service of Brazil's foreign debt, and what it saw as his subservience to the IMF and the United States. It was because they felt that the economic model was the main obstacle to agrarian reform that the MST leadership began targeting economics-related ministries with the group's pressure tactics in 1998. They hoped to drive home the point that real reform would only be implemented when Brazil had abandoned neoliberalism.

35. Interview with João Pedro Stedile, member of the MST National Directorate, December 15, 2000, São Paulo, SP. The negative impact of Cardoso's liberalizing policies on small farmers was a major issue of editorials and articles in the *Jornal Sem Terra*.

In late 1997, the MST launched an initiative called the Popular Consultation, aimed at forming a national activist network to curry public support for a leftist, nationalist alternative to neoliberalism. Although the MST sought to bring other leftist groups into the campaign, the CUT and PT largely stayed away. In August 1998, the consultation launched a two-month march from Rio de Janeiro to Brasília. Unlike the 1997 march, this one received little media coverage. What attention it did garner was critical, stressing the MST's involvement in issues distant from agrarian reform.

Movement Organizations

The Cardoso years brought a major increase in the number of actors involved in the landless movement. Most of them focused more or less exclusively on organizing land occupations. As in the past, rural unions were behind many land occupations. A rural union leader from Pará said that during the mid-1990s union activists increasingly moved toward proactively organizing occupations, rather than supporting spontaneous efforts.[36] In Pernambuco, unions in the sugarcane zone had traditionally been involved in struggles for better wages and working conditions rather than for land reform, but in the mid-1990s many of them began organizing land occupations.[37]

In addition, many new groups sprang up devoted exclusively to organizing rural workers to press for land redistribution. Although most were exclusively local actors, organized by politicians, party activists, or union leaders, some came to operate in multiple states.[38] These include the Workers' Movement (MT), active in Pernambuco and Alagoas; the Struggle for Land Movement (MLT), in Bahia and Pará; the Brazilian Landless Movement (MBST), in Maranhão, Pará, and the Federal District; and the Movement for the Liberation of the Landless (MLST), in Maranhão, Minas Gerais, Pernambuco, Rio Grande do Norte, and São Paulo (Fernandes 1999, 255).

Although some of these organizations had a strongly leftist bent, non-MST actors were in general less ideologically motivated and more willing to settle for marginal properties. They often had a clientelistic character,

36. Interview with Airton Faleiros, president of the state rural union federation, FETAGRIPA, April 26, 2000, Brasília, DF.
37. Interview with Januário Moreira, president of the Federation of Agriculture Workers of Pernambuco (FETAPE), May 23, 1998, Recife, PE.
38. Fernandes found twelve such entities operating in the Pontal do Paranapanema alone, almost all founded after 1995 (Fernandes 1999, 254–55).

functioning as vehicles for politicians or union leaders to deliver patronage to their followers. In fact, media reports suggested that, as expropriations accelerated under Cardoso, there arose many instances in which landowners with properties they could not sell profitably made deals with landless "activists." The latter would organize an occupation of the property, provoking an expropriation that would result in financial benefits for the landlord.[39]

The strategy of combining occupations with roadside camps became more generalized during the late 1990s. Even in regions where the struggle for land was influenced by an older squatter tradition that largely ignored the idea of appealing to public opinion and the media, camping showed signs of catching on (Ondetti, Wambergue, and Afonso forthcoming). By the late 1990s, the landless camps strewn across the Brazilian countryside could no longer be assumed to reflect MST activity.

Nevertheless, in the public mind the MST remained virtually synonymous with the grassroots struggle for land reform. Most Brazilians seemed to be unaware that many occupations were not organized by the MST. This perception was a product of the MST's unrivaled capacity to mobilize workers nationally, its boldness and flare for the dramatic, and its role in some of the most publicized social conflicts of the mid-1990s, including the Eldorado incident and the struggle in the Pontal do Paranapenema.

The MST's basic characteristics as an organization did not change greatly during 1995–99, but its ability to mount protest campaigns was enhanced by an inflow of organizational resources. In part, these were of a human variety. The growth of land occupations and settlements provided a larger base from which to recruit activists. However, as the MST grew, it arguably became less solid in terms of human resources. Activists in the Northeast, for example, complained that the sugarcane workers who made up much of the MST's social base in the region were not easily transformed into quality activists, because of their low literacy, lack of initiative, and deference to authority.[40] Ironically, activists sometimes also complained that the acceleration of settlement activity had negative effects on their organization. A shorter, easier camping process meant that families were less likely to become politicized and to feel loyalty toward the MST.

The inflow of material resources was possibly more impressive and had less ambivalent effects. Sympathy and publicity generated by the massacres

39. "Aliança do barulho," *Veja*, January 14, 1998, 22–24.
40. Interview with MST activist Dirce Salete Ostroski, February 2000, João Pessoa, PB.

of the mid-1990s helped give the MST greater access to NGO funding (Cadji 2000). In particular, help came from established European groups, such as Frères des Hommes of France and Mani Tese of Italy. In two northeastern states I visited, Alagoas and Paraíba, European NGO grants accounted for at least half the budget of the state secretariat. The MST was even awarded a large grant, reportedly worth several hundred thousand dollars, from the European Commission for legal expenses. Access to public funds also grew. Federal outlays on settler credit increased greatly, because of both the growing number of settlers and increases in the volume of credit per settler. Settler contributions meant that some of this money found its way into MST coffers. The MST also required agronomists hired under the INCRA's technical assistance program to contribute part of their salaries. In addition, the MST was able to obtain substantial funding from a number of other federal agencies, including the ministries of labor and education. The MST also benefited from the sale of books and compact discs produced by famous Brazilian artists to promote the cause of agrarian reform.[41]

The CUT and PT continued to be important MST allies at the local and national level. PT legislators were active in Congress pressuring for agrarian reform legislation and criticizing the government's claims about its land reform program. The CUT organized thousands of workers to attend the MST demonstration in Brasília in April 1997, helping to make it a major success. Nonetheless, relations between the MST and both the CUT and PT seemed to cool somewhat over the course of the late 1990s.[42] The MST's criticism of their moderation, crystallized in the Popular Consultation, was one source of stress. In addition, some PT politicians were at least privately critical of certain MST tactics, such as looting. Since the MST and PT were strongly associated in the public mind, they felt these actions could hurt their electoral prospects.

Responses to Protest Activity

The growth of protest activity for land reform did not, of course, go unnoticed by other sectors of Brazilian society. Not surprisingly, one group that

41. Renowned Brazilian photographer Sebastião Salgado donated part of the revenues from a striking book of photos, many of them documenting the MST's struggle. Pop singer Chico Buarque did the same with a CD.

42. Interview, Altemir Tortelli, vice president of the CUT, April 15, 2000, São Paulo, SP.

was particularly concerned were large rural landowners, especially those whose properties were vulnerable to being seized to provide land to the landless.

Although landowners did not engage in a national campaign against land occupations, these actions did provoke countermobilization efforts at the local and state level. The one that drew the most attention was in the Pontal, where landowners refounded the UDR in 1996. The major complaint of landowners in a number of states was that state authorities were not executing judicial orders of expulsion or were doing so in a slow or timid manner. Pará was probably the most extreme example. Landowners there told me that the state government had essentially stopped sending the Military Police to expel land occupiers after the killings at Eldorado.[43] They argued that the lack of police repression tended to encourage new occupations. Landowners also criticized the INCRA for settling land occupiers, rather than conducting reform according to more universalistic criteria. Responding to landowner pressure, in July 1997 Cardoso issued a decree prohibiting the INCRA from assessing for expropriation properties under occupation. However, this measure had little practical effect in terms of limiting occupations.

The major exception to the rule of relatively modest official repression of land occupations was the state of Paraná. There, the Military Police force launched a major campaign against the MST in 1999, clearing numerous land occupations and arresting dozens of campers and movement leaders (Branford and Rocha 2002, chap. 8). Ironically, Governor Jaime Lerner of the Democratic Labor Party (PDT) had generally been seen as relatively progressive. The activist community attributed the onslaught to a political pact they said Lerner had made with the state's landowners in order to guarantee his reelection in 1998.

Despite the high level of protest in the countryside, land-related violence did not return to anywhere near the levels of the mid-1980s (CPT 1986, 1987, 1988b, 1989a, 1990, 1991, 1992, 1993a, 1994, 1995). This apparent paradox would seem to have two explanations. First, even in frontier regions, land conflicts more frequently took the form of large land occupations and camps than in the past. These sometimes elicited strong reactions from landowners and police. However, large groups were generally less vul-

---

43. Interview with Carlos Xavier, president of the state agricultural federation, FAEPA, November 7, 1999, Belém, PA.

nerable to repression than were the isolated squatters of the 1980s. Second, and perhaps more important, the tremendous public attention focused on the land question, especially after Eldorado dos Carajás, made it more likely that violence against the landless would be punished.[44]

Another politically important actor was the news media. Media coverage of the landless movement in the mid-1990s was mixed. Coverage focused overwhelmingly on the MST. Articles and editorials often expressed sympathy for its cause and the discipline and commitment of its activists, but they were often critical of land occupations, sometimes describing them as "illegal" and "violent." Criticism grew visibly more virulent as the Cardoso era wore on. The 1997 National March received relatively positive coverage. However, the MST's building and toll plaza occupations and its involvement in looting seemed to provoke even more criticism than land occupations. By the late 1990s, both *Veja* and the official editorials in the *Folha de São Paulo* had adopted an aggressively anti-MST stance. Despite its generally moderate politics, the latter publication called insistently for Cardoso to take sterner measures against the MST's "criminal radicalism" and cautioned that other groups might follow its example, generating a rising tide of social chaos.[45]

Opinion polls taken in the mid-1990s suggested substantial public support for both land occupations and the MST. In a late 1996 poll, 59 percent of respondents said they always or usually approved of the MST.[46] In a March 1997 poll by the major firm IBOPE, 74 percent of those interviewed agreed with the statement, "The policy of invasions is important in order to call the attention of the government to the problem of the landless."[47] Later polls, however, seemed to indicate lower levels of public support. In an IBOPE poll taken in March 1998 only 30 percent of respondents evaluated the MST's actions as excellent or good, while 26 percent saw them as bad or

44. Interview with Plínio de Arruda Sampaio, April 3, 2000, São Paulo, SP. Sampaio, a former PT federal deputy and a longtime ally of the MST, argued that repression against the landless tends to be worse when the agrarian question is ignored by the media and (consequently) the urban public.

45. *Folha de São Paulo*, May 15, 1998.

46. The study was reported in the *Jornal Sem Terra*, July 1996. It was conducted by the polling firm Vox Populi in May 1996 in eight major state capitals. The MST's approval level was similar to that of the public universities and higher than that of the Military Police, the Civil Police, the CUT, the state industrial federations, and the Brazilian Congress.

47. Reported by the *Jornal Sem Terra*, April/May 1997. The study was commissioned by the National Confederation for Industry (CNI) and was based on more than two thousand interviews.

terrible.[48] Support for land "invasions" was down to 59 percent. A survey commissioned by the federal government in June 1998, following the MST's campaign of looting in the Northeast, produced even more negative results.[49] Sixty-six percent characterized the MST as "violent," rather than "pacific" and 67 percent felt that the group was more interested in the "political" than the "social" results of its actions. Seventy-two percent of those interviewed said they disapproved of looting and 57 percent said they did not support the MST.[50] Polls taken in the early 2000s (some of which are cited in Chapters 5 and 6) would generally confirm the erosion of public support for the MST relative to the mid-1990s.

Cardoso, Jungmann, and other federal officials were highly critical of land and, especially, building occupations, qualifying them as politically motivated, lawless, and an obstacle to reform. They said the MST had arisen for a good cause, but had lost its way and was now more interested in overthrowing the elected government than in achieving land reform. Why else, they asked, would the MST insist on its aggressive protest actions, when the government was settling landless families at an unprecedented rate? By the late 1990s, there was little or no direct contact between Jungmann or Cardoso and the MST leadership. Nonetheless, lower-level officials generally responded to MST protest actions by sitting down to negotiate and granting some concessions. This provoked substantial criticism of the Cardoso government, especially among more conservative commentators.

Explaining Movement Takeoff

As the preceding discussion suggests, the landless movement grew exponentially during 1995–99, transforming itself into a social phenomenon of massive proportions. The movement's sprawling camps became a routine part of the rural landscape in many regions. What was behind this abrupt change in the intensity of protest for land reform in Brazil?

48. "Pesquisa de opinião pública sobre a reforma agrária," IBOPE, March 1998.
49. "Pesquisa telefônica: Brasil—19 Junho 1998," Instituto de Pesquisas Sociais, Políticas e Econômicas (IPESPE). Unlike the IBOPE polls cited above, this one was done by telephone. The sample size was one thousand.
50. An article published in Veja would appear to confirm this trend. It refers to polling data showing a decline in support for the MST from close to 80 percent in 1996, to 58 percent in 1998 and 28 percent in August 1999. Sources are not cited for these data. See "Marchando para trás," Veja, October 20, 1999.

Organizational capacity played some role in the process. Grassroots organizational structures in the communities where landless workers were recruited probably did not get any stronger, but new resources to support protest activities were channeled into the movement by actors external to the landless population. The MST, in particular, experienced a major new influx of material resources from both the federal government and foreign NGOS. Nevertheless, an increase in organizational capacity was not the key factor behind the movement's expansion. The timing of resource flows into the MST suggests that they were not a major cause of movement growth. When MST occupations began to intensify in late 1995, the distribution of land, credit, and other sources of government funding was just beginning. The new influx of NGO funding also occurred only after protest had increased dramatically. These changes probably helped the MST mount its campaigns of the late 1990s, but they cannot explain the initial upsurge of protest.

Activist strategy is even less convincing as an explanation of the movement's abrupt rise. It is hard to find any way in which strategic choices by activists affected the takeoff of the landless movement, independent of other, more contextual factors. During the period of rapid acceleration, in the mid-1990s, there were really no innovations in tactics, goals, organizational forms, or framing strategies to speak of, either by the MST or by other landless SMOS. The MST did make some tactical changes in the late 1990s, with its National March, occupations of the Ministry of Finance, looting, and other actions. It arguably also shifted its goals somewhat, by elevating the struggle against neoliberalism to the status of a major immediate priority. However, these innovations followed the major upsurge in protest, rather than preceding it, and were largely a response to the fact that it had not produced a deeper and more lasting change in government policy.

The grievance/discontent perspective offers somewhat more leverage on this question. As I mentioned at the outset of this chapter, some informal analyses have focused on the effects of rising absolute necessity, related to deteriorating employment conditions. Fernandes (1998, 2000) takes this position, stressing the impact of liberalizing policies under Collor and Cardoso on both rural and urban employment. The argument is not extensively developed, but the basic idea is simple: given declining opportunities for gainful employment in either agriculture or the urban sector, poor workers increasingly pursued agrarian reform as a substitute. "Unemployment generates a growing demand, particularly in small and medium-sized cities. An important option for rural and urban wage workers is the struggle for land," writes Fernandes (1998, 48).

There would seem to be reason to question why, in the face of declining conditions for family agriculture, workers would chose participation in agrarian reform as an economic strategy. Nevertheless, wage laborers facing poor employment opportunities might see in land reform a way to at least guarantee their subsistence, by providing an area to plant food crops. This could possibly be combined with other strategies, such as wage labor. Although Fernandes does not mention this factor, the prospect of receiving government-funded housing and highly subsidized credit (much of which was ultimately not paid back) was undoubtedly also attractive to many poor workers. Although selling agrarian reform plots was technically illegal, it was a common practice in some areas.

With regard to agricultural employment, the evidence for this explanation is mixed. There is at least some reason to believe that the growing crisis of employment in agriculture did create increasingly favorable conditions for the landless movement's growth, particularly in its impact on certain labor-intensive crops. However, the crisis cannot explain either the abruptness or the magnitude of the increase.

The contention that employment opportunities became scarcer in agriculture during the early and mid-1990s is supported by the fact that the labor force shrunk substantially during the 1992–97 period, despite the relatively slow growth of urban jobs. In addition, it is striking that 1996, the year that land occupations exploded, also brought easily the largest decline in agricultural employment. Nevertheless, comparing across regions, there seems to be no clear relationship between employment losses and occupation activity. For example, the Northeast, which experienced the largest increase in occupying families during 1995–99, was the region that saw easily the smallest decline in its agricultural workforce. Meanwhile, the South, which had the second-largest drop in agricultural jobs, saw the smallest increase in families and the second-smallest increase in occupations.

This lack of cross-regional correspondence between declining employment and increasing protest would seem to be a strong argument against a causal link, but we must consider extenuating factors. First, not having employment data for the North undermines the comparison somewhat. Second, the internal heterogeneity of the regions may hide the impact of job losses in agriculture on landless protest.[51] In addition, evidence of a more anecdotal kind seems to provide solid support for the link between the agricultural employment crisis and movement growth, especially with regard to certain labor-intensive crops. In particular, it has often been argued that the growth of occupations in the sugarcane areas of the Northeast was encouraged by the painful restructuring forced by the decline in federal subsidies beginning under Sarney (Wolford 2004). Because it brought a reduction in the area planted, and encouraged greater mechanization, the crisis of the sugar sector undercut farm employment in states such as Pernambuco and Alagoas.[52] Even in some states that are not major sugarcane producers, underemployed cane cutters were often a major presence in landless camps.

The movement's rapid growth in Paraná, to offer another example, appears to have been fed by the crisis of cotton cultivation. Trade liberalization dealt a major blow to the state's cotton sector, exposing it to competition from more efficient producers (Lunardon 2000). This change had a negative impact on sharecroppers, tenant farmers, and wage laborers. Since many (if not most) of the families involved in MST occupations in the Pontal do Paranapanema were actually recruited in northern Paraná, the rural employment crisis in that state arguably also contributed to the acceleration of protest in São Paulo.

However, even if we accept that the diminishing capacity of Brazilian agriculture to absorb labor increased the potential for movement expansion, it is clear that this factor cannot fully explain the abruptness or magnitude of the movement's growth in the second half of the 1990s. The crises of northeastern sugarcane and southern cotton were already a number of years old when the movement surged in the mid-1990s. Moreover, the magnitude of the decline in agricultural employment pales in comparison to the growth of land occupations. The agricultural workforce in 1999, for example, was about 10 percent smaller than in 1992, but the number of families involved in occupations was more than 400 percent greater.

As I noted, Fernandes also stresses the impact of growing unemployment in the cities on the landless movement's growth. It is true that many people

51. A statistical analysis using *município*-level employment and occupation data would probably help to shed more light on this question.
52. This process also contributed to the intensification of land occupations by leaving many former sugar plantations virtually abandoned, facilitating expropriation. The drought of the late 1990s aggravated this effect.

who joined the movement in the 1990s were living in urban areas and thus would have been directly affected by changes in urban employment conditions. It is also true that inconsistent growth and neoliberal restructuring made the 1990s, on the whole, a poor decade for urban employment in Brazil. This situation helped create a relatively favorable social climate for the movement's recruiting efforts. However, the trajectory of urban employment during the 1990s does not parallel the movement's growth trajectory. Job creation during the mid-1990s, when land occupations exploded, was more robust than during either the early or late 1990s, both periods of gradual movement growth. Hence, the evidence does not support a tight causal link between urban unemployment and landless protest.

There is also little evidence for an explanation based on relative deprivation. Analysts of rural movements, as referred to in Chapter 1, have sometimes seen protest as a response to modernizing initiatives that failed to produce the promised results. The upsurge of protest in the second half of the 1990s in Brazil, however, came after a number of difficult years in agriculture, and the economy as a whole, during which government resources and protection were steadily withdrawn. Relative deprivation analyses of rural protest have also shown it to be a result of the exposure of rural dwellers to urban influences, which makes clear their own relative poverty, but this explanation implies a rural sector much more backward and isolated than the contemporary Brazilian one.

As this discussion suggests, a growing crisis of agricultural employment in the first half of the 1990s helped create a somewhat more favorable social context for the landless movement's expansion. Job growth in the urban sector was not robust enough to counteract this situation. Nevertheless, in itself, growing necessity at the grassroots cannot explain either the abruptness of the landless movement's takeoff in the second half of the 1990s, or its impressive magnitude.

In my view, the key factor in the landless movement's expansion during this period was a shift in the political opportunity structure. Protest grew mainly because workers and activists perceived that the Cardoso government was more likely to respond positively to pressures for land reform than were its predecessors. That protest responded to a shift in federal policies rather than to grievances is suggested by the fact that every region of the country experienced a major increase in land occupations during the 1995–99 period, despite important differences in agricultural economies, land distribution, employment conditions, and other socioeconomic variables. The major increase in land occupations between 1995 and 1996 was also geographically diffuse.

Another piece of evidence that supports this view is that, as Figures 7 and 8 suggest, protest surged most strongly directly in the aftermath of the two major instances in which Cardoso sought to signal his commitment to agrarian reform, in large part by taking control of the INCRA away from conservative forces. Occupations surged in late 1995, when Cardoso made Francisco Graziano president of the INCRA, and then again in April and May 1996, when he created a new ministry for agrarian reform and committed himself to pushing forward a number of important land reform–related bills.

Because they suggested that Cardoso was indeed going to accelerate the pace of land reform, and because the INCRA had historically prioritized people already involved in camps and occupations, these announcements motivated activists to intensify their efforts to organize new protest actions. That these changes were perceived as improving the prospects for land distribution is suggested, for example, by the November 1995 *Jornal Sem Terra* editorial cited above, which portrayed Graziano's rise to the presidency of the INCRA as a critical advance for agrarian reform, making it the only government policy "of interest to the workers." By increasing the pace of protest, landless workers and activists sought to take advantage of the government's anticipated largess. The more politicized actors, especially the MST, also sought to apply additional political pressure in order to make sure that Cardoso at least made good on his commitments.

Most of the MST leaders I interviewed in the late 1990s would only grudgingly admit that the acceleration of land reform had encouraged movement expansion, preferring to emphasize the impact of neoliberal policies on employment. They sometimes did admit, though, that Cardoso's settlement policy had contributed to the rise of other, less politicized landless organizations.[53] Rural union activists, who were generally less virulently antigovernment than their MST counterparts, were often more willing to acknowledge this relationship.[54] Some INCRA officials also acknowledged it.[55]

53. Interview with Gilmar Mauro, member of the MST National Directorate, May 11, 2000, São Paulo, SP.

54. Interview with Sebastião Neves Rocha, secretary for land and environmental policy, CONTAG, May 2, 2000, Brasília, DF.

55. Interview with José Rui, chief, Settlement Division, INCRA-RS, September 3, 1999, Porto Alegre, RS.

My analysis of the movement's rise thus supports, in general terms, the political opportunity perspective's take on the causes of change in protest intensity over time. However, up to now, this discussion has left out an important aspect of the political opportunity context, one that has also escaped extant interpretations of the movement's takeoff during this period. This is the impact of the Corumbiara and Eldorado massacres. Because they abruptly focused public attention and concern on the agrarian question, these incidents had an indirect but critical role in the movement's expansion during the 1990s.

The influence of the massacres on protest activity occurred through two main channels. The most important of these was their impact on federal land reform policy. When Cardoso moved to demonstrate his commitment to agrarian reform in late 1995 and mid-1996 he was, as was argued earlier in this chapter, responding mainly to the public outcries provoked by the massacres. The upsurge in protest that followed each of these announcements was thus an indirect product of the impact of the massacres on Brazilian public opinion and foreign observers, which forced the government into action. Graziano himself has argued that he was appointed president of the INCRA to remedy the political damage caused by the killings at Corumbiara (Graziano 1996).

The second way in which the massacres affected the opportunity context for landless protest was their effect on repression. Landowners frequently complained during the second half of the 1990s that state authorities were not obeying judicial orders to expel occupiers. Although some left-leaning governors behaved this way for ideological and partisan reasons, another motive was clearly the fear of provoking a new Eldorado. The decline in police repression in Pará is only the clearest example; my field research uncovered evidence of this effect in others states also.[56]

An objection that may be raised to this argument is that the impact of the massacres on public opinion and government policy was itself a by-product of the expectations of progressive change created by Cardoso. What was really important was the electoral change itself. This perspective is not wholly without substance. Cardoso's personal image as an enlightened intellectual sensitive to Brazil's social problems probably helped to sway urban, centrist voters who might otherwise have hesitated to cast their

---

56. For example, in Alagoas both rural activists and human rights activists commented to me that the example of Eldorado had contributed to changes in the Military Police's approach to dealing with land occupations.

ballot for a coalition involving the PFL and other conservative parties. His election created expectations among these sectors that he would introduce significant social reforms, and his failure to do so in the early going created a gap that agrarian reform, in a sense, ended up filling.

It would be a major mistake, however, to reduce the impact of the massacres to a product of the character of the government in office. To begin with, it is important to underscore that, in terms of reducing conservative influence on federal policies, the major transition of the 1990s was the fall of the Collor government, not Cardoso's election. It was at that point that the more purely conservative governing coalitions of the late Sarney and Collor years gave way to ones in which more urban-based centrist forces played a bigger role. It was largely for this reason that landless protest started to show tentative signs of intensifying under Itamar Franco. Cardoso's election represented continuity with this moderate shift toward the center. Consequently, it was interpreted by the Left as a defeat.

It is also important to stress that the massacres were quite unusual in their magnitude and public visibility. This is especially true of Eldorado. Murders related to conflicts over farmland have been quite common in Brazil, but I know of no other such instance in which so many people were killed and injured at the same time. Just as important, the fact that the incident was captured on video and that its product, a flatbed truck laden with mangled bodies, was the subject of many powerful photographic images, was very unusual. Deadly land conflicts had generally occurred deep in rural areas, far from reporters and television cameras. The availability of images was critical in a society in which more than 80 percent of households possess television sets (Power and Roberts 2000, 237). It helped transform the massacre at Eldorado do Carajás from an obscure incident in the backlands into a powerful symbol of social injustice in the countryside.

Although this account of the landless movement's takeoff supports the basic dynamics of the political opportunity perspective, it also lends some support to two aspects of the current conceptual critique of this perspective, regarding the character of the political opportunity structure and how it can be shaped by a movement's own actions.

As I argued in Chapter 1, discussions of the components of the political opportunity structure have tended to focus mainly on relatively concrete phenomena, such as changes in institutional structures and partisan alliances, the mobilization of elite groups, or defeats in interstate wars. Scholars have paid scant attention to more purely subjective changes, or explicitly argued that these should not be considered an aspect of the political opportunity structure. McAdam (1996), for example, acknowledges that events that "dramatize a glaring contradiction between a highly salient cultural value and conventional practices"—a fairly good description of the massacres at Corumbiara and Eldorado dos Carajás—can contribute to movement growth (25). Yet he asserts that they should be seen as "cultural" rather than "political" opportunities. "The kinds of structural changes and power shifts that are most defensibly conceived of as political opportunities," he writes, "should not be confused with the collective process by which these changes are interpreted and framed" (25–26).

To the extent that such events provoke protest directly, by spurring outraged people to take to the streets regarding some issue that has just become more salient to them, McAdam is correct. In such a case, the event affects protest by intensifying grievances. The process analyzed in this chapter exhibits a different dynamic. Although massacres did provoke some street protests by people outraged that public functionaries had murdered innocent people, their major effect on movement activity was indirect. They influenced the intensity of protest mainly by affecting authorities' political vulnerability to pressure by landless workers for agrarian reform. Therefore, it seems hard to deny that the "cultural" or subjective effect of the massacres gave rise to a "political" opportunity for protest.

Some scholars have also taken the political opportunity literature to task for exaggerating the extent to which politics shapes social movements (Goodwin and Jasper 1999). The causal relationship between movements and their political environments, they argue, is more reciprocal and fluid than this literature suggests. Although mainstream political opportunity analyses have acknowledged that movements shape their political opportunity structure, they have not paid much real attention to this notion.

My account of the impact of the landless massacres of the mid-1990s on the intensity of protest for land reform provides some support for the idea that the political opportunity structure can be partly a product of a movement's own actions. Landless activists did not consciously seek to provoke these incidents. Nor, for the most part, were activists able to control their influence on public perceptions and state policy once they had occurred. Nevertheless, this transformation of the political opportunity structure was not altogether independent of the landless movement's own actions. The massacres in rural Rondônia and Pará would surely not have come about had the movement not been using mass protest to press for land reform. Its aggressive tactics threatened the interests of landowning elites and their conservative allies within the state. They also challenged the ability of local police forces to maintain public order. As a result, they had the effect of encouraging these actors to resort to violence on a large scale.

Conclusion

The landless movement grew extremely rapidly during the 1995–99 period relative to the preceding decade. Land occupations multiplied quickly, especially during the mid-1990s. From 1997 on, other forms of protest became increasingly common and provoked a great deal of attention and controversy. In this chapter I have sought to explain the upsurge of landless protest and to use the findings to evaluate the relative capacity of existing theoretical perspectives to explain temporal variation in movement intensity.

The grievance/discontent perspective finds some support in this analysis. A growing unemployment crisis in the agricultural sector, aggravated by slow job growth in the cities, helped provide an underlying potential for expansion. However, the key to the landless movement's takeoff lies in the political opportunity structure. Protest grew mainly because the prospects for gaining land through occupations and other pressure tactics improved, motivating existing movement organizations to accelerate the pace of protest activity and stimulating the entrance of many new actors into the movement.

The improvement of the political opportunity structure was partially tied to the moderate progressive shift in governing coalitions that came with the fall of Collor, as well as President Cardoso's enlightened personal image. However, the key to understanding the rapid increase in protest for land in the mid-1990s lies in the political impact of the massacres at Corumbiara and Eldorado do Carajás. These not only forced the Cardoso government to accelerate the pace of settlement activity, they also brought a decline in police repression of land occupations, at least in some states. Together, these effects created powerful incentives for activists to accelerate mobilization and protest for agrarian reform.

Although this account of the movement's takeoff generally supports the political opportunity perspective, it also underscores the value of some of the recent critiques of how political opportunity has been conceptualized. Specifically, it demonstrates the potentially powerful impact of purely subjective changes in the political context on protest activity, and it illustrates the notion that major changes in the political opportunity structure can be partially a consequence of a movement's own protest actions.

FIVE   Decline, 2000–2002

During the second half of the 1990s the landless movement had became the largest and most influential
rural movement in Brazilian history. Hundreds of thousands of people had participated in its
protest actions. Directly or indirectly, its pressure tactics had
played a central role in bringing about the most significant agrarian reform program ever carried out in Bra-
zil. Then, beginning in 2000, the movement entered a period of decline.
Land occupation activity dropped sharply, reaching levels comparable to
those of 1995. Although other tactics seem to have intensified somewhat,
the critical role of occupations in the movement's tactical repertoire made
the decline of such actions a major blow. With the falloff in occupation
activity, the prospects for recruiting new families into the movement grew
increasingly dim. At the same time, the government's commitment to land
reform deteriorated further. Only the triumph of the PT in the national
elections of 2002 served to brighten an otherwise bleak scenario.

My aim in this chapter is to explain why the incidence of land occupations in Brazil suffered a major decline during 2000–2002, the last three
years of the Cardoso presidency. I use this empirical episode to evaluate
competing theoretical perspectives on temporal variation in movement intensity and, in particular, on the issue of movement decline.

As they have with emergence, adherents of the political opportunity
perspective have staked a strong claim to being able to explain movement
decline. They view decline as a reflection of the diminishing efficacy of
protest in producing concessions or the intensification of repression. Griev-
ance/discontent theory has not had much to say about decline, but the
logic of this perspective suggests that movements may enter into crisis if
the grievances that gave rise to it are attenuated. The organizational capac-

ity perspective would lead us to suspect a deterioration of the grassroots organizational structures underlying protest or the withdrawal of resources previously supplied by some external group. From the standpoint of the activist strategy perspective, decline may result from poorly chosen tactics, unfortunate framings, or other choices that go awry or fail to respond to changing circumstances.

To my knowledge, there are no in-depth studies of the decline of land occupations in Brazil during this period. My account is consistent with informal commentaries on this question, but I work out the argument more systematically and also discuss its theoretical significance.

The decline of land occupations in 2000–2002 was not a product of diminishing grievances or falling organizational capacity, although the latter did occur to some extent during this period, as I discuss below. Its central cause, rather, was a series of new repressive measures adopted by federal authorities in mid-2000, which made the land occupation largely useless, if not counterproductive, as a strategy for seeking access to farmland. The Cardoso government sought to demonstrate (and was largely successful in doing so) that it would no longer respond to this type of pressure, except to punish the perpetrators. In this sense, the episode clearly supports the political opportunity perspective on the question of social movement decline.

Nevertheless, activist strategy must also be seen as playing an important role in the movement's crisis. Although its proximate cause was a transformation in the political opportunity structure, this change was itself partly a product of a shift in movement tactics. In particular, Cardoso's turn toward stronger legal repression was influenced by the growing boldness of MST protest actions, a phenomenon that began to take shape in the late 1990s and arguably peaked in early 2000. Tactics such as looting and the occupation of public offices helped provoke a stern response, both because they challenged the president's authority and because they undermined the MST's public support, making a crackdown politically easier. The MST's ambitious attempts to lead the opposition to neoliberalism also helped pave the way for the crackdown by contributing to its political isolation.

As this brief discussion suggests, the argument I develop in this chapter provides further support for the idea that a social movement's political opportunity structure may be influenced by its own actions. Cardoso's 2000 crackdown clearly brought a sharp change in the receptivity of the state to protest for land reform, one that activists had little power to revert, at least in the short term. Nonetheless, this change may well have been delayed or not occurred at all had it not been for the movement's own protest initiatives, which threatened authorities and undermined support for the movement.

I begin the chapter with a concise overview of the major political and socioeconomic developments in Brazil during this three-year period. Then I discuss the evolution of state policies relevant to the landless movement, focusing particular attention on the new measures introduced in 2000 to stop land occupations. In a third section I analyze the basic patterns in landless protest activity in 2000–2002. In the final part of the chapter, I flesh out the arguments mentioned above regarding the causes of the movement's decline.

Hard Times for the PSDB

An economic recovery in 2000 helped Cardoso regain some of the public support he had lost in 1999 with the economic crisis. However, the government soon encountered new problems. Social protest erupted in March, April, and May, involving truckers, indigenous groups, the landless, and public employees. These protests troubled and embarrassed the government, because of both the popular discontent they expressed and the occasionally excessive repression they provoked from public security forces. I discuss the landless and indigenous protests further below.

Later in the year, the government was dogged by a corruption scandal involving a former top Cardoso aide. Adding to the government's worries was the stellar performance of the PT in the October 2000 local elections. PT victories in a number of major state capitals seemed to position the party well for the 2002 national election campaign. In 2001, new corruption scandals affected the PSDB's major political allies, the PMDB and PFL. Although these scandals did not directly affect the president, they divided his legislative coalition and increased the public perception of generalized official corruption. To make matters worse, a substantial energy crisis emerged at midyear, requiring electricity rationing and slowing down economic growth.

Overall, the performance of the economy was a liability for the government during Cardoso's last three years in office. After a strong 4.4 percent expansion in 2000, the economy grew by only 1.3 percent in 2001 and 1.9

percent in 2002 (IPEADATA, PIB). Social indicators do not suggest major changes during this period. Urban unemployment dipped in 2000, with the economic recovery, but tended to rise again in subsequent years (IPEADATA, Taxa de Desemprego Aberto nas RMS). Poverty, which had increased in 1999 with the economic crisis, returned to lower levels gradually in 2000–2002 (Neri 2006, 3). Average household income, which had dipped in response to the 1999 crisis, increased slowly throughout this period (18). Agriculture was a bright spot in the generally gloomy economic picture. Growth in this sector was the mirror image of the economy as a whole, falling slightly in 2000 then growing by 4.7 percent in 2001 and by a whopping 11.5 percent in 2002, driven by high international commodity prices and a favorable exchange rate (CNA 2003). Rural poverty held steady in 2000 and 2001, then declined in 2002 (Neri 2006, 19), presumably because of the agricultural boom.

The employment performance of the farm sector was less impressive, reflecting the central role of capital-intensive activities, especially soybean cultivation, in driving the expansion in farm output. The number of people active in agriculture had spiked up in 1999, probably because of the economic recession, which undermined the urban job market. It faded thereafter, despite rapid agricultural sector growth. If we exclude 1999, the size of the agricultural labor force remained basically stable between 1996 and the end of the Cardoso era, although it declined very substantially as a proportion of the total Brazilian labor force (IBGE 1996, 2002).[1] The composition of the farm labor force, in terms of the relative weight of wage workers, small producers (including independent smallholders, tenant farmers, sharecroppers, and squatters), and unpaid family laborers, also did not change very substantially.[2]

The poor economic conditions and high unemployment of Cardoso's second term took its toll on the government's popularity and created the opportunity the PT had been waiting for to end its status as a permanent opposition party. Running in his fourth presidential race, Lula finally emerged victorious, defeating José Serra, the lackluster candidate of the

1. PNAD data show that the number of people involved in agriculture was 2.2 percent smaller in 2002 than in 1996. As a percentage of the total Brazilian labor force, the agricultural workforce declined from 24.5 percent to 20.6 percent. The rural population also shrank substantially, by 13.8 percent, during this period.

2. The most significant change in this sense was a gradual decline in unpaid family labor, which probably reflected the growing incorporation of labor-saving technologies.

PSDB-PFL coalition, in a runoff. The PT also did well in legislative elections, becoming the largest party in the Chamber of Deputies for the first time in its history. The electoral campaign contributed to Brazil's sluggish economic performance in 2002. Worried that the election would bring an anti-market radical to power, investors began pulling out of Brazil. Only a series of IMF-endorsed stabilization measures, combined with repeated public pledges by Lula that he would pursue sustainable, market-friendly economic policies, averted a deeper financial crisis (Giambiagi 2005).

Cardoso Cracks Down

Cardoso's second term in office had started off poorly for the landless movement in 1999, with cuts in the agrarian reform budget and the policy changes marketed as the "New Rural World." This negative trend only deepened during the 2000-2002 period and took on additional, equally troubling characteristics.

On the surface, land redistribution seemed to continue at full tilt. The Ministry of Agrarian Development announced impressive settlement totals: 92,986 families in 2000, 82,449 in 2001, and a projected 60,000 in 2002 (INCRA 2002). These tallies raised Cardoso's two-term total to a figure exceeding 608,000 families, more than double that of all the previous governments combined. As in earlier years, the ministry launched high-profile initiatives. In 2000 Jungmann announced a "war" on land grabbing. The INCRA canceled the titles of thousands of suspicious properties, placing the onus on landowners to provide proof of ownership. Illegitimately held properties would be used for land reform, officials said. In early 2001 the INCRA also began allowing people to register for agrarian reform by mail. Families interested in receiving land could pick up a form at a post office, fill it out, and return it to the INCRA. If they met the necessary criteria, officials claimed, they would eventually receive land. Camping, in other words, was no longer necessary.

The appearance of continuity masked an important retrogression relative to Cardoso's first term. Spending on agrarian reform never recuperated from its sharp decline in 1999. The second PSDB term brought a significant fiscal adjustment, but the reduced investment in this policy area reflected a change in priorities and not simply the impact of the general belt-tightening. This is suggested by the fact that INCRA spending shrank from an average of 0.48 percent of total federal outlays during Cardoso's first term to only 0.20 percent during his second (Ondetti 2006a, 30). Reflecting this change, the amount of private land expropriated for agrarian reform fell by more than half (IPEA 2003, 109).

Given these trends, the official settlement figures appeared suspiciously high. In 2002 they came under increased scrutiny. A series of reports in the *Folha de São Paulo* beginning in April suggested that the government had inflated its 2001 settlement count by including expropriated areas lacking houses, infrastructure, and (in some cases) even settlers.[3] The newspaper also suggested that the INCRA had included families that had been granted land by previous governments but received some service or infrastructure under Cardoso. The MST, CPT, and other groups had long expressed skepticism about official figures, as noted in the preceding chapter, but Cardoso's second term seems to have brought a deepening of questionable accounting practices. The IPEA settlement data suggest that the number of families effectively settled during Cardoso's second term was barely more than half that of his first (IPEA 2006, statistical annex, table 7.1).

Declining land redistribution was only part of the bad news for the landless. A more visible change was the hardening of the government's stance toward the movement's protest tactics. This occurred rather abruptly, in early May 2000. First, Cardoso issued a "provisional measure" (a kind of decree) rendering occupied rural properties ineligible for expropriation for two years. If occupied a second time, the prohibition would be extended to four years. People and organizations involved in the "invasion" of rural lands or public property would be ineligible to receive any kind of public funding. Resources already disbursed, including land, could be taken back. The government also announced that henceforth the federal police force would be used to protect federal buildings from occupation. A special division of agrarian conflicts, moreover, would be created within this force (PT 2000).

These measures came in response to MST protest actions. Early in 2000, the MST had vowed to counter the government's commemoration of the five hundredth anniversary of the Portuguese discovery of Brazil by organizing five hundred land occupations. In mid-April the MST launched a "day of struggle," involving land occupations, demonstrations, and other tactics. In Belém, capital of Pará, MST activists protesting the still-unpunished mur-

3. The first story appeared on April 21, 2002.

ders at Eldorado do Carajás entered and allegedly vandalized the state Secretariat of Security.[4] Even the local PT issued a statement criticizing this action. Another controversial initiative occurred in Pernambuco, where the MST occupied a sugar plantation that authorities had already conceded to the state rural union confederation. CONTAG leaders were furious and, for perhaps the first time, publicly criticized the MST.

The action that probably drew the most fire from authorities was the MST's protest march during official ceremonies in Porto Seguro, Bahia, where the Portuguese had landed in 1500. Anticipating the MST's arrival, local authorities had made extensive security arrangements to bar marchers from the ceremony site. The most controversial aspect of the ensuing conflict, though, was that police ended up beating and teargassing a large group of indigenous protestors. For obvious reasons, the violent repression of indigenous protestors on precisely this occasion held great symbolic resonance. It made front-page news in Brazil and abroad and was deeply embarrassing to the Cardoso government.[5] Officials seemed to hold the MST responsible for the crisis. In the wake of this incident Cardoso made some of his most strongly worded pronouncements against the MST, warning that he would not tolerate more "troublemaking."

A few days later, at the beginning of May, the MST launched one of its largest days of struggle ever, which included occupations of federal buildings in thirteen state capitals, as well as Brasília. Some thirty thousand people participated. In some cases, windows, doors, and other property were damaged in the occupation process. Most of the building occupations involved the Ministry of Finance. The MST refused to leave the buildings until the government agreed to negotiations involving either Cardoso himself or one of his economic ministers. It demanded a major increase in the agrarian reform budget. The situation was tense. Military police in Paraná, attempting to block the MST from entering the state capital, shot and killed a settler.

In contrast to earlier MST protest campaigns, this time Cardoso refused to make even minor concessions. He quickly issued the anti–land and building occupation measures mentioned above and said he would not allow any negotiations as long as federal buildings remained under occupation. Cardoso's spokesperson suggested to reporters that the death in Paraná should

4. *Folha de São Paulo,* April 18, 2000.
5. "De nau a pior," *Veja,* May 3, 2000, 44–50.

"serve as an alert to those who opt for provocation and disrespect to democracy and citizenship."[6] In the end, it was the MST that backed down,
abandoning its occupations. About a week later, in what was universally
interpreted as an attempt to isolate the MST, Cardoso greeted the CONTAG's
annual "Cry of the Land" day of protest with unusually generous concessions.[7]

In the immediate aftermath of the MST occupation campaign, federal
authorities announced the creation of a new intelligence service, which
would be devoted to public security issues. Critics accused the government
of recreating a military-era intelligence service used for political repression.[8] Although officials claimed that this initiative had nothing to do with
the MST, commentators suggested that it reflected the government's growing concern about its inability to prevent MST protest tactics and that the
timing of the announcement had been affected by the May building occupation campaign. Some thirty MST militants who participated in these actions were arrested. In at least one case, police invoked the military-era
Law of National Security in detaining MST activists.

Critics were not altogether lacking, but the media's coverage of the government's offensive against the MST was generally quite positive.[9] Commentators underscored the growing threat the MST posed to "democracy" and
the "rule of law" and applauded the fact that Cardoso was "finally" getting
tough on the MST's unruly tactics. According to an article in the May 10
edition of *Veja*: "The government took a long time to conclude that the
invasions promoted by the landless in public buildings, some with vandalism, required a severe reaction from authorities. Last week the [presidential
palace] showed signs that it had suddenly discovered that you cannot negotiate with the MST. The truth is that the government, loath to be accused
of social insensitivity, has avoided using its authority against members of
the MST, who scoff at the country's laws."[10]

The cover of this issue of the magazine featured the MST's red flag and
the headline "The Tactic of Troublemaking: The MST Uses the Pretext of
Agrarian Reform to Preach Socialist Revolution." Coverage in the *Folha de
São Paulo*, though not as blatantly anti-MST as in *Veja*, also favored the

---

6. "Sem terra e sem lei," *Veja*, May 10, 2000, 42–49.
7. "Suspiro no campo," *Veja*, May 17, 2000, 48–50.
8. *Latin American Brazil Report*, May 30, 2000.
9. "Mídia, mentira e ditadura," *Caros Amigos*, June 2000.
10. "Sem terra e sem lei," *Veja*, May 10, 2000, 42–49.

government's position. Public opinion studies suggested a strong rejection of the MST's tactics. For example, a week after the occupation campaign, the *Folha* published a poll taken in the city of São Paulo, showing that 70 percent of respondents were against land "invasions" and 75 percent against the "invasion" of public buildings.[11]

A few days after the end of the MST occupations, the INCRA launched a nationwide investigation of the MST's use of government credit to fund its operations. The initiative was announced the day after the *Folha de São Paulo* ran an investigative report on the MST's use of public credit in Paraná.[12] The report accused the MST of charging its settlers a "tax" on their credits and using strong-arm tactics to get money from those unwilling to donate it freely. It also accused MST cooperatives of using a variety of schemes to funnel off official funds. Although framed as a new revelation, the "tax" had been common knowledge to the INCRA for many years and had even been mentioned in media coverage. These accusations were reproduced in newspapers, magazines, and television news programs all over Brazil and frequently echoed by government officials.

The apparent increase in settlement activity in 2000 appears to have been an effort to soften the hard image generated by the government's repressive measures. Catholic Church organizations, including the CPT and CNBB, were critical of Cardoso's hard line toward the MST. However, other actors on the left were rather quiet. The PT put a statement on its Web site criticizing the "invasions of public property."[13] News reports said the PT, gearing up for the 2000 municipal elections, was eager to distance itself from the MST's radicalism. Lula did not attend the MST's 2000 congress, though he had attended some of the MST's previous congresses. In an interview with *Veja* in December, Minister Jungmann said the government had expected that its crackdown on the MST would meet considerable resistance from the Left, but had been surprised by the timid response.[14]

In July and August 2000, INCRA officials and MST leaders met for negotiation sessions mediated by the Catholic Church; this meeting did not produce an agreement. The government unilaterally announced an increase in settlement goals, but denied one of the MST's major demands, for more and cheaper credit. After these meetings, the two parties hardly spoke at the

11. *Folha de São Paulo,* May 13, 2000.
12. *Folha de São Paulo,* May 14, 2000.
13. *Latin American Brazil Report,* May 30, 2000.
14. "O MST se perdeu," *Veja,* November 15, 2000, 11–15.

national level during the rest of the Cardoso era. The MST sometimes pressured for new negotiations, but officials did not seem very interested.

Cardoso's measures against land occupations appear to have been implemented rather consistently after their mid-2000 announcement.[15] Properties made ineligible for expropriation were listed on the INCRA's Web site. The site also listed the names of settlers excluded from the program, although only about two dozen people were included. The investigation into financial wrongdoing in MST cooperatives and the "tax" or "toll" charged on settler credits continued into at least early 2001, although it is not clear what its result was. The *Jornal Sem Terra* reported that federal technical assistance and primary education programs for land reform settlements had been cut off entirely.[16]

The MST devoted a great deal of effort in 2000 to trying to stem the damage to its reputation caused by the corruption charges made by the media and government. It published special editions of the *Jornal Sem Terra* and released to the media letters of support from foreign luminaries, including Rigoberta Menchú and Noam Chomsky. The MST claimed that the government was attacking it to cover up its own corruption and flagging support. MST leaders argued that the government was bent on destroying the organization altogether.

Reversing the trend visible in the late 1990s, press coverage of the land question intensified in 2000, mainly as a result of reports on the MST's April and May offensives and the government's responses to them. Nevertheless, this revival fell far short of the peaks in coverage seen in 1996 and 1997 and proved to be fleeting. Relatively little attention was devoted to this issue during the balance of Cardoso's presidency. The number of articles and editorials on the agrarian question in *Veja,* for example, dropped from an average of 14.5 in Cardoso's first term to only 5 in his second.[17]

For the MST and other pro-land reform groups the only good political news of Cardoso's second term came at its very end, with the PT's electoral triumph. MST activists had campaigned for Lula in a number of states. The media suggested that the MST had also instituted a "truce" in its protest

---

15. Oral presentation, Bernardo Mançano Fernandes, Congress of the Latin American Studies Association, Washington, D.C., September 9–12, 2001.

16. *Jornal Sem Terra,* September 2001.

17. In the *Folha de São Paulo,* the number of items making reference to some aspect of the agrarian question declined from an average of 2,246 a year in Cardoso's first term to 1,303 in his second.

tactics during the election campaign in order to foster a climate of calm in the countryside and thus help ensure Lula's victory. The MST itself steadfastly denied this. Evidence from the CPT land occupation data is mixed, suggesting some slowdown in occupations during the months leading up to the election, but certainly not a full-fledged halt.[18] The MST celebrated the PT's victory, but they were also wary of the PT's growing political moderation and what that might mean for the future of agrarian reform. I discuss this issue at greater length in the following chapter.

Movement Decline

Land occupation activity dropped quite sharply all over Brazil during the 2000 to 2002 period. Although other tactics appear to have maintained or perhaps even exceeded the intensity of past years, the decline in land occupations was a major blow to the movement, since it changed the incentive structure for movement participation, making the prospects for maintaining the previous pace of mobilization seem quite dim.

Relative to 1999, in 2000 there occurred a 32.9 percent decline in the number of occupations and a 16.9 percent drop in occupying families (see Figs. 11 and 12). Occupation activity began quite vigorously, but slowed down visibly after May (Fig. 13). As a result, the first four months accounted for almost 80 percent of the year's occupations. Activity declined even more sharply in 2001, as occupations dropped by 50.6 percent and

Fig. 11 Land occupations in Brazil, 1995–2002

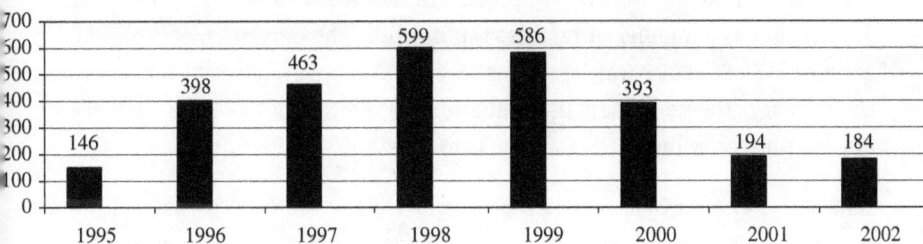

Source: CPT 1996a, 1997, 1998, 1999, 2000, 2001, 2002, 2003.

18. Only fourteen of the MST's ninety-eight occupations in 2002 occurred in the three months before the presidential runoff on October 27 (CPT 2003). However, it must be remembered that since about 1997 MST occupations have tended to be heavily concentrated in the first half of the year, particularly March and April, in commemoration of the Eldorado do Carajás incident.

Fig. 12   Occupying families in Brazil, 1995–2002

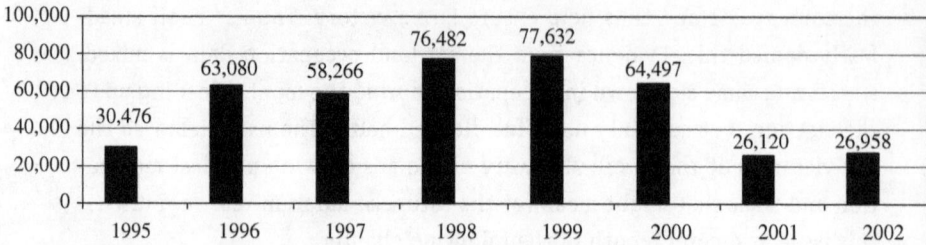

Source: CPT 1996a, 1997, 1998, 1999, 2000, 2001, 2002, 203.

Fig. 13   Land occupations by month in Brazil, 2000

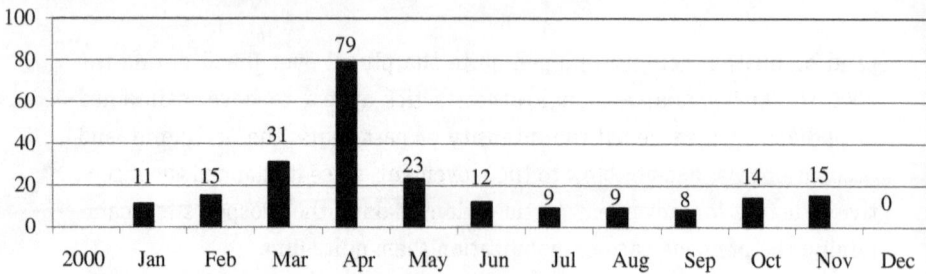

Source: CPT 2001.

occupying families by 59.5 percent relative to 2000. The following year brought a similar level of activity.

Overall, land occupations in 2000–2002 declined by 53.2 percent relative to the preceding three-year period, while the number of families involved in them declined by 44.6 percent. Compared with the figures for 1995, Cardoso's first year in office, the number of occupations in 2002 was still greater, but the number of families was smaller. The decline in occupation activity in 2000–2002 was, as Tables 11 and 12 suggest, generalized across the country. The MST's share of occupations rose during 2000–2002, reflecting its greater willingness to defy Cardoso's anti-occupation decree. For

Table 11   Decline in land occupations by region, 1997–1999 to 2000–2002

Region	1997–1999	2000–2002	% Decline
Center-West	322	135	58.1
North	125	84	32.8
Northeast	632	314	50.3
South	279	65	76.7
Southeast	290	173	40.3

Source: CPT 1998, 1999, 2000, 2001, 2002, 2003.

Table 12 Decline in occupying families by region, 1997–1999 to 2000–2002

Region	1997–1999	2000–2002	% Decline
Center-West	43,800	22,189	49.3
North	19,383	10,752	44.5
Northeast	79,220	46,488	41.3
South	34,550	13,921	59.7
Southeast	35,427	24,225	31.6

Source: CPT 1998, 1999, 2000, 2001, 2002, 2003.

the period as a whole, the MST accounted for 48.9 percent of the total, a substantially larger share than in the late 1990s.

The fact that occupations faded did not mean that existing camps disappeared. In late 2001 the MST estimated that there were more than eighty thousand families camped all over Brazil.[19] Officials tended to put the number at around fifty thousand. Even this figure meant that somewhere in the neighborhood of two hundred thousand people were still involved in the camping process. The MST managed to make headlines by repeatedly threatening to occupy (and finally occupying) a *fazenda* in the state of Minas Gerais owned by President Cardoso's family, forcing federal authorities to send army troops to defend the property. The MST had used this tactic before, but turned to it with greater frequency in 2000–2002. It drew a great deal of media attention and undoubtedly embarrassed the government.

Other forms of protest for land also continued and, to a limited extent, may have intensified to compensate for the decline of occupations.[20] In some cases, groups of landless camped in areas adjacent to targeted properties instead of occupying them. The MST also continued to organize marches, demonstrations, and even occupations of public buildings, although notably not those of the Ministry of Finance. National days of struggle were held regularly, as in past years. In early September 2001 the MST formed a semipermanent camp in Brasília, dubbed the Eldorado do Carajás camp. It grew to around one thousand workers, who engaged in almost daily protests. The camp also included participants from other organizations, such as the CPT.[21] MST activists urged landless families to fill out the

19. *Jornal Sem Terra,* September 2001.
20. The CPT began publishing data in 1998 on forms of rural protest other than land occupations. Unfortunately, particularly for the early years, it is not possible to distinguish between protest for agrarian reform and protest aimed at achieving other objectives. In addition, data collection early on seems to have been less comprehensive than in later years, diminishing the data set's usefulness for evaluating the trajectory of protest.
21. *Jornal Sem Terra,* October 2001.

official agrarian reform registration cards and mail them to the INCRA en masse, to demonstrate that land-reform-by-mail was really a hoax.

Nevertheless, the apparent demise of land occupations as a tactic seemed to bode ill for the future of the movement. Occupations had been an important instrument of pressure on authorities, particularly at the subnational level. Just as important, as I argued in Chapter 3, the landless movement's relatively successful use of this tactic had created strong individual, material incentives for landless families to participate in the movement, making it less dependent on other types of incentives to recruit new members. With the decline of land occupations, it appeared that the landless movement would find itself in the same position as that of other movements. Given the general paucity of movement activity in contemporary Brazil, it seemed unlikely that the landless movement would be able to maintain for long the impressive level of protest achieved since the mid-1990s.

The MST showed few external signs of crisis or self-doubt. Nevertheless, there were indications that a certain pessimism was beginning to take hold of the organization. An MST activist on a speaking tour of the United States told me in June 2002 that, given the intensity of the government counteroffensive and the difficulty of occupying land, some of her colleagues were beginning to suggest that the MST's future might be in doubt.[22]

Explaining Movement Decline

The landless movement entered a new phase in 2000, characterized by the marked decline in its traditional core tactic, land occupations. Although other forms of protest for land reform seemed to continue with the same intensity as in earlier years, the decline of land occupations was a major blow. How do we explain this change, and what do the findings suggest about the ability of existing theoretical perspectives to explain temporal variation in movement intensity and, especially, movement decline?

The evidence does not provide much support for the idea that the fading of protest activity was a direct reflection of diminished social grievances. Brazil's economic recovery in 2000 could potentially have contributed to declining land occupations by opening up alternative opportunities for poor workers, but the decline continued in 2001 and 2002 despite subpar

22. Personal communication, Wanusa Pereira dos Santos, June 3, 2002, Chapel Hill, NC.

economic growth. Agricultural growth, moreover, moved in the opposite direction, from stagnation in 2000 to rapid expansion in later years. Trends in the agricultural workforce also do not seem to provide much explanatory leverage on the decline in occupations in 2000–2002. As noted earlier, with the exception of 1999, which brought a temporary increase in agricultural work, the size and composition of the farm labor force did not change much between 1996 and the end of Cardoso's second term.

If declining demand for land reform was not a direct trigger of the drop-off in land occupations, perhaps it was an underlying or background factor. It is provocative in this sense that the growth of occupations began to stagnate in 1999, even before the sharp decline in 2000. Did occupations plateau in 1999 because of declining grievances? Government officials sometimes suggested that the slowdown in movement growth in 1999 was a result of Cardoso's land reform program, implying either that the government had shown the landless that it was no longer necessary to engage in occupations in order to receive land or that reform efforts were beginning to exhaust existing demand for land.

In my field research in late 1999 and early 2000, I saw no sign that the INCRA had stopped prioritizing campers in its settlement efforts. Some INCRA officials freely acknowledged that, given their limited resources, expropriation and settlement efforts still occurred mainly in response to land conflicts.[23] Nor is there reason to believe that Cardoso's program had significantly reduced the demand for land redistribution. Officials often claimed that there were only some 2.5 million families left in agriculture that could be considered even potential candidates for land reform.[24] However, by the early 1990s the movement's camps included many people not currently working in agriculture. If one takes the movement's actual social base as defining the potential client base for agrarian reform, the resulting count would surely be higher than 2.5 million families. It is therefore unlikely that Cardoso's settlement efforts were enough to make a major dent in demand for land. This would become even more evident in 2003, with the vigorous revival of landless protest under the PT government, which I discuss in the following chapter. If the leveling off of land occupations in

23. Interview with José Rui, chief, Settlement Division, INCRA-RS, September 3, 1999, Porto Alegre, RS.

24. These claims were based on an academic study published by the INCRA. The study estimates potential demand for land and makes projections through 2003. It is based on data from the agricultural censuses of 1985 and 1995/1996. See INCRA (2000a).

1999 was a reflection of state policies at all, it was in all probability a response to the sharp cuts in INCRA funding and the consequent slowdown in settlement efforts, which diminished the prospects for rapid settlement. In other words, it was a product of the deterioration of the political opportunity structure.

The sharp decline in land occupations beginning in 2000 was also not caused by a collapse in the grassroots social networks and institutions through which landless families were recruited into the movement, as the organizational capacity perspective would suggest. There is no reason to suspect a change in such organizational structures and, as I suggested in Chapter 3, by the early 1990s bloc recruitment through secondary associations was no longer the norm for the landless movement. Movement participants were often recruited on an individual basis, through knocking on doors in poor neighborhoods.

However, organizational resources are not necessarily indigenous to the communities from which movement members are recruited. Social movement theorists have sometimes seen the decline of popular social movements as resulting from the withdrawal of resources by elite groups that had previously supported the movement. Did such a change affect the landless movement's ability to organize occupations in 2000–2002? The landless movement, and especially the MST, did in fact lose access to much of the government funding it had formerly benefited from. Although the end of the PROCERA credit program in 1999 may have had a negative effect on the MST's finances, the withdrawal of public funds occurred mainly after the federal crackdown of mid-2000. The MST was deprived of many of the explicit funding agreements it had with agencies such as the ministries of labor and agriculture. Moreover, its ability to extract contributions from settlers was undoubtedly impeded by the INCRA's investigation into this issue and negative publicity the affair generated in the media.

However, if this effect were really very strong, there should have been a decline in all types of MST protest for land reform. Based on the available evidence, there does not seem to have been a decline in nonoccupation tactics. More important, it is notable that the drop in land occupations became visible rather immediately after the government's crackdown in May 2000. If this drop were principally a result of a growing resource deficit, one would reasonably expect a certain time lag between the closing of the financial spigot and the drying up of the flow of protest.

Rather, the evidence clearly suggests that the sharp drop-off in land

occupations was mainly a direct consequence of a change in the movement's political opportunity structure. Occupations declined because the
federal government went out of its way to make clear, beginning in May
2000, that it would no longer respond to such actions with concessions and
might even punish those involved by making them ineligible for land reform. This shift made it largely counterproductive to occupy land. Land
occupations might potentially still be used as a way of pushing authorities
to settle the families involved on a different property, but it is arguably
harder to motivate people to occupy a piece of land that they will definitely
not be able to settle on. Moreover, to avoid exhausting the stock of unproductive land by rendering it ineligible for expropriation, activists would
have to target productive properties, a tactic that is highly controversial
and would put them into confrontation with more powerful landowners.

The government's new policy that those participating in land occupations, including existing settlers, would be ineligible for land reform may
have also served to discourage occupations. The INCRA's agrarian-reform-by-
mail campaign may have helped in a small way to keep the number of
occupations low, by suggesting to the landless that they could gain land
without the sacrifices involved in camping. However, this program would
not have been successful in preventing occupations in the absence of a
political will on the part of authorities to ignore or punish occupations. As
long as people who engaged in occupations received priority in settlement
activities, there would always be an incentive to occupy.

That the drop in occupation activity was a result of Cardoso's 2000 anti-
occupation measures is generally accepted by movement leaders and scholars of the landless movement alike. Writing in the CPT's report on rural
conflicts for 2000, for example, a well-known Brazilian academic and MST
activist said of these measures, "It is evident that with this policy of crimi-
nalizing the struggle for land, the government was able to diminish the
number of occupations" (CPT 2001, 33). As I argue in Chapter 6, moreover,
the nonenforcement of the anti-occupation decree by the Lula government
would play a central role in the revival of occupations beginning in 2003.

The decline in land occupations thus clearly responded to a change in
the degree of receptivity of federal authorities to this type of protest action. Yet to stop the analysis there and proclaim victory for the political
opportunity perspective would be to ignore the important role of strategic
choices made by the MST in bringing about the intensification of repressive
measures in 2000. The landless movement's new political opportunity

structure beginning in mid-2000 was in part the product of its previous actions.

President Cardoso had a clear interest in stopping land occupations and other types of aggressive protest for land reform. These activities caused friction within his political coalition and generated a sense of social chaos and instability. During much of his presidency, however, the political risks of taking strong measures to clamp down on protest outweighed the potential benefits. The massacres of the mid-1990s focused public attention on the land problem and ceded to the landless the moral high ground. To act aggressively against occupations during this period would have smacked of blaming the victim and would have cast doubt on Cardoso's determination to address the underlying causes of unrest in the countryside. Over time this effect seemed to fade somewhat. As the public opinion data presented in Chapter 4 suggest, the landless movement's public image became somewhat less favorable during the course of the late 1990s. People came to see its protest actions as excessive and politically motivated. As a result, the pressure on the president to respond positively to its pressures tended to wane.

To some extent, this change was independent of the movement's own actions. When the MST first captured the nation's attention in the mid-1990s it did so under conditions conducive to eliciting widespread public sympathy. The Eldorado do Carajás incident, in particular, cast it in the role of pacific victim of an oppressive system and heroic defender of the oppressed peasantry. As the MST became more familiar, though, the public and the media became more conscious of its character as a radical, Marxist-influenced group that uses confrontational tactics to force the hand of public officials. This side of the struggle for land was bound to be more controversial. Aware of this, the government and much of the media frequently went out of their way to point out aspects of the MST that might be objectionable to the average Brazilian, including its links to radical groups in other countries and its political indoctrination of camper and settler children. Cardoso's agrarian reform program and the propaganda surrounding it may have also helped to turn public opinion against the movement to some degree. At least to those who took the government's more inflated claims seriously, they suggested that the MST's continuing use of aggressive protest tactics was unnecessary and motivated by broader political goals.

Nonetheless, the crackdown was also a product of the MST's own strategic choices. The MST's urban protest initiatives in March and April 2000 were particularly massive and unruly. They helped to trigger increased repression in two ways. First, they directly challenged Cardoso's authority and his ability to maintain social order. They lent additional credence to the criticism that Cardoso was too timid in dealing with movement and risked encouraging other groups to adopt similar approaches. That the 2000 offensive occurred during a period of generalized protest in Brazil exacerbated this effect. Second, the aggressiveness of the MST's actions provoked a strong media and public rejection, as the *Folha de São Paulo* poll cited above suggests. This rejection made it easier for Cardoso, from a political standpoint, to adopt stern repressive measures.

Pivotal as they proved to be, the 2000 protests were only part of a more general strategic shift that began earlier, in the late 1990s, with the turn to increasingly bold pressure tactics, including looting and occupations of the Ministry of Finance, highway toll plazas, and productive estates. As I discussed in the preceding chapter, for the MST this change was a question of necessity, brought on by Cardoso's unwillingness to undertake a major land reform, as well as the steady reduction in funding for this policy after 1997. Yet these tactics seemed to provoke increasingly strident media criticism and, in all probability, helped to damage the MST's public image. The decay of the MST's public support also made it harder for other leftist organizations, particularly the PT, to come to its aid.

The MST's growing involvement in the struggle against neoliberalism under Cardoso probably also contributed to this trend. Nominal public support for agrarian reform, as mentioned in the preceding chapter, was quite strong, remaining in the 80 percent range throughout the 1990s. Suspending foreign debt payments, reversing privatizations, and breaking ties with the IMF were more controversial issues. By involving itself visibly in these struggles, the MST "politicized" its image and isolated itself from a good many potential supporters, ones who favored land reform but were not leftists in a broader sense.

Thus, although the direct precipitant of the steep decline in land occupations during 2000–2002 was Cardoso's crackdown, this shift in policy was influenced by the concrete decisions taken by movement activists, with regard to both tactics and, to a lesser extent, goals. Over time, these choices increased the government's desire to repress the movement and made it politically easier to do so by undermining public support for the MST.

It can be argued that by avoiding this bolder approach, the MST would have been resigning itself to the reality of a superficial land reform. It is certainly true that a tactical approach based purely on land occupations would surely have resulted in fewer official concessions. However, some initiatives taken by the MST beginning in the late 1990s only served to undermine its image, without having much impact on agrarian reform policy. The clearest example was its high-profile leadership of looting in the Northeast. Although these actions may have yielded short-term concessions, the damage they caused in public relations terms surely outweighed the benefits. The MST's ostentatious engagement in the battle against neoliberalism also achieved little except to drain off organizational resources from the struggle for land and hand critics additional ammunition to attack the MST for becoming "politicized" and no longer being interested in land reform.

The MST leadership appear to have believed that Cardoso would not be able to muster the political will to take a harder line against the movement. Their miscalculation stemmed at least in part from the visible upsurge in public concern about the land issue in the mid-1990s, which was reflected in growing support for the MST and its cause, at least among more progressive domestic sectors and many foreign observers. This led them to overestimate their own political invulnerability. The MST sometimes appeared to believe that its support was unconditional and that, consequently, the government would never be able to act decisively against its protest actions.[25] Clearly, they were wrong.

My interpretation of the landless movement's temporary decline in 2000–2002 thus provides substantial support for the activist strategy perspective on social movement development. In addition, it provides yet another good illustration of how a social movement's political opportunity structure can be shaped by its own protest actions, underscoring the reciprocal character of the causal relationship between movements and their larger political environments.

Once Cardoso's crackdown was set in motion it represented a new structural reality for the landless. Activists were essentially powerless to revert it in the short term. Indeed, it would ultimately take a change in the president and governing coalition to bring a relaxation of the anti–land occupa-

25. A top MST leader, Jaime Amorim, told me that repression would not work against the MST, because the more authorities repressed, the more the public supported the MST. Interview, February 27, 2000, Caruaru, PE.

tion measures, as I discuss in the following chapter. Yet it is hard to deny that the political opportunity structure the landless faced after mid-2000 was itself partially a product of the movement's own actions and the tactical decisions taken by the MST leadership beginning in the late 1990s. Had the MST not escalated its protest tactics and broadened its political strategy, Cardoso might well have found it less necessary and, in particular, less politically feasible to implement strong measures against land occupations. If a crackdown occurred at all during the president's second term, it would probably have happened later and in a less decisive fashion.

Conclusion

By the late 1990s, the Brazilian landless movement had become a vast social phenomenon, with perhaps two hundred thousand people actively engaged in the struggle to conquer new lands. During the 2000 to 2002 period, the movement entered a new phase in its development, as its core tactic, land occupations, suffered an abrupt decline. In this chapter I have offered an explanation of this decline in light of existing theories on social movement development and discussed what the empirical findings suggest about the relative explanatory power of the various theoretical perspectives.

I have argued that neither the grievance/discontent perspective nor the organizational capacity perspective provides much explanatory leverage on this question. Land occupations declined, rather, as a direct consequence of a rapid change in the political opportunity structure for this type of action. Decisive new repressive measures introduced by the Cardoso government in May 2000 rendered land occupations largely useless, if not counterproductive, as a means for obtaining land. Although the episode confirms the value of political opportunity in explaining rapid fluctuations in protest intensity, it also suggests an important caveat. The change in the political opportunity structure was, to a substantial extent, a consequence of strategic decisions taken by the leadership of the movement's major organization, the MST. As a result, the case must also be seen as fortifying the activist strategy perspective on social movements. In addition, it suggests that the political opportunity structure is not altogether independent of the choices made and the actions taken by movement activists.

SIX   Resurgence, 2003–2006

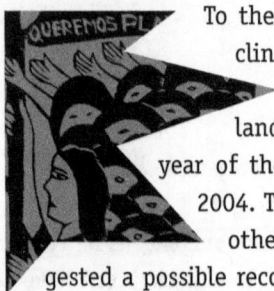

To the relief of activists, the landless movement's decline during the late Cardoso years turned out to be temporary, rather than terminal. Protest for land rebounded strongly beginning in 2003, the first year of the PT government, and continued to increase in 2004. There was a moderate fall in land occupations and other tactics in 2005, but partial data for 2006 suggested a possible recovery. Although protest for agrarian reform grew during Lula's first term, it usually did not take on the markedly aggressive, disruptive character often seen during the late Cardoso years. While land reform activists expressed deep discontent with Lula's policies, state-movement relations were more cordial than under the PSDB, reflecting the mutual interest of the movement and PT in avoiding sharp conflict.

In this chapter I explore the revival of the landless movement in the context of theoretical discussions of the causes of social movement growth. The theoretical notions guiding my analysis here are the same as those employed in Chapters 2 and 4, which also covered periods of rapid movement expansion. I seek to evaluate the relative effectiveness of explanations of the landless movement's expansion based on rising grievances; increasing organizational capacity; strategic innovations by activists; and finally, expanding political opportunities.

Explanations of the movement's resurgence based on grievances, organizational capacity, and activist strategy are all unconvincing. Socioeconomic variables that might be causally related to protest for land reform moved in contradictory directions during this period and some of them would seem to favor a decline, rather than an increase, in protest. The external resources available to landless groups did increase, as Lula renewed the flow of federal funds to the MST (and probably other groups as well). However, as I explain below, it is unlikely that this change was the primary factor behind the resurgence of protest. Finally, although the movement did adjust its tactical repertoire in some ways, there were no major changes in the area of activity strategy that could reasonably explain the sharp resurgence of protest activity early in the Lula presidency.

My analysis shows that protest for land reform revived under Lula essentially because of an improvement in the structure of political opportunities facing the movement. The PT's shift toward the political center detracted from the significance of its electoral victory, but the arrival in power of a center-left party with a historic commitment to land reform and strong ties to pro–land reform groups created expectations of greater settlement activity relative to the late Cardoso years and an end to the anti–land occupation policies adopted in 2000. Although the Lula government's performance in this area was generally disappointing, some of those expectations were fulfilled. Perhaps most important, during Lula's first term the Ministry of Agrarian Development largely failed to enforce Cardoso's anti–land occupation decrees.

The chapter is divided into five sections. It starts off with a general discussion of Lula's first term, including his economic and social policies and their results, in which I focus particular attention on Lula's land reform program and his policy toward land occupations. In the section that follows I discuss the general increase of protest activity for agrarian reform in 2003–6. The third section centers on more qualitative aspects of the movement's approach to pressuring the state under Lula, in particular, the relative restraint exercised by the MST and the rural unions. In the fourth I examine the reaction of landowners to landless protest, which was initially quite strong, reflecting both the growth of land occupations and the broader political context. Finally, in the fifth section, I flesh out my explanation of the movement's resurgence during this period.

The Lula Government: High Expectations, Mixed Results

Despite signs that he would hew to a moderate path, Lula's election as president in November 2002 fed hopes for progressive change. The experiences of Lula's first term were sobering for many PT activists and sympathizers, as the government in essence followed the neoliberal development strategy that the PT had vehemently rejected while in the opposition. Nevertheless, Lula made important advances in some social areas, while achieving a solid economic performance. In terms of land reform, his government was, in general, disappointing to the activist community. Nevertheless, it brought some positive changes in relation to the late Cardoso years.

Neoliberalism with a Gentler Face

Lula's victory was not an endorsement by the Brazilian electorate of radical change. Led by Lula's Articulação faction, the PT had edged closer to the political center during the 1990s, softening its discourse and solidifying its commitment to electoral politics. Its transformation into a center-left party was consolidated during the 2002 campaign. Lula's early lead in the polls had provoked unease, if not panic, among investors, who feared that under his leadership the Brazilian government would default on its debts (Sallum and Kugelmas 2004). As the year progressed, capital began to flow out of the country and inflation surged, raising the specter of a new economic meltdown. Seeking to seal his victory and ensure that he would not inherit an economy in collapse, Lula made a number of gestures signaling his commitment to moderation. In June he chose as his running mate José Alencar, a wealthy industrialist and leader of the conservative Liberal Party (PL), and issued a "Letter to the Brazilian People," which stated his intention to honor the state's debts and maintain fiscal discipline. Another document, issued in August, promised that the PT would respect an agreement President Cardoso had negotiated with the IMF to stave off the crisis.

Lula's institutional power base also should have served to temper hopes for fundamental change. The PT made important advances in the national Congress, becoming the largest party in the lower chamber for the first time. However, given the fragmentation of the Brazilian party system, the PT remained a minority party, with only 17.7 percent of the seats in the House of Deputies and 17.2 percent in the Senate (where it was the third-largest party). Its alliances with other left parties and the PMDB gave it working majorities in both chambers, but they were clearly rather fragile ones.

These signals did not altogether dampen hopes for progressive change. Given Lula's humble origins as a shoeshine boy and factory worker and his party's long-standing leftist credentials, many Brazilians continued to believe that the Lula government would do more than its predecessors to help Brazil's poor. In a late 2002 poll, for example, about 70 percent of respondents expressed confidence that the Lula government would reduce poverty and unemployment (Hunter 2003, 161). MST leader Stedile probably expressed the view of more hopeful leftists when he suggested in the weeks prior to the elections that Lula's moderation represented more of a tactical maneuver than a permanent shift to the political center: "Lula is creating a discourse within the parameters of an electoral campaign. . . . It is a discourse in the center of the ideological spectrum. But as I already stated, the most important thing is not the discourse. The most important thing is the social forces that gather around this or that candidate. The candidacy of Lula has the symbol of change."[1]

In retrospect, Stedile's judgment was too optimistic. During his first term in office, Lula followed in the footsteps of his nominally more conservative predecessor to an extent that few would have predicted. Lula's economic program reinforced Cardoso's emphasis on fiscal and monetary discipline. He also pushed forward some structural reforms associated with neoliberalism, including an attempt to trim the state pension system, and approved the use of genetically modified seeds in agriculture, a move deeply opposed by many leftist groups, including the MST. The government's adherence to a liberal economic program reflected the PT leadership's awareness, strengthened as a result of the 2002 financial crisis, that investor suspicions regarding their true policy intentions left them with little room to maneuver (Giambiagi 2005). Ironically, Lula's background as a leftist put more pressure on him to follow a conservative economic policy in order to reassure capital of his good faith.

His management of the economy won Lula high praise from much of the private sector, as well as international financial institutions, but it caused acute tensions within his party. Although many PT loyalists seemed resigned to this policy tack, the left wing of the party did not take it lying down. The unwillingness of a number of PT legislators to follow the government's lead in Congress led to their eventual expulsion from the party. Others left voluntarily. In mid-2004 dissidents formed a new party, the Party for Socialism and Liberty (PSOL). Its presidential candidate, former PT senator Heloísa Helena, captured 7 percent of the vote in the first round of the 2006 election.

Lula's tight fiscal policy, combined with modest economic growth, limited resources for social programs. Overall social spending remained essen-

1. *Folha de São Paulo,* September 16, 2002.

tially stable relative to the late Cardoso years in real, per capita terms (Pochmann 2006). Nevertheless, spending on programs targeted directly at the poor grew. Easily the most visible social policy initiative under Lula was a series of direct cash transfer programs to the poor that are now known collectively as Bolsa Família, or Family Grant. Some of these programs had been established under Cardoso, but Lula expanded them greatly and made them part of a broader antipoverty plan called Zero Hunger. By late 2006, the Ministry for Social Development and the Fight Against Hunger claimed that Family Grant was reaching more than 11 million families throughout the country.[2] Although it was sometimes criticized for inefficiency and clientelism, Family Grant was extremely popular and by 2006 was clearly one of the PT's biggest political assets.[3]

Another way in which the PT government tried to assert its progressive (and nationalist) credentials was through its foreign policy. Early on, Lula sought to establish Brazil as a leader among less developed countries, especially in multilateral trade negotiations, where it took a strong position in pressuring rich nations to reduce their agricultural subsidies. At the same time, however, Lula sought to distance himself from the more radical, anti-American position of Venezuelan president Hugo Chávez.

During Lula's first term the Brazilian economy experienced a modest revival, growing faster than during Cardoso's second term and at about the same rate as during his first. Growth rates were 0.5 percent in 2003, 4.9 percent in 2004, and 2.3 percent in 2005 percent (IPEADATA, PIB). In 2006 the economy was expected to expand by about 3 percent. Unemployment tended to decline after 2004 but was still at higher levels in late 2006 than before the financial crisis of the late 1990s (IPEADATA, Taxa de Desemprego Aberto nas RMs). Poverty increased in 2003, when the economy was stagnant, but declined substantially in both 2004 and 2005 as a consequence of renewed economic growth; a rising minimum wage; and targeted social programs, especially Family Grant (Neri 2006, 3). Overall, poverty fell by 15.0 percent between 2002 and 2005, the largest decline since the Real Plan was instituted in 1994.

Agriculture went against the grain of the economy as a whole. Propelled

2. Programa Bolsa Família (PBF), "Principais resultados," Ministério do Desenvolvimento Social e Combate à Fome, http://www.mds.gov.br/bolsafamilia/o_programa_bolsa_familia/principais-r esultados (accessed December 29, 2006).

3. The best evidence of its popularity is the fact that all the major candidates in the 2006 presidential election campaign promised to preserve it.

by strong international prices and a favorable exchange rate, the sector boomed in 2003, expanding at a pace of almost 12 percent for the second consecutive year. The area planted in crops expanded rapidly (Figueiredo and Corrêa 2006, 9). There were reports of accelerating deforestation in frontier states as farmers sought new land to plant soybeans. A bust soon followed, however. Production stagnated in 2004 and fell by almost 10 percent in 2005 as a result of an appreciating currency, weaker international demand, and a domestic drought (CNA 2006a). The year 2006 was expected to bring a further reduction (CNA 2006b).

In spite of the rapid growth in output, employment in the agricultural sector expanded by only 1.7 percent in 2003, underscoring agriculture's inability to absorb labor (IBGE 2002, 2003). It remained essentially stable in 2004 and 2005.[4] The composition of the agricultural workforce also did not change significantly during this period. Poverty in rural areas was stable in 2003 relative to 2002, but fell in both 2004 and 2005, despite the mounting problems of the farm economy (Neri 2006, 19). The overall decline in rural poverty between 2002 and 2005 was 12.9 percent. The fact that this variable did not follow the performance of the agricultural sector reflects both the weight of nonagricultural employment in the rural sector and, perhaps more important, the growing impact of federal social programs, especially Family Grant.

A comparatively solid economy and improving social indicators helped buoy Lula's chances for reelection in 2006. These advantages, however, were counterbalanced by a series of scandals. The biggest erupted in mid-2005 when top PT leaders were found to have channeled generous payments to members of other parties to ensure their support for the government's agenda in Congress. The Mensalão (or "big monthly payment") scandal caused serious damage to one of the PT's most valuable political assets, its reputation for honesty. Another scandal, involving the PT's illicit purchase of a report that supposedly implicated PSDB leaders in acts of corruption, arose only two weeks before the October elections. At least partly as a result of the "dossier-gate" incident, Lula was forced into an unexpected runoff with PSDB candidate Geraldo Alckmin, governor of the state of São Paulo. Although Lula was ultimately reelected by a wide margin, these inci-

---

4. Unlike previous PNAD surveys, the 2004 and 2005 versions included the North. In assessing the extent of change in agricultural employment between 2004 and 2003, I excluded the northern states in order to make the results comparable.

dents eroded his personal prestige and caused the PT to lose seats in both chambers of the Brazilian Congress.

Lula and Land Reform

Pro–land reform groups had ambivalent feelings about the PT's electoral triumph in 2002. On the one hand, no major Brazilian party had ever been a more consistent and ardent defender of land reform than the PT. Moreover, the trends of the late Cardoso years—the legal repression of land occupations, the cutoff of federal funds to the MST, and the sharply reduced fiscal commitment to land redistribution—suggested that another PSDB-PFL victory could easily spell the end of the landless movement as a major phenomenon. Realizing this, the MST and other groups had campaigned actively for the PT in many states and had held back on protest to some extent during the 2002 race to increase Lula's chances of being elected.

On the other hand, the nature of the PT campaign was a source of concern. Lula's alliance with the PL, his "Letter to the Brazilian People," and his commitment to honoring the IMF agreement suggested a relatively conservative, market-oriented policy tack. In addition, the party's position on land reform was more ambiguous than in earlier campaigns. After promising to settle 800,000 landless families in the 1994 election campaign and 1 million during the 1998 race, the PT leadership decided not to commit itself to an exact figure in 2002. This reflected substantial disagreement within the PT about the priority it should assign to this policy.[5] Although MST leaders sometimes suggested that Lula's moderation was partly a tactical ploy, they were nonetheless concerned about what it might mean in terms of policy.[6]

In some ways their doubts proved quite justified. The final results for Lula's first term are not yet available; nevertheless, it is clear that the PT government did not make major advances in the land reform area. In particular, expropriation of private farmland slowed considerably relative to the Cardoso years. The average number of hectares expropriated annually in 2003–5 was only about two-thirds the 1999–2002 figure (IPEA 2003; INCRA 2004, 2005, 2006). The difference is larger if we include Cardoso's first term,

---

5. A document drafted by the party's National Agrarian Secretariat, which advises the leadership on land reform, expressed this conflict, noting the "considerable divergences" and "irreconcilable" differences among party activists (PT 2001, 1).

6. Personal communication, Wanusa Pereira dos Santos, June 3, 2002, Chapel Hill, N.C.

when expropriations proceeded at a much faster rate. Landless groups pressured the government to change the indexes of agricultural production used to judge whether a property is unproductive and thus vulnerable to expropriation.[7] These date back to the 1970s and reflect the technological standards of that period. Changing them would facilitate expropriation, making many new properties available. Through the end of 2006, Lula had not been willing to implement this reform, which requires no new legislation, but is vehemently opposed by landowner groups.

Nevertheless, in other ways the PT government brought positive change for the movement, at least in relation to Cardoso's second term. First, by most accounts Lula accelerated the pace at which the INCRA grants land to the landless and land poor. The IPEA's settlement data indicate an increase in the average number of families granted land each year from 34,945 in 1999–2002 to 42,323 in 2003–5 (IPEA 2006, statistical annex, table 7.1). The intensification of settlement activity was accomplished, despite the slowdown in expropriations, by placing many families in vacant plots in existing settlements and creating settlements on public land. Easily the most productive year was 2005, which accounted for more than half the 2003–5 total.

A second positive change, from the point of view of landless activists, involved the legal repression of land occupations. During Lula's first term in office, the INCRA essentially ignored the tough anti-occupation measures adopted by Cardoso in 2000 (CPT 2006, 102). Lula did not officially revoke these measures, but they were generally not enforced. This change, which was apparent by mid-2003, benefited all the groups involved in the struggle for land, enhancing their ability to recruit new members. It was undoubtedly politically costly for Lula, since Cardoso's crackdown had been deeply appreciated by landowners and other conservative groups. Partly as a result of this shift, landowners mobilized intensely against occupations in 2003, helping to prompt a wave of rural violence, as I discuss below.

Lula's mixed performance on land reform reflected a compromise response to contradictory pressures. On the one hand, Lula and the PT undoubtedly felt an obligation to live up to their longtime commitment to land reform. Pro-land reform groups, as I make clear below, used protest actions and statements in the media to remind them and the public of this

7. This was one of the key demands of the MST's National March in July 2005, discussed below (*Jornal Sem Terra,* July/August 2005). Lula agreed to change the indexes, but has thus far not made good on his promise.

obligation, and of the continuing relevance of the land problem. On the other hand, the tight fiscal policy limited resources for this and other programs, and the government's desire to reassure a skeptical private sector probably worked to impede faster progress on expropriation. Land prices were also somewhat higher under Lula, making expropriation of private farmland more costly.[8]

In addition, there were few signs that land reform was a priority issue for the Brazilian press and public, as it appeared to be during Cardoso's first term, in the wake of the Corumbiara and Eldorado do Carajás massacres. Media coverage of the agrarian question increased somewhat relative to the late Cardoso years, but it did not return to the levels seen during the mid-1990s. Figure 14, which shows the number of articles and editorials on this question in *Veja* between 1996 and 2005, illustrates this trend. Coverage in the *Folha de São* exhibits a similar pattern. Land reform, moreover, was largely a nonissue during the 2006 election campaign. These trends underscore the exceptional and temporary character of the sharp upsurge in media and public interest in this question during the mid-1990s.

Movement Resurgence

Protest for land experienced a strong revival during Lula's first term. Even before he took office, in the weeks following his electoral victory, landless

Fig. 14   Coverage of the agrarian question in *Veja*, 1996–2005

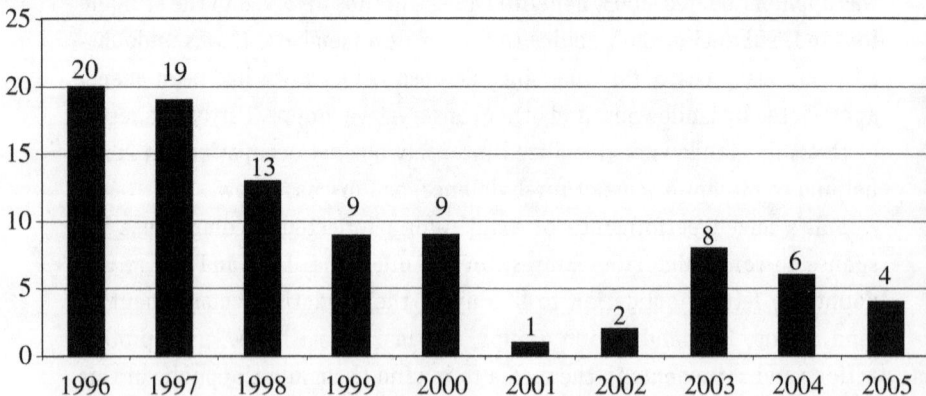

Source: *Veja*.

8. Interview with INCRA president Rolf Hackbart, June 29, 2005, Brasília.

camps began growing in size and number.[9] Occupations began to surge visibly in March and April, traditionally the key months for landless protest. By early June the number of land occupations nationally had already exceeded the 2002 total. Occupations increased by 112.5 percent in 2003 relative to the previous year (see Fig. 15). They increased again, by 26.9 percent, in 2004, before declining somewhat in 2005. Complete data for 2006 are not available at the time of this writing, but partial numbers suggest an outcome roughly similar to 2005 (MDA 2006). Overall, land occupations in 2003–5 increased by 71.7 percent relative to 2000–2002. The pattern of expansion was the same for the number of occupying families and the overall increase for 2003–5 was very similar at 69.7 percent. From a longer-term perspective, occupation activity under Lula returned to levels

Fig. 15 Land occupations in Brazil, 2000–2005

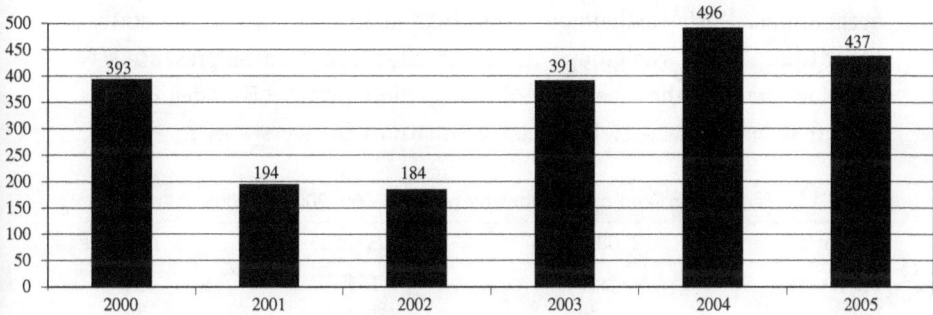

Source: CPT 2001, 2002, 2003, 2004, 2005, 2006.

Fig. 16 Occupying families in Brazil, 2000–2005

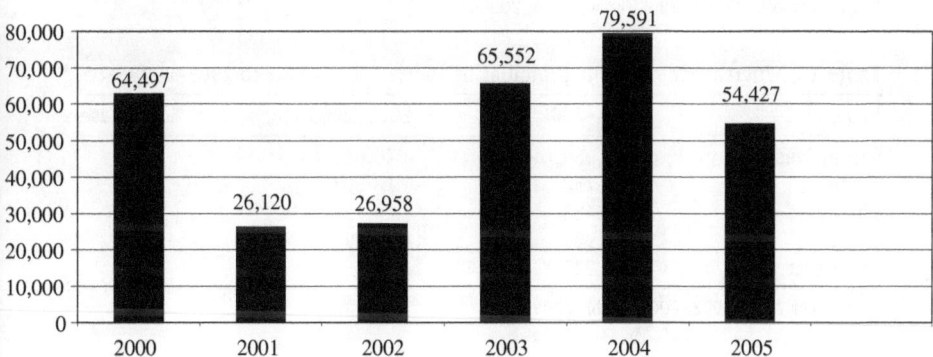

Source: CPT 2001, 2002, 2003, 2004, 2005, 2006.

9. *Folha de São Paulo,* February 23, 2003.

comparable to those of 1996 and 1997, but shy of the peaks attained during the 1998–99 period.

The revival of occupations under Lula was a national phenomenon. Every region experienced a substantial increase in occupation activity in 2003–5 relative to 2000–2002 (see Tables 13 and 14). The South, however, stood out in the extent of the upsurge. This region's leadership was largely a result of the rapid escalation of occupations in Paraná, where the repressive Lerner government was replaced by a left-leaning PMDB administration led by Roberto Requião.

As it had during the previous period of expansion, the movement grew more diverse under Lula. The number of entities organizing at least one occupation increased from thirty-three in 2000–2002 to forty-two in 2003–5 (CPT 2006, 102). Many of these, it should be underscored, existed for only a short period of time and were associated with only a handful of occupations. Most, furthermore, were limited to only one or two states. Other than the MST, the group with the broadest geographical presence was the Movement for the Liberation of the Landless (MLST).[10] Founded in 1998 in Pernambuco, the MLST launched occupations in five states in 2003–5,

Table 13   Increase in land occupations by region, 2000–2002 to 2003–2005

Region	2000–2002	2003–2005	% Increase
Center-West	135	166	23.0
North	84	113	34.5
Northeast	314	557	77.4
South	65	188	189.2
Southeast	173	300	73.4

Source: CPT 2001, 2002, 2003, 2004, 2005, 2006.

Table 14   Increase in occupying families by region, 2000–2002 to 2003–2005

Region	2000–2002	2003–2005	% Increase
Center-West	22,189	40,661	83.2
North	10,752	18,507	72.1
Northeast	46,488	74,154	59.5
South	13,921	27,790	99.6
Southeast	24,225	38,458	58.8

Source: CPT 2001, 2002, 2003, 2004, 2005, 2006.

10. The CONTAG was easily the second-most-important actor in organizing land occupations, if one combines all the initiatives by its associated unions and federations (CPT 2006). However, as I discussed in Chapter 3, the CONTAG cannot readily be considered a unitary actor, since the STRs and state federations linked to it are not really obligated to follow its lead.

with the bulk of its activity being in the Northeast. Its key leader, Bruno Maranhão, is a longtime PT activist. At the state level, the most diverse movements were in Minas Gerais, Pernambuco, and São Paulo. The large number of groups active in these states reflects not only the overall size of the movement, but also the considerable strength of the Left and the fact that the MST had not established a dominant position early on in the movement's development.

As the number of groups involved in the struggle grew, the proportion of total occupations organized by the MST declined. However, the fall was quite modest, from 61.9 percent to 57.1 percent. One reason for the small decline relative to the late Cardoso years was that occupations by rural unions linked to the CONTAG grew fairly slowly under Lula. Their proportion of the total thus fell from 17.5 percent to 10.5 percent. As it did during most of the Cardoso era, in 2003–5 the MST intensified its land occupations in or around the month of April, in commemoration of the Eldorado do Carajás killings. In recent years, the media has taken to calling this surge "red April."

Land occupation activity continued to be broadly distributed geographically in 2003–5. Table 15, which lists the top ten states in terms of the number of land occupations, demonstrates this pattern. Each of the major regions of Brazil is represented by at least one state and no region has more than three representatives on the list. In terms of the number of occupying families, each of the top five states (Pernambuco, São Paulo, Paraná, Goiás, and Pará) represents a different region of the country. The landless movement thus continued to be a truly national social movement, albeit one with points of unusual strength in certain states.

Table 15 Occupation activity: Leading states, 2003–2005

State	Occupations	Occupying Families
1. Pernambuco	272	34,563
2. São Paulo	157	19,525
3. Paraná	132	18,752
4. Minas Gerais	106	13,071
5. Bahia	106	14,731
6. Pará	79	14,969
7. Goiás	78	16,172
8. Alagoas	63	7,575
9. Mato Grosso do Sul	45	11,173
10. Mato Grosso	33	11,394

Source: CPT 2004, 2005.

Protest tactics other than land occupations also appear to have picked up during the Lula years. Data compiled by the CPT show, for example, that the number of nonoccupation protest events in which the MST was involved rose from 203 in 2002, to 256 in 2003, to 284 in 2004 (CPT 2003, 2004, 2005). It dipped somewhat, to 260 events, the following year, but 2005 brought the single most ambitious MST protest initiative of the Lula years. In May some twelve thousand activists participated in the National March for Agrarian Reform. The marchers took seventeen days to make the two-hundred-plus-kilometer trip from the city of Goiânia to Brasília. In the capital they met with the president, and they extracted from officials a series of commitments. The most controversial was a promise to change the production indexes used to judge whether a private estate can be expropriated. In late September, when it became apparent that government was fulfilling almost none of its promises, the MST launched a national day of struggle, its second of the year.

Signs of Restraint

Although the MST did not hold back from using protest to pressure Lula, the unruliness that often seemed to characterize its tactics in the late 1990s and early 2000s was less evident. In their 2005 march to Brasília, for example, MST leaders were determined not to enter into skirmishes with police, as had happened many times under Cardoso. When the MLST invaded the Chamber of Deputies in June 2006, provoking a confrontation with police and negative publicity for the PT, the MST's Stedile publicly criticized the initiative, arguing that the "the deputies need to be our allies; they shouldn't be attacked."[11] Instances of MST involvement in looting and vandalism of public property also seemed to die down.[12]

The MST's tactical moderation was accompanied by a certain restraint in publicly criticizing the Lula government. Particularly in the early years of the government, MST leaders were generally measured in expressing their displeasure about the slow pace of expropriation and the overall conservativeness of federal policies. They refrained from criticizing Lula himself and when they criticized his land reform policies, they often made clear that

11. *Folha de São Paulo,* June 9, 2005.
12. The decline of looting probably also has to do with the lack of a drought in the Northeast similar to the one that afflicted the region in the late 1990s.

they were not opposed to his government. Even when Stedile suggested to a reporter that the MST would intensify its protest efforts in 2005, he was careful to point out that the protests would not be "against the government, but to force the government to change its economic policy."[13]

This combination of pressure and restraint reflected the strategic dilemma presented by the Lula government. On the one hand, the MST grew increasingly discontented with Lula's moderation and his willingness to accept the dictates of the IMF and market forces. On the other hand, they were conscious that the alternatives to the PT would probably be worse and that their efforts to exert pressure could be used by the Right to weaken Lula and divide the Left. They were loath to serve as confirmation of the conservative prediction that a PT government would bring social chaos. As Valmir Rodrigues Chaves, a top MST leader in São Paulo, put it, "The MST can't enter into the war of the press and the UDR against Lula."[14]

Early on, the MST adopted a more pragmatic attitude toward the government than did some other groups associated with the left wing of the PT. The leadership seemed to believe that, despite the party's conservative turn, Lula could still end up making important progressive advances. They argued that the struggle between the forces of change and the defenders of the status quo to capture the government's loyalties was still unresolved. According to Chaves, "We don't know where he is, but we know that if the poor do not get organized, he will go in the direction of the rich. But we don't think Lula's government is lost, we think it is still in dispute. Lula still has the smell of the people from which he came. We don't agree with the 'radicaloids' of the urban Left who don't believe in the government anymore. They don't think Lula can be redeemed. We disagree. We think he can be redeemed."[15]

The MST's relative restraint also reflected the goodwill the Lula government had expressed toward the organization in a number of ways. In a July 2003 meeting with the MST leadership, Lula had donned a red MST cap in front of television cameras, a gesture that earned him harsh criticism from conservative sectors and much of the major media.[16] Unlike its predecessor, Lula's government had accepted the MST's right to use protest tactics and was always open to negotiation. At the level of policy, the government had

13. *Folha de São Paulo,* January 7, 2005.
14. Interview, August 9, 2003, Teodoro Sampaio, SP.
15. Ibid.
16. "O bone é apenas um detalhe," *Veja,* July 9, 2003.

failed to implement Cardoso's anti-occupation measure and restored the flow of federal funds to the MST. In fact, grants to the MST by federal agencies increased threefold during Lula's first three years in office.[17]

Over time, however, the slow pace of land expropriations caused the MST's patience with Lula to grow thin. This is reflected in the national protest campaigns of 2005, as well as in the organization's discourse. When the INCRA announced its 2005 results, the MST responded with a press release of its own arguing that the agency's activities did not affect the concentration of farmland and alleging that its settlement figures were "distorted and inflated."[18] Its newspaper compared minister of agrarian development Miguel Rossetto's "manipulations" to those of the reviled Raúl Jungmann and chided the government for preferring to "continue the neoliberal economic policy adopted by the previous government instead of daring to make the changes endorsed by the 53 million votes it received."[19] Gilmar Mauro, a veteran member of the National Directorate, said that, given its disappointing performance in office, the PT could not expect his organization to participate in the 2006 electoral campaign the way it had in past races.[20]

Other pro-land reform groups varied in their approach to the Lula government. In its public rhetoric, the CPT was quite critical. Its president, Bishop Tomás Balduino, was one of the harshest commentators on Lula's policies for the countryside. The CONTAG, meanwhile, was more hesitant to pressure or reprove the PT administration. As noted earlier, land occupations tied to its member federations and unions declined as a proportion of total occupations, a trend that helped keep the MST's share of the total higher than during the late 1990s. This trend reflected a more accommodating attitude toward the Lula government on the part of union leaders. The CONTAG's moderation was in line with its traditional approach to politics, but it was also a product of its support for a number of PT initiatives that helped small farmers, including the expansion of the PRONAF rural credit program, Family Grant, and a number of other programs targeted at the rural sector.

17. During the last three years of the Cardoso administration, the MST received about R$7 million in federal funds. In contrast, during the first three years under Lula they received about R$30 million (*Folha de São Paulo,* April 30, 2006).

18. MST, "Reforma agrária do governo Lula não desconcentra a terra, diz MST," posted on the Web site of PSOL federal deputy Ivan Valente, http://www.ivanvalente.com.br/CN02/noticias/nots_det.asp?id = 647 (accessed December 29, 2006).

19. *Jornal Sem Terra,* December 2005/January 2006.

20. Interview, June 29, 2005, São Paulo, SP.

Landowner Resistance

Early in the Lula government, resistance to land occupations and expropriation from landowners and their political allies took on a more aggressive
and visible character than during the late Cardoso years. This was a product
of the acute threat landowners initially perceived, given the PT's socialist
origins and links to the MST. Two phenomena most clearly reflect their
alarm.

One was the rapid escalation of violence in the countryside in 2003.
Murders related to rural social conflict quadrupled relative to 2002, reaching a level not seen since the late 1980s (CPT 2004). As has always been the
case, the vast majority of these incidents were linked to conflict over land.
In part, this phenomenon was a consequence of the swelling number of
land occupations and landless camps in the vicinity of vulnerable properties. However, the intensification of violence far outstripped the increase
in land occupations. Thus, it also seemed to reflect a panicked reaction on
the part of landowners to the new political context.

Early 2003 brought news of a variety of initiatives by landowners aimed
at preventing land occupations (CPT 2004, 200–201). The most notorious
was in Paraná, where landowners faced the twin threats of a leftist president and a governor friendly to the MST. Landowners in the central part of
the state formed the First Rural Command (PCR). The name was derived from
that of a violent criminal organization in neighboring São Paulo and implied what some members openly suggested: that it would use armed force
to defend its interests. Pro-landowner activists alleged that the INCRA was
becoming a "political arm of the MST within the government" and that Lula
planned a state takeover of agricultural lands along the lines of what was
seen in the Soviet Union.[21] Undoubtedly, they were also worried about
signs that Lula would revoke or ignore Cardoso's anti-occupation measures.[22] Their initiatives were motivated by a combined desire to galvanize
other landowners, frighten landless workers, and warn authorities that if
they did not do something to prevent occupations, blood would be spilled.

The second phenomenon that expressed landowners' sense of threat was

21. *Folha de São Paulo*, March 12 and June 29, 2003.
22. For example, in an interview with the *Folha de São Paulo* in December 2002, future
minister of agrarian development Miguel Rossetto refused to state his support for maintaining
the decree, prompting the paper to publish a highly critical editorial (*Folha de São Paulo*,
December 27, 2002).

an initiative by leaders of the *bancada ruralista* in August 2003 to form a special commission, the Bicameral Congressional Investigating Commission (CPMI), to investigate land occupations. This was a direct response to Lula's controversial meeting with the MST in July 2003, in which he donned the MST cap. In particular, conservative legislators sought to use the "CPMI of Land" to call attention to the MST's use of federal funds to bankroll its struggle.[23] PT legislators were able to force a broadening of the agenda, to include land-related violence, but the report ultimately adopted by the commission in 2005 clearly favored conservative interests (IPEA 2006, 177–80).

Although it was not publicly at the forefront of struggles against land reform, the CNA also seemed to intensify its efforts in this area in 2003.[24] For example, it hired an official to work exclusively on the land reform issue, something it had not done during the Cardoso years. The CNA also commissioned a top polling firm to conduct a national survey on the public's view of agriculture and, in particular, the land question. Its findings, reported by some newspapers, showed that 58 percent of the respondents considered the MST to be a violent organization and 68 percent believed that it was more motivated by the political than the social results of its actions.[25]

Signs of landowner countermobilization declined over time. Despite some prominent incidents in subsequent years, land-related violence fell greatly after 2003.[26] There were also no new political initiatives along the lines of the CPMI of Land. The slackening of landowner resistance had to do with two factors. First, the relatively small number of land expropriations, combined with Lula's failure to change the standards for expropriation, was undoubtedly reassuring to owners of rural estates. Second, and just as important, the attention of the *bancada ruralista*, CNA, and other entities was diverted by the economic crisis facing the agricultural sector since late 2004, which negatively affected even the most productive farmers.

23. Interview with Deputy João Alfredo, the top PT representative on the commission, July 1, 2005, Brasília.
24. Interview with Anaximandro Doudement de Almeida, advisor for land affairs, CNA, June 27, 2005, Brasília.
25. "Visão da sociedade sobre o setor agropecuário," CNA/Vox Populi, 2003.
26. Two incidents of land-related violence received substantial press coverage. The first was the murder of five people in an MST encampment in Felisburgo, MG, in November 2004. The second, which received wider coverage, was the murder of Dorothy Stang, an American-born nun who worked with *posseiros* in violence-ridden rural Pará. Stang was killed by hired gunmen in February 2005.

Explaining Movement Resurgence

Under the first PT government, the relationship between pro-land reform groups and the state was in some ways less openly conflictive than when Cardoso's PSDB-led coalition was in office. Nevertheless, protest for land redistribution clearly intensified relative to the late Cardoso years, in both land occupations and other tactics. How can we explain the landless movement's resurgence?

There is little evidence that would favor an explanation based on absolute grievances. Economic and social trends in agriculture and the rural sector do not point in any clear direction. Growth in farm output boomed in 2003, but declined sharply thereafter. Farm employment, meanwhile, was essentially stagnant throughout the period. Rural poverty was stable in 2003, but dropped rather sharply thereafter, contradicting the trends in agriculture. Changes in the overall economy also do not provide a solid foundation for a grievance-based argument. The moderate revival of economic growth under Lula could logically have been expected to work against the movement's resurgence by creating new opportunities for employment outside agriculture.

It is also difficult to formulate a causal account based on relative deprivation. One could potentially find a relative deprivation–type scenario in the trajectory of agricultural sector growth, with sustained increases in prosperity being followed by a sharp decline. However, the primary beneficiaries of the upward trend were mainly well-off farmers, and in any case, protest actually began to revive when agricultural output growth was still rapid. The grievance/discontent perspective thus does not seem to provide the key to the landless movement's recent resurgence.

Changes occurring during the Lula years did increase the landless movement's organizational capacity in significant ways. Most important, there was a renewed inflow of money from a variety of federal programs into MST coffers. Other organizations involved in the movement with close ties to the PT may have also benefited from such an influx. As landowners have long complained, these flows help the landless movement to wage its struggle. Nevertheless, the upsurge of protest during this period began in the first several months of 2003, which is probably too early for it to have been decisively affected by an increase in funding. Federal funding may have helped to sustain the heightened intensity of protest and facilitated major events such as the MST's 2005 National March and the CONTAG's annual "Grito

da Terra" campaign, but it cannot easily account for the early revival of the
movement.

Likewise, there do not appear to have been any important innovations
in the movement's strategy or tactics capable of explaining the increased
level of protest activity under Lula. There were some modest tactical modi-
fications by the MST leadership relative to the Cardoso years in terms of
avoiding sharp confrontations with the government, but these cannot account for the greater level of activity. Otherwise, the landless movement
generally used the same tactics, organizational forms, and framing strategies as in previous periods.

Rather, the movement's resurgence was a product of a change in its
political opportunity structure. Lula's election emboldened the landless to
increase their pressure on authorities because of the improved prospects
for positive results relative to the difficult late Cardoso years. Despite the
PT's shift toward the political center and its failure to announce a specific
settlement goal during the 2002 campaign, activists and the landless expected to receive more favorable treatment from this historically pro–
agrarian reform party. A few weeks after Lula's victory, the MST demanded
publicly that he start to make good on his party's commitment to land
reform immediately, by settling eighty-five thousand camped families in
his first 150 days in office. Landless leaders assumed, moreover, that Lula
would revoke Cardoso's reviled anti–land occupation decree.[27]

Because of these expectations, landless camps began to swell in size
and number even before Lula's inauguration on January 1, 2003, and land
occupations began to surge in the first half of the year. According to the
CPT (2004), "The year 2003 began with the euphoria of the 'hope that overcomes fear' [a PT campaign slogan]. Workers of the countryside thought
the hour of profound change had arrived. That's why they multiplied their
actions" (7).

In office, Lula was rather disappointing. In particular, as was discussed
earlier in the chapter, through the end of 2005 he had expropriated farmland at a slower rate than that of his predecessor, relying mainly on public
sources of land. But expectations of positive change were not totally un-
founded. First, the government did not implement Cardoso's anti–land occupation measures, the central factor behind the decline of this tactic
beginning in 2000. Second, although it was very slow to get started, the

27. *Folha de São Paulo*, November 29, 2002.

government appears to have granted land to the landless at a somewhat faster pace than Cardoso did during his second term in office. These policies (combined with the renewed flow of financial resources to the MST and other landless groups) helped to sustain protest for agrarian reform at a much higher level than during 2000-2002. The decline in legal repression of occupations, in particular, is seen by most commentators as the major reason for the revival of occupation activity during the Lula years.[28]

Conclusions

During Lula's initial term in office mobilization and protest for land reform in Brazil rebounded strongly. Land occupations and other tactics grew in number all over the country, reversing the trend of the last three years of the PSDB government and reasserting the vitality of the movement and its key organization, the MST.

Explanations of the landless movement's resurgence rooted in social grievances, organizational capacity, and strategic innovation by activists are all unconvincing. Protest intensified, rather, because the Lula government was viewed by the landless as more vulnerable to pressure. Although many aspects of Lula's agrarian reform policy proved disappointing to the activist community, trends in both the number of families granted land by the INCRA and, in particular, the degree of legal repression of occupations were more positive than during the late Cardoso years. Expectations that the landless would receive better treatment at the hands of the Lula government were therefore not completely off base.

28. See the discussion by scholars Anderson Antonio da Silva and Bernardo Mançano Fernandes in the CPT report on land conflicts for 2005 (CPT 2006, 96-108). See also *Folha de São Paulo*, June 3, 2006.

Conclusion

The landless movement is undoubtedly the largest and most successful grassroots rural social movement in Brazilian history and one of the most influential popular movements in contemporary Latin America. It has existed continuously for close to three decades, and during that time, it has mobilized hundreds of thousands, if not millions, of poor Brazilians to pressure the state for land redistribution. It has succeeded in reviving agrarian reform as a political issue and pushing authorities to implement by far the most extensive agrarian reform the country has ever seen.

In this book I have sought to add to our knowledge of the forces shaping the movement's development. I have focused on explaining the four major changes in protest intensity that occurred as the movement evolved: its emergence as a significant actor during the late 1970s and early 1980s (Chapter 2); its takeoff during the mid-1990s (Chapter 4); its crisis beginning in 2000 (Chapter 5); and finally, its resurgence since 2003 (Chapter 6). In addition, I have sought to clarify why the movement continued to grow in the late 1980s and early 1990s, when virtually every other important movement born during the transition from authoritarian rule was showing signs of decline (Chapter 3). In this exploration I have been guided by the major theoretical perspectives on social movements, while also seeking to evaluate them. In particular, I have tried to reassess political opportunity, an important theory that today finds itself under fire.

In this concluding chapter I take on three tasks. First, I briefly review the key findings of the preceding chapters. Second, I contextualize these findings by discussing some of their broader theoretical implications for our understanding of social movements. What do they mean beyond the particular case of the landless movement? The third task also takes us beyond the previous chapters, but in a more empirical direction. I examine the results of the movement's efforts in terms of agrarian reform policy output and the welfare of settler families. Partly on the basis of this analysis, I discuss what positive roles agrarian reform can play in contemporary Brazil given adequate state support.

Findings of the Study

In this book I have sought to account for two broad types of variation: longitudinal variation in the intensity of protest within a given social movement and variation in the growth trajectories of different movements that emerged within the same protest cycle. Chapters 2, 4, 5, and 6 all dealt with the first type. My aim in each was to explain an instance of relatively rapid change in the intensity of protest within the landless movement. Political opportunity theorists have argued that movements surge and decline largely in response to changes in the political opportunity structure. My findings were supportive of this notion. In all four episodes of change examined in these chapters, political shifts that affected the receptivity or vulnerability of governing authorities to the movement's protest actions played a critical role. In none of them was there a variable at work that was clearly more important than political opportunity.

My analysis of the landless movement's initial emergence in Chapter 2 presented the most complex causal picture. I argued that the rise of a significant movement for agrarian reform beginning in the late 1970s was a product of a combination of rising social grievances, increasing organizational capacity, and an improving political opportunity structure. No single factor was clearly predominant.

With regard to grievances, I argued that rapid agricultural modernization under the military tended to erode popular access to farmland. Although this trend had potentially welfare-reducing consequences, its impact was offset for a time by rapid urban job creation, increasing wage work in agriculture, and frontier expansion. In the early 1980s, these countervailing trends stalled or went into reverse. Pressure on land resources increased and rural welfare declined, helping to generate demands for agrarian reform. Increasing organizational capacity among the landless was mainly a product of the popular church movement that arose during the course of the late 1960s and 1970s. Political activists inspired by liberation theology played a key role in the movement's initial rise through their grassroots organization and consciousness-raising efforts.

The landless movement's emergence must also be understood as a product of the institutional liberalization and political weakening of the conservative military dictatorship, in power since 1964. This process reduced the threat that social protest would be met with overwhelming repression and improved the prospects for gaining concessions from authorities in land redistribution. As a result it provided incentives for landless rural workers and their supporters to get organized to press for land reform.

An improvement in the political opportunity structure was more clearly the dominant factor in the rapid expansion of the landless movement in the mid-1990s, which I examined in Chapter 4. Rising absolute grievances played some role in bringing about this increase. In particular, a crisis of agricultural employment, caused by the withdrawal of government subsidies and trade protection, as well as the impact of the 1994 Real Plan, made it harder for poor rural workers to make ends meet and thus may have increased the attractiveness of struggling for land. However, as my analysis suggested, the key cause of the upsurge was clearly the growing disposition of authorities to respond to protest for land with concessions, rather than repression. The shift began with President Collor's removal at the end of 1992, which initiated a period of less conservative, more urban-based governments. It was deepened in late 1995 and 1996 by the rapid ascension of land reform as a public issue, propelled mainly by the shocking massacres at Corumbiara and Eldorado do Carajás. By forcing authorities to accelerate land redistribution and treat the movement with (in relative terms) kid gloves, this transformation promoted the movement's expansion.

Just as the takeoff of the landless movement was caused principally by a change in the political opportunity structure, so was its decline beginning in 2000. As I argued in Chapter 5, the key cause of the sharp drop in land occupations during 2000–2002 was the Cardoso government's decision in mid-2000 to crack down on these actions by declaring all occupied farms legally ineligible for expropriation for two years and establishing penalties for those found to be participating in land occupations. These change had a chilling effect on the movement's core tactic, casting doubt on its future. Although a shift in the political opportunity structure was clearly the proximate cause of the movement's crisis, shifts in activist strategy played a role by contributing to this change. In particular, as I discuss further below, the MST's tactical initiatives during the late 1990s and 2000 helped to bring about the movement's decline by encouraging Cardoso to take a harder line on protest.

Finally, as Chapter 6 made clear, the revival of protest for land reform beginning in 2003 was essentially the product of a more favorable political opportunity structure relative to the late Cardoso years. The elections of 2002 put the PT, a center-left party historically committed to radical land redistribution, in control of the national government. Although the first PT government was rather disappointing in terms of land reform, it did bring an easing of legal repression against land occupations and a somewhat faster pace of settlement, both of which served to encourage the growth of landless protest. No other variable played a significant role in this expansion.

While in the four chapters that examined instances of relatively rapid change in the pace of protest activity I provided strong empirical support for the basic dynamics of political opportunity theory, I also underscored the value of some aspects of the evolving critique of how political opportunity has been conceptualized. In particular, I pointed to the importance of both subjective political shifts and social movement agency in shaping the opportunity structure for protest.

As I noted in Chapter 1, critics of political opportunity theory have sometimes complained about its excessive focus on certain types of factors, such as institutional openings, coalition shifts, and defeats in foreign wars. Political changes of a more purely subjective or cultural character are neglected or even explicitly excluded. My analysis of the landless movement's takeoff in Chapter 4 underscores the potentially powerful role of subjective political shifts in shaping the political opportunity structure for movement activity. I argued that the upsurge of landless protest in the mid-1990s was caused in large measure by the impact of the massacres at Corumbiara and Eldorado do Carajás on the perceptions of the general public and key actors in civil society regarding the urgency of the agrarian question. By abruptly focusing public concern on this issue, the massacres forced the federal government to be more responsive to grassroots pressure for land reform, creating incentives for increased movement activity.

Critics of political opportunity theory have also claimed that it overemphasizes the external determination of protest activity, underestimating the extent to which movements shape their own political environments. It would be a mistake, as I stated in Chapter 1, to assert that political opportunity analyses ignore the reciprocal causal relationship between states and social movements, but the idea that movements can affect their own political opportunity structures has not received much attention. Two chapters in this book helped to address this lacuna by showing how the landless movement's present political opportunity structure was shaped by its own past actions.

My argument in Chapter 4 addressing the influence of the major landless massacres of the mid-1990s on the political opportunity structure gets at this issue. Landless activists did not purposely provoke these actions and had little control over their interpretation or political impact once they occurred. Nonetheless, the massacres were in part a product of the movement's own aggressive protest strategy, which threatened the social and political status quo in rural areas. The analysis I developed in Chapter 5 of the movement's temporary decline in 2000–2002 also illustrates how movements can affect their own political opportunity structures. As I noted above, the decline in land occupations was a direct result of a transformation in the state's response to protest. The movement had little power to revert this change once it occurred. Nonetheless, the crackdown on protest was in part a consequence of the MST's own initiatives. The adoption of increasingly bold pressure tactics during the late 1990s and 2000 both raised the costs to President Cardoso of continuing to tolerate the movement and made it politically easier for him to repress it. The crackdown was also facilitated by the MST's adoption of the struggle against neoliberalism as one of its major banners. This decision had the effect of "politicizing" its image further and isolating it from some potential supporters.

The second kind of variation this book has addressed is, as I mentioned, variation in the trajectories of different social movements that arise within the same general cycle of movement activity. More specifically, in Chapter 3, I tried to explain why the landless movement continued to expand gradually following the return to civilian, democratic rule in 1985, despite the general decline of protest activity in Brazil. My findings provided support for both the activist strategy and political opportunity perspectives.

With regard to strategy, I argued that the adoption of land occupation as the landless movement's core tactic was critical because it meant that the movement was less affected than others by the free-rider problem identified by Olson (1965). Since authorities typically responded to occupations by settling only those involved, and not others, the movement was not for the most part struggling for a public good, as defined by Olson. The possibilities for free riding were thus greatly reduced. Unlike most other movements, which relied on normative incentives to overcome the free-rider problem, the landless movement could depend largely on the narrow desire of each family to gain a plot of land and accompanying benefits. As a result, it was less vulnerable than other democratic transition–era movements to the fading of the ethical, political grievances that had helped to motivate protest under the military dictatorship.

The MST was particularly important in reaping the benefits of land occupations, since it employed this tactic aggressively and played a central role in diffusing it nationwide. The leadership's creative use of land occupations and the resulting camps also provided other benefits that help explain the movement's survival. In particular, the MST exploited the social contexts created by the camping process to foment ideological commitment to the struggle for land, create bonds of group solidarity, and promote loyalty to the MST as an organization. Partly as a result, it enjoyed a steady influx of new activists and the continuing contributions of people who had already gained land, in both monetary donations and participation in protest actions.

Nevertheless, the movement's exceptionalism cannot be reduced to a question of strategy. The tactic of occupying the good that is the target of the movement's demands was not available to other movements to the same extent. Some goods that Brazilian movements sought simply cannot be occupied. Many others, such as urban land or housing, potentially could be occupied, but their occupation is not widely considered legitimate. What set farmland apart was its special constitutional status as the only type of private property whose ownership is clearly conditional on its productive utilization. This status made Brazilian authorities vulnerable to the strategy of occupying unproductive farmland. Since the constitution is a political document, the movement's exceptional trajectory during this period must be seen as partly a function of its unusual political opportunity structure. Chapter 3 thus provided further support for the political opportunity perspective.

Some Broader Implications

What do these results mean for social movement theory? In addressing this question I focus in particular on two especially important and controversial issues: the role of political opportunity in shaping the rise and decline of social movements over time, and the role of the free-rider problem in collective action.

The most obvious implication of my findings is that the political opportunity perspective is not a paper tiger. As I discussed in Chapter 1, critics have argued that the apparent power of the political opportunity structure concept with regard to explaining the rise and fall of social movements is related to the license scholars have taken in defining it and the failure to test it against other potential explanations. In this study, however, I have adopted a relatively narrow definition of the concept, one that excludes phenomena that other scholars have seen fit to include under the political opportunity rubric. I have applied it to a movement that appeared to provide a challenging case for political opportunity, judging from the emphasis that previous writings have placed on activist agency in shaping its development. Finally, I have systematically tested it against three other theoretical perspectives derived from the literature. This approach increased the chances that the theory would be falsified. Nevertheless, my results demonstrate strong support for it.

I would stop short of endorsing some of the stronger claims about political opportunity, particularly the idea that shifts in the political opportunity structure are a virtual prerequisite for movement rise or decline. The empirical evidence for such a claim is still shaky. Moreover, no one has so far articulated a sound theoretical justification for believing that political opportunity is, in general, a more powerful explanatory tool than the other perspectives. Nevertheless, my analysis of the landless movement's development in this book supports the idea that political opportunity structure constitutes a powerful heuristic for understanding why social movements surge and decline.

Future research should continue to test political opportunity–based accounts against other explanations of social movements. In fact, one of the weaknesses of the social movement literature is that it has too often been willing to settle for illustrations of the usefulness of a particular theory for explaining protest activity, without actually pitting one explanation against another. By rigorously testing one theory against another we can gain a better understanding of the forces that shape social movements. The examination in this study is of the development of a single movement over time, but qualitative comparisons of multiple movements and large-N statistical analyses can also make an important contribution.

My interpretation of the landless movement's exceptional trajectory following the return to civilian rule also runs contrary to trends in social movement theory, particularly in how I relate my findings to Olson's theory of the dynamics of collective action. As I explained in Chapter 1, although movement scholars have often disagreed with Olson's account of how the free-rider problem is overcome, they have not questioned the idea that collective action necessarily involves the pursuit of a public good: one that must be provided to everyone in a given group if it is provided to anyone. This notion is critical to Olson's theory because if noncontributors are excluded from the benefits of collective action there is an inherent individual incentive for participating and thus no free-rider problem. My analysis in Chapter 3, however, suggests that under certain conditions movements may actually pursue objectives that are not public goods. In such cases, the issue of how a movement overcomes the free-rider problem, whether through normative incentives or material ones, is largely irrelevant.

The question that remains, however, is, How widespread is this phenomenon? Is the landless movement an isolated case, or is it part of a broader category of social movements? This is not the place for a truly in-depth analysis of this issue, but I believe that even a cursory look at social movement activity suggests that the landless movement is not a sui generis phenomenon in this sense. I focus here on Latin America, because that is the region of the world that I am most familiar with.

Although they have rarely, if ever, achieved comparable geographical scope or longevity, land occupation–based movements exhibiting a relationship to the state roughly similar to that of the Brazilian landless movement have actually appeared in many Latin American countries. Examples can be found, for example, in Venezuela during the late 1950s and early 1960s, Peru in the early 1960s, Chile in the late 1960s, Colombia in the late 1960s and early 1970s, Honduras in the late 1970s, and sporadically in Mexico since the 1930s (Huizer 1972; Zamosc 1986; de la Peña 1994). These movements have been aided by provisions in several Latin American constitutions permitting expropriation of privately owned farmland when it is not fulfilling what is considered to be its social function (De Janvry and Sadoulet 2002).

As I mentioned in Chapter 3, occupation of urban land by the poor has frequently been a nonmovement process, in which people occupy unused space in peripheral areas with comparatively little resistance from authorities. However, it has occasionally taken on more of a social protest character, involving well-organized and highly visible occupations of urban lots aimed at pressuring the state to turn them over to participants. Such movements have in some cases become significant political phenomena (Castells 1982).

A common aspect of such rural and urban "squatter" movements is that the individuals and families involved seek access to land and view participation in mass occupations as a vehicle for improving their chances of achieving this goal. Occupation-based movements have sometimes contributed to broad policy changes that benefit even people who did not participate in protest initiatives. Usually, though, authorities have responded to them in much the same largely piecemeal fashion exhibited in Brazil, appeasing some groups with official grants of land while failing to enact a more universalistic program of land redistribution. The absence of a free-rider problem in this type of situation arguably helps to explain why land occupation–based movements have been such a widespread and occasionally influential phenomenon in Latin America.

Occupation-based movements are the most common examples of Latin American social movements that skirt the free-rider problem by pursuing a nonpublic good, but they are not alone. One that is worth citing because of its recent prominence is the *piquetero* movement in Argentina, which arose in the mid-1990s and then became a major national phenomenon during the economic crisis of the early 2000s (Svampa 2003). There are a number of different organizations within the movement, but their tactics are quite similar. Groups of *piqueteros* block public roads to pressure authorities to provide them with jobs or monetary assistance. The benefits are channeled through *piquetero* organizations, and those who do not participate in the movement's activities do not usually receive benefits.[1]

As this discussion suggests, the Brazilian landless movement may be a particularly striking example of a movement that largely avoids the free-rider problem by pursuing a nonpublic good, but it is by no means an isolated one. A promising avenue for future research would be a broader and more systematic examination of the social and political conditions under which this type of situation arises, as well as of the implications of the lack of a free-rider problem for the intensity and frequency of protest activity.

Agrarian Reform in Brazil, Present and Future

So far in this book I have talked mainly about protest for agrarian reform. Agrarian reform as a policy and an instrument of social change has received

---

1. *Clarín*, September 26, 2002.

only passing attention. I would be remiss, however, if I closed the book without some discussion of the concrete results the landless movement's efforts have yielded and what land reform is capable of contributing to Brazilian society in the future. I begin by looking at what has actually been done in both land redistribution and supporting policies, such as the provision of settlement infrastructure and agricultural credit, during the landless movement's lifetime. Then I examine the impact of these policies on the welfare of settler families. Finally, partially on the basis of this assessment, I discuss the positive roles agrarian reform can play in contemporary Brazil, as well as the roles it should not be expected to play.

One important question, of course, is, How much land reform has actually occurred? Data compiled by the federal research agency IPEA from INCRA records show that by the end of 2005 there were 7,381 federal land reform settlements in Brazil, covering an area of 60,689,941 hectares. A total of 667,230 families were living in those settlements (IPEA 2006). About a third of the land was obtained by expropriation of private holdings. Most of the rest was already owned by the federal government or one of the state governments. Although this data set includes some settlements created prior to the landless movement's emergence, the amount of land redistributed before the return to civilian rule in 1985 was by all accounts very modest. Expropriation of private land, in particular, was quite rare. Using data from the 1985 agricultural census and assuming that four members of the agricultural workforce equal one family, one may conclude that these totals represent 11.4 percent of all agricultural families and 16.2 percent of all the land in farms.

Not all the settlements the INCRA has established were a direct response to land occupations or other forms of organized pressure. Particularly in frontier areas, where land can be obtained more cheaply, settlements are sometimes created by the state in a more proactive fashion. Nonetheless, it seems safe to assume that very little land redistribution would have been accomplished in the absence of substantial mass protest. Even when the state is creating settlements that are not direct concessions to particular groups of landless workers, they are responding to the more diffuse political pressure the movement creates by generating a sense of disorder and drawing public attention to the problem of landlessness.

Table 16 shows a comparison of this effort with the other significant agrarian reforms in Latin American history. As the table suggests, the Brazilian reform process so far pales in comparison to the major reforms in the

Table 16   Brazilian agrarian reform in comparative perspective

Country (Years)	Land Redistributed (% total farmland)	Beneficiary Families (% total farm families)
Cuba (1959–65)	60	60
Mexico (1917–76)	43	50
Nicaragua (1979–89)	40	Not available
Chile (1962–73)	40	20
Peru (1963–76)	42	32
Guatemala (1952–54)	34	33
El Salvador (1980–84)	25	22
Bolivia (1952–70)	18	39
Venezuela (1959–70)	16	15
Brazil (1985–2005)	**16**	**11**
Colombia (1961–72)	10	4
Dominican Republic (1972–78)	5	6
Panama (1968–73)	4	Not available
Honduras (1972–81)	4	14
Costa Rica (1962–80)	2	3
Ecuador (1964–69)	1	4

Sources: De Janvry 1981; Priestly 1986; Stanfield 1989; Sobhan 1993; Thiesenhusen 1995; Brockett 1998; El-Ghonemy 2001.

region, such as those of Cuba, Mexico, and Nicaragua. These, however, were all products of violent upheavals, or of regimes that allowed little organized political dissent. If we focus only on the agrarian reforms accomplished under democratically elected regimes and without a violent national political conflict, a somewhat different picture emerges. Among this group, only the Chilean, Guatemalan, and Venezuelan reforms surpass the Brazilian version. Tellingly, the first two of these were partially rolled back as the result of military coups that sought to restore the status quo. Land reform, in other words, has been very difficult to achieve in Latin America under democratic conditions. Thus, although it by no means represents a fundamental restructuring of land ownership in the countryside, Brazil's democratic land reform should be considered a significant political achievement.

One of the major complaints of land reform activists in Brazil (as in most other countries in Latin America where land reform has been undertaken) is that settlements lack the infrastructure and support services needed for settlers to prosper. The MST, in particular, has made the expansion of such programs an important objective. There is little information available on infrastructure conditions in Brazil's settlements. Easily the most comprehensive and current data come from a national settlement survey conducted in 2004 and cosponsored by the ministries of Education and

Agrarian Development (MEC/MDA 2005). Researchers focused on INCRA settlements created beginning in 1985. They visited 5,595 settlements. In each one they interviewed three categories of people: school teachers or principals, presidents of agricultural associations, and rank-and-file settlers. A total of 10,200 settler households were interviewed.

Some of the most favorable results had to do with housing. The researchers found that the vast majority (83.5 percent) of settler families lived in permanent dwellings, rather than shanties or huts. Dwellings generally had four or more rooms, and more than 85 percent of settlers characterized their house as either "good" or "average." Similarly, the vast majority of settlements (79.3 percent) had their own schools and many others had access to schools nearby. In some cases, settlement schools even attracted students from neighboring rural communities. More than 70 percent of settlers considered access to schools to be either "good" or "average." Although relatively plentiful, settlement schools often lacked electricity and generally did not offer instruction beyond the elementary level. Thus, young people who want to pursue their education further must study outside their settlement, which sometimes means living outside it, as well.

Performance on other infrastructure variables was generally worse. For example, 45.9 percent of settler families lacked electric power (other than from a private generator), 37.9 percent lived in dwellings with no bathroom or outhouse, and 42.5 percent had no system for disposing of sewage. Based on interviews with association leaders, the survey's findings showed that only 24.5 percent of settlements had running water, 16.9 percent had telephone service, and 4.2 percent had trash collection. Getting to and from the settlement was widely considered a problem. Only 22.3 percent considered access to their settlement good. Generally speaking, settlement infrastructure was worst in the North and best in South and Southeast. Table 17 displays a comparison between infrastructure conditions in land reform

Table 17 Infrastructure conditions in agrarian reform settlements (% of Households)

Variable	Brazil	Rural Brazil	Settlements
Electric power	96.3	80.4	54.1
Sewage treatment	93.5	72.2	57.5
Bathroom	93.5	72.2	62.1
Telephone	64.3	24.4	16.9
Trash collection	82.9	20.1	3.4

Sources: IBGE 2004, MEC/MDA 2005.

settlements and those in the rural sector and Brazil in general. As the data suggest, rural conditions are generally inferior to those in urban areas, but the situation in land reform settlements is particularly bad.

Agricultural support programs have generally reached only a fraction of the settler population. The PROCERA subsidized credit program for settlers existed between 1986 and 1998, but I have only had access to data for the Cardoso years. Between 1995 and 1998, about 25 percent of Brazil's settler families received a PROCERA loan each year (INCRA 2000c, 15).[2] PROCERA was abolished in 1999 and replaced by PRONAF, which also serves smallholders who are not agrarian reform settlers. Under PRONAF, the average number of loans conceded to settlers each year has grown modestly, but the proportion of the total settler population receiving them has declined, to an average of about 13 percent (PRONAF Web site: www.mda.gov.br/saf/index .php?sccid = 812). State-sponsored technical assistance for settler families, which appears to have been rare before Cardoso, increased with the introduction of a new federal program in 1997. In 1999 the program (called Lumiar) reached around 30 percent of the settler population (INCRA 2000c, 199). It was eliminated that same year and no other national program took its place. Lula introduced a new technical assistance program in 2004 called the Program for Technical, Social, and Environmental Advising (ATES), which appears to have achieved broader coverage than Lumiar. INCRA data suggest that ATES reached about half the settler population in both 2004 and 2005 (INCRA 2005, 2006).

How, then, are Brazil's agrarian reform beneficiaries actually doing according to key socioeconomic welfare indicators? Although data are still rather scarce, a number of recent surveys of settlements provide some preliminary evidence. I look first at indicators of agricultural production, then at measures of overall settler welfare.

Information on agricultural production is particularly limited, but some studies offer relevant data. Two compare settlement production to that of farms in the *municípios* where the settlements are located. Probably the most positive findings come from a survey of 92 settlements in six states conducted in 2001–2 (Heredia et al. 2002). Focusing on a number of major

2. This figure comes from dividing the total number of loans by the accumulated number of families settled, using the IPEA settlement data cited above. It is an approximate figure because the IPEA data, as I mentioned earlier, are not comprehensive, and because the number of families in a given settlement can vary over time. In particular, families sometimes end up abandoning their plots, thus reducing the number of settlers.

products, the authors compared average crop yields for settlements with those of farms in their *município*. In 42 percent of the cases, settlements had a higher yield than did the *município*, in 10 percent they were close to the *município* average, and in 48 percent they were well below the average.[3] Medeiros and Leite (2004), in a study of twenty-six settlements in six states conducted in 1997–98, compare the average value of total agricultural production on individual settler plots with that of farms in the *município*. In two states settlers tended to produce more than farmers in their *município*, in one they were close to the average, and in three they were significantly below the average. Settlers generally performed better relative to their local area in states with more backward agricultural sectors.

It should be noted that these findings probably overstate significantly the competitiveness of settler agriculture relative to the Brazilian farm sector as a whole, because settlements tend to be concentrated in *municípios* (many of them in the underdeveloped North and Northeast regions) where land can be readily expropriated or purchased at an affordable price by federal authorities. For obvious reasons, these are not usually the areas with the most dynamic agricultural economies.

Another aspect of settlement agricultural production for which we have data is the extent of settler participation in the marketplace. This arguably serves as a rough proxy for productivity (since competition presumably promotes more efficient use of resources) and gives a sense of how much settlers are contributing to the larger economy. An analysis by Sparovek et al. (2005), which is based on a survey of more than four thousand settlements nationwide conducted in 2002, is easily the broadest study on this issue. The authors characterize the predominant trend among settler families in a particular *município* according to their level of market participation. In the majority (56 percent) of *municípios* studied, settlement production consisted basically of subsistence farming: families tended to sell only what they could not consume. These *municípios* were present in every region, but were particularly common in the North and Northeast. In 21 percent of the *municípios*, meanwhile, market-oriented production was the predominant type. The remaining 23 percent occupied an intermediate category.

Although they do not permit definitive conclusions, these data suggest

3. A "case" here is a particular product in a particular *município*. There were 146 such cases.

that agricultural production in Brazil's land reform settlements is currently modest in terms of productivity and is dedicated mainly (although by no means exclusively) to family consumption. Broader indicators of settler welfare tend to confirm this idea, although data are, once again, somewhat limited.

Monetary income is the most commonly used measure of a population's overall welfare. Findings on this variable, however, are inconsistent. The most positive recent numbers come from Medeiros and Leite (2004). The authors found average monthly family incomes ranging from R$307 in the state of Acre to R$959 in Mato Grosso. Acre was the only state in which the average fell below a standard poverty line. Heredia et al. (2002) yielded more modest results on this question. The overall average for the 1,568 settler families interviewed for this study was R$312. State averages ranged from R$117 in the arid northeastern state of Ceará to $439 in Santa Catarina, in the more prosperous South. As a frame of comparison, the average monthly family income in 2001 was R$451 in rural areas and R$993 in Brazil as a whole (IBGE 2001).[4]

Another indicator of welfare is the possession of durable consumer goods. The 2004 settlement survey cited above also collected data on this question. Table 18 compares the frequency of ownership of a series of goods among settler families with the frequency among households in the rural sector and Brazil as a whole. As the data suggest, even by rural standards, settlers tend to be rather poor. The differences are particularly great with regard to the more expensive goods, such as automobiles. Ownership of consumer durables varies considerably by region. In general, settlements in the South and Southeast are the best endowed, while those in the North and Northeast were the worst. The Center-West occupies a middle position.

Table 18 Possession of durable consumer goods (% of Households)

Variable	Brazil	Rural Brazil	Settlements
Stove	97.5	92.4	84.4
Television	90.3	69.2	46.5
Refrigerator	87.4	61.5	42.2
Automobile	32.7[a]	19.0[a]	8.0
Washing machine	34.5	10.6	7.3

Source: IBGE 2004, MEC/MDA 2005.

[a] From IBGE 2000.

4. In U.S. dollar terms, these values were equivalent to about $150 and $330, respectively, at the time. During Lula's first term, the real appreciated somewhat relative to the dollar.

These findings are sobering, but it is very important to note that, despite their generally modest means, settlers clearly feel that their lives have improved since gaining land (Heredia et al. 2002, 35–36). When asked to assess the change in their overall "living conditions," no less than 91 percent stated they were better off. Findings on more specific questions were also quite positive: 79 percent said they had better housing, 70 percent said that the education available to their children was better, 66 percent said they were eating better, and 62 percent said they had more purchasing power. Medeiros and Leite (2004) report very similar results. The findings on food consumption and purchasing power presumably reflect the fact that settler families can supply much of their own food. This advantage, not reflected in the income data, improves nutrition and frees up resources to purchase other goods.

Taking into consideration these results, what can we expect this policy to contribute to Brazilian society in the foreseeable future if authorities continue to pursue it at roughly the level of the last decade? Let me begin by discussing the bad news, or in other words, what land reform probably cannot achieve.

One of the most traditional arguments in favor of land redistribution is that it can increase agricultural production and thus contribute to economic development. Proponents of agrarian reform in Brazil today often make the same argument (Schönleitner 1997; Wright and Wolford 2003). If large, unproductive estates are subdivided and distributed to landless families, they suggest, their land resources will be used more intensively, expanding agricultural production. Although the logic of this argument is not unreasonable, claims about the macroeconomic value of land reform in contemporary Brazil should, in my view, be downplayed. Land redistribution can certainly help stimulate agricultural production and economic development in local areas where the farm sector is depressed, as I argue below. Nonetheless, at this stage in the country's development process it is unlikely to have a major effect on total farm output.

As the data presented above tentatively suggest, Brazilian land reform settlements are currently functioning at modest levels of productivity and market integration. This situation reflects in part the newness of many settlements and the deficits they suffer in terms of credit, infrastructure, and technical assistance. With time and at least moderate improvements in state support, advances will undoubtedly occur. However, there are at least two other factors that are likely to continue to limit agricultural output on Brazil's land reform settlements in the future.

First, the farmland settlers receive is generally not of good quality. The soils are often poor or degraded, rainfall is insufficient, and the settlements are in many cases located in remote areas not served by good roads, making market access problematic. This is the case mainly because in today's highly developed Brazilian agricultural economy, good, physically accessible farmland is usually in production and thus not vulnerable to expropriation under the current constitution. As a recent analysis put it, "Although Brazil still has large idle agricultural areas, many are located either in infertile regions (such as the Northeast's semi-arid areas) or in the remote Amazonian regions, which are far from markets" (Baer and Filizzola 2005, 22).

Some improvement in the quality of land redistributed could be made on the margins without new legislation, but a major change would require a constitutional reform relaxing the restrictions on the expropriation of private landholdings, especially the ban on seizing productive land. It is very hard to envision such a reform gaining approval in the foreseeable future. Even if it were approved, the impact on agricultural output might not be positive and could potentially be negative, since settlements established on formerly productive land might well produce less than the large estate that preceded them.

Second, many of the people who are being settled have little or no experience in running a farm. In the more economically successful agrarian reform experiences, such as those of South Korea and Taiwan, land redistribution was often based on granting legal ownership to tenant farming families, many of whom had generations of experience deciding what crops to plant, when to plant them, and how to care for and harvest them. In contemporary Brazil the situation is different. Especially outside the South, where there is a stronger smallholder tradition, many of the beneficiaries of agrarian reform have never operated a farm. They have worked mainly as wage laborers in agriculture or other sectors of the economy. In some cases they are basically urban people who must make a transition to country life. It is, of course, possible for them to learn the skills necessary to thrive as small independent farmers. The state, moreover, can play an important role in this process by providing quality technical assistance. Nevertheless, it is undoubtedly a considerable disadvantage to arrive on the land lacking such skills.

It is not realistic, then, to expect that agrarian reform will contribute very substantially to the growth performance of Brazilian agriculture, much less the economy as a whole. I should emphasize, though, that land redistribution undertaken within the current constitutional parameters poses no threat to the dynamism of the agricultural sector. The ban on expropriating productive land effectively shields large commercial producers, and smaller ones are doubly protected, since the constitution does not allow small properties to be seized. It is important to stress, furthermore, that the Cardoso years brought both the most intense expropriation activity in Brazilian history and among the most impressive gains in agricultural productivity. Evidently, there was no conflict between the two.

Expectations about agrarian reform's ability to transform Brazilian politics should also not be set very high. MST activists have sometimes argued that redistributing farmland will undermine the political power of landowning elites by weakening rural clientelist networks and strengthening popular political organization in the countryside. Some students of the movement and agrarian reform concur with this assessment (Sparovek 2003; Wright and Wolford 2003). This process may be occurring to a modest extent in some local areas, but land reform's independent impact on Brazilian politics is unlikely to be great.

To begin with, under the existing constitutional framework, land expropriations mainly serve to transform one source of political power, the control of a large estate, into another, money. Those whose properties are expropriated receive compensation in cash and government bonds. Barring a return to the unsustainable macroeconomic policies of the past, the latter should tend to retain much of their real value. A few decades ago, when Brazil was a predominantly rural society and agricultural production basically involved combining land and labor, the political importance of land arguably went beyond its monetary value. Today, with big agriculture highly capitalized and the vast bulk of the labor force working outside the farm sector, it is harder to make that case.

In addition, it is not clear that agrarian reform settlements will become a bulwark of support for the Left in the countryside, as activists often hope. We lack studies of the political behavior of settlers. However, a survey of landless encampments in four states conducted in 1996 found that as many campers (35 percent) had voted for Cardoso as for Lula in the 1994 elections.[5] MST settlers in all probability tend to support leftist candidates, but today they are no more than a quarter of the total settler population.[6] The Left is only likely to become a hegemonic force among settlers if the Lula government (or future PT governments) greatly increases its commitment to redistributing farmland and helping existing settlements. Such a move is not impossible, but it does not seem very likely at the moment.

Having discussed some of the things land reform should not be expected to accomplish, let me turn to what it can achieve, which is quite considerable. First, land reform can be an effective tool for stimulating local economic development, at least in rural *municípios* where the agricultural sector is weak. Where many large holdings lie fallow, dividing them and putting them into the hands of even inexperienced and undercapitalized smallholders will strengthen agricultural production. This, in turn, will increase the supply of food and deliver a boost to commercial activity. In addition, if there are enough settlers concentrated in a given area, the grants and subsidized loans that the federal government makes available to settler families can inject a significant amount of cash into the local economy, further stimulating commerce. Thus, while not an economic development policy at the national level, land reform in contemporary Brazil can be an effective rural development policy, one that can deliver much-needed assistance to depressed areas.

However, undoubtedly the most important role that agrarian reform can play in Brazil today is to increase in a sustainable way the living standards of the families it directly benefits. As the data I presented above indicate, settlers tend to be rather poor, even by the standards of rural Brazil. Nevertheless, they are in general substantially better off than they were before being settled. The evidence suggests that they are eating better and have better housing and schools. The extremely high proportion of settlers who report having better "living conditions" probably also reflects the sense of security, autonomy, and simple dignity that comes with having land and a house of one's own and not being dependent on rural or urban landlords. A greater state commitment to providing infrastructure, credit, and ag-

5. *Folha de São Paulo,* June 30, 1996. These results may well have exaggerated the level of support for Lula, since 28 percent of those interviewed were from Rio Grande do Sul, which was at that time the most pro-Lula state.

6. According to the MST Web site, in 2004 there were 1,649 settlements loyal to the MST, containing 105,466 families (http://www.mst.org.br/mst/pagina.php?cd=1010, accessed December 31, 2006). This was roughly 27 percent of the total number of settlements and 20 percent of the settler families.

ricultural extension services would undoubtedly strengthen these results further. Agrarian reform is thus an effective vehicle for attenuating poverty among rural or recently urbanized families and helping their children acquire the education necessary for them to prosper as adults, whether it be in the rural or urban sector.

It is true, as some critics of agrarian reform emphasize, that the costs associated with this policy are at least initially far higher than those of other antipoverty programs. With the money it takes to provide a family with land, infrastructure, and agricultural credit, for example, the federal government could give them Family Grant benefits for many years.[7] However, it does not follow that agrarian reform must be an inefficient way of tackling rural poverty. Land redistribution is qualitatively different from most other social programs in that it provides beneficiary families with a durable resource in which they can invest and around which they can structure their family economy for many years, or even generations. Settlers do need some ongoing support in terms of credit and technical assistance, but the costs of such programs are relatively modest, and if well administered, their effect will be to increase agricultural production and prepare settler families to eventually make ends meet without the INCRA's assistance.

Alleviating poverty and promoting economic development in the Brazilian interior are major challenges, which can only be met through a coordinated set of economic and social policies that deal with different aspects of the problem. Agrarian reform, in other words, cannot be expected to work miracles on its own. However, given a reasonably strong state commitment to making it work in the long term, this policy can serve as the structural core around which a broader strategy is built. It can thus play an important role in making Brazil a better place for its poorer citizens.

---

7. The group of experts President Lula charged with drafting an agrarian reform plan in 2003 calculated the per-family cost of settling a family at R$24,180, or about U.S.$10,000 at the prevailing exchange rate. In comparison, the monthly Family Grant benefit for the poorest families ranges from R$50 to R$95.

APPENDIX: INTERVIEWS

Afonso, José Batista Gonçalves, southeast region coordinator, CPT-PA, and member, CPT National Coordination, October 11, 1999, and July 11, 2005, Marabá, PA.

Alfredo, João, federal deputy (PT-CE), July 1, 2005, Brasília, DF.

Almeida, Alvaro, vice president, Agricultural Federation of the State of Alagoas (FAEA), February 17, 2000, Maceió, AL.

Almeida, Anaximandro Doudement de, advisor for land affairs, National Confederation of Agriculture (CNA), June 27, 2005, Brasília, DF.

Alves, Cicero da Silva, MST militant, May 11, 1998, Ribeirão, PE.

Alves, Eva Vilma Bezerra, MST militant, February 2000, Sapé, PB.

Amaral, Carlos Guedes do, Jr., legal advisor to the MST, November 3, 1999, Marabá, PA.

Amaro, MST militant, May 1998, São Luís do Quitunde, AL.

Amorim, Jaime, member, MST National Directorate, May 9, 1998, and February 27, 2000, Caruaru, PE.

Andrade, Manoel Correia de, expert on agriculture in northeastern Brazil, Fundação Joaquin Nabuco, May 22, 1998, Recife, PE.

Andrade, Tânia de, president, Land Institute of the State of São Paulo (ITESP), May 24, 2000, São Paulo, SP.

Araújo, Flademir, former CPT activist and editor, *Jornal Sem Terra*, March 5, 1998, Porto Alegre, RS.

Araújo, João Batista, federal deputy (PT-PA), November 9, 1999, Belém, PA, and June 29, 2005, Brasília, DF.

Barbosa, Antonio Raimundo, MST militant, February 1999, Atalaia, AL.

Barbosa, Joaquim Daniel, president, Rural Workers' Union of Conceição do Araguia, October 28, 1999, Conceição do Araguaia, PA.

Barros, Antonio Esras Alves, MST militant, Lagoa Grande, PE, May 1998.

Britto, Glauco, INCRA agricultural extension agent and MST militant, November 1999, Marabá, PA.

Britto, Joaquim, president, Urban Public Service Workers' Union, June 3, 1998, Maceió, AL.

Bueno, Jandir, member, MST State Coordination, March 12, 1998, Ronda Alta, RS.

Campos, Roberson Pinheiro de, MST militant, May 16, 2000, Teodoro Sampaio, SP.

Campos, José, MST militant (former member, MST National Directorate), September 14, 1999, Porto Alegre, RS.

Canova, Father Hermínio, coordinator, CPT Northeast region, May 24, 1998, Recife, PE.

Carvalho, Eurival Martins, member, MST State Directorate, October 10, 1999, Marabá, PA.

Carvalho, Francisco Ferreira, Southeast region vice coordinator, Federation of Workers in Agriculture of the State of Pará (FETAGRI-PA), October 1999, Marabá, PA.

Chaves, Valmir Rodrigues, MST activist (former member, MST State Directorate), May 17, 2000, and August 9, 2003, Teodoro Sampaio, SP.

Choinacki, Luci, Federal Deputy (PT-SC), April 27, 2000, Brasília, DF.

Cícero, MST militant, May 1998, São Luís do Quitunde, AL.

Correa, Ciro Eduardo, MST activist and agronomist for INCRA technical assistance program, September 18, 1999, Hulha Negra, RS.

Correa, Sebastião, MST militant, March 8, 1998, Ronda Alta, RS.

Correia, Daniel, member, MST National Coordination, February 2000, Maceió, AL.

Correia, Sérgio, member, Agricultural Union of Marabá, November 3, 1999, Marabá, PA.

Costa, Francisco de Assis Soledade da, Southeast region coordinator, Federation of Workers in Agriculture of the State of Pará (FETAGRI-PA), October 9, 1999, and July 15, 2005, Marabá, PA.

Costa, Florisvaldo Alexandre, president, State Center for Settler Associations and Smallholders (CEAPA), June 6, 1998, and February 2000, Maceió, AL.

Delira, Jonas Ferreira, member, MST State Directorate, May 11, 1998, Ribeirão, PE.

Elias, member, MST State Coordination, May 9, 1998, Caruaru, PE.

Engelmann, Irineu, member, MST State Coordination, September 16, 1999, Hulha Negra, RS.

Erisvalda, member, MST State Directorate, June 7, 1998, Maceió, AL.

Faleiros, Airton, president, Federation of Workers in Agriculture of the State of Pará (FETAGRI-PA), April 26, 2000, Brasília, DF.

Fernandes, Bernardo Mançano, professor, State University of São Paulo–Presidente Prudente, August 8, 2003, Presidente Prudente, SP.

Fernando, Paulo, state deputy (PT), June 4, 1998, and February 13, 2000, Maceió, AL.

Fillippi, Regiane, former superintendent, INCRA-RS, September 21, 1999, Porto Alegre, RS.

Freire, Eduardo, census director, INCRA, May 2, 2000, Brasília, DF.

Gasparin, Geraldo, member, MST State Coordination, September 19, 1999, Hulha Negra, RS.

Geraldo, INCRA agricultural extension agent and member, MST State Directorate, May 1998, São Luís do Quitunde, AL.

Gilmar, MST militant, Lagoa Grande, PE, May 1998.

Gomes, Claudemir, MST militant, May 16, 2000, Teodoro Sampaio, SP.

Görgen, Friar Sergio, CPT activist, March 18, 1998, Porto Alegre, RS.

Gouveia, Raimundo dos Santos, member, MST State Directorate, October 1999, Eldorado do Carajás, PA.

Graziano, Francisco, federal deputy (PSDB-SP), April 3, 2000.

Guedes, Automar, INCRA agricultural extension agent and member, MST State Directorate, February 2000, João Pessoa, PB.

Guedes, Jânio, former superintendent, INCRA-RS, August 31, 1999, Porto Alegre, RS.

Hackbart, Rolf, advisor to PT congressional caucus (named INCRA president in October 2003), April 25, 2000, May 2, 2000, and June 29, 2005, Brasília, DF.

Hein, Nestor, legal advisor to Agricultural Federation of Rio Grande do Sul (FARSUL), September 3, 1999, Porto Alegre, RS.

Jesus, Renato Rodrigues de, MST militant, May 16, 2000, Teodoro Sampaio, SP.
Junior, Fetter, federal deputy (PTB-RS), May 4, 2000, Brasília, DF.
Lagoia, Carla, MST militant, November 1999, Belém, PA.
Lara, Augusto, state deputy (PTB), September 14, 1999, Porto Alegre, RS.
Lemos, Araceli, state deputy (PT), November 1999, Belém, PA.
Lima, Edmilson Vitorino de, former employee, Land Institute of the State of São
Paulo, May 23, 2000, São Paulo, SP.
Lima, José Carlos da Silva, coordinator, CPT-AL, February 2000, Maceió, AL.
Lewy, Milton, member, MST State Directorate, May 17, 1998, Lagoa Grande, PE.
Lins, Marcos, former president, INCRA, April 28, 2000, Brasília, DF.
Mandinho, José Armando, MST militant, February 2000, Sapé, PB.
Manfron, Volnei, MST militant and city councilmember (former member, MST State
Directorate), September 16, 1999, and April 22, 2000, Hulha Negra, RS.
Marangon, Antônio, former CPT activist and former federal deputy (PT-RS), September 1999, Porto Alegre, RS.
Marquezelli, Nelson, federal deputy (PTB-SP), April 26, 2000, Brasília, DF.
Marinho, Reinaldo, vice president, Association of Sugarcane Planters of Alagoas
(ASPLANA), February 22, 2000, Maceió, AL.
Martins, Ademir, city councilmember (PT), November 1999, Marabá, PA.
Martins, Edivaldo, member, MST State Directorate, February 2000, Sapé, PB.
Martins, Leônidas, coordinator, CPT-Xingu region, November 7, 1999, Belém, PA.
Maschio, Darci, MST activist (former member, MST National Directorate), March 10,
1998, Ronda Alta, RS.
Matheus, Delwek, member, MST National Directorate, June 2, 2000, São Paulo, SP.
Matos, Deusamar Sales, member, MST State Directorate, October 1999, Parauapebas,
PA.
Matos, Valdinei Roque de, MST activist (former member, National Coordination), September 16, 1999, Hulha Negra, RS.
Mattes, Antônio, MST activist (former member, MST National Directorate), March 18,
1998, Porto Alegre, RS.
Mauro, Gilmar, member, MST National Directorate, May 11, 2000, May 22, 2000, and
June 24, 2005, São Paulo, SP; August 14, 2003, Cajamar, SP.
Medeiros, Hinamar Araujo, MST militant, PB, February 2000.
Mello, Elisvânia, MST militant (former member, MST State Directorate), October 1999,
Parauapebas, PA.
Mendes, Cledison, member, MST State Directorate, Teodoro Sampaio, SP, May 15,
2000.
Mendonça, Antônio Haroldo Pinheiro, regional coordinator, Caritas, November 5,
1999, Belém, PA.
Micheletto, Moacir, federal deputy (PFL-PR), May 5, 2000, Brasília, DF.
Mifarreg, Elias Ralim, member, board of directors, Agricultural Federation of the
State of Pará (FAEPA), November 1999, Marabá, PA.
Milan, Arnaldo Luiz, member, MST State Directorate (former member, MST National
Coordination), October 7, 1999, Marabá, PA.
Montenegro, Pedro, lawyer and human rights activist, June 2, 1998, Maceió, AL.
Monteiro, Alcenir, MST militant, November 1999, Belém, PA.
Monteiro, Raquel, MST militant, September 19, 1999, Hulha Negra, RS.
Moreira, Januário, president, Federation of Agricultural Workers of Pernambuco
(FETAPE), May 23, 1998, Recife, PE.

Moreira, Telmo, member, MST State Directorate, September 19, 1999, Hulha Negra, RS.

Moura, Francisco, member, MST State Directorate, November 1999, Belém, PA.

Moura, José Antônio de, member, MST State Directorate, February 2000, AL.

Muniz, Orlando, president, INCRA, December 13, 2000, Brasília, DF.

Nan, Luciene, MST militant, February 2000, Sapé, PB.

Nascimento, Edivaldo Bastista de, member, MST State Directorate, February 2000, João Pessoa, PB.

"Neide," MST militant, May 9, 1998, Caruaru, PE.

"Neno," member, MST National Coordination, May 30, 1998, Maceió, AL.

Neri, Jorge, member, MST National Directorate, October 11, Marabá, PA, and November 10, 1999, Belém, PA.

Nunes, Paulo, state deputy (PT), February 1999, Maceió, AL.

Oliveira, Erinaldo Bastista de, MST militant, February 2000, AL.

Oliveira, Geraldo de Fatima de, member, MST State Directorate, May 19, 2000, Promissão, SP.

Oliveira, Luiz Lima de, member MST State Coordination, October 1999, Eldorado do Carajás, PA.

Oliveira, Maria de, director for land conflicts, INCRA, May 5, 2000, Brasília, DF.

Oliveira, Miram Farias de, member, MST State Directorate, August 9, 2003, Teodoro Sampaio, SP.

Oliveira, Valdecir de, member, MST State Directorate, May 10, 1998, Ribeirão, PE.

Oliveira, Valdemar, MST settler (former member, MST National Coordination), March 12, 1998, Ronda Alta, RS.

Oliveira, Valdirene de, member, MST State Directorate, May 20, 2000, Promissão, SP.

Olsson, Augusto, member, MST State Directorate, March 24, 1998, and September 5, 1999, Porto Alegre, RS.

Ostroski, Dirce Salete, MST militant (former member MST National Commission), João Pessoa, PB, February 2000.

Pacheco, Reginaldo, member, MST National Directorate, June 6, 1998, and February 2000, Maceió, AL.

Padilha, Fábio Jesus, MST militant, April 16, 2000, Teodoro Sampaio, SP.

Paixão, Victor Hugo, superintendent, INCRA–Southeastern PA, November 1999, Marabá, PA.

Pantaleão, Sergio, member, MST State Directorate, May 16, 2000, Teodoro Sampaio, SP.

"Parazinho," member, MST State Directorate, November 1999, Marabá, PA.

Parente, José Vaz, director, National Confederation of INCRA Employees (CNASI), June 27, 2005, Brasília, DF.

"Dona Pel," member, MST State Coordination, May 1998, São Luís do Quitunde, AL.

Pereira, Gedeão, president, Commission on Land Affairs, Agricultural Federation of Rio Grande do Sul (FARSUL), September 8, 1999, Bagé, RS.

Pereira, José, MST militant, February 2000, Sapé, PB.

Pereira, Valdomiro Costa, member, MST State Coordination, October 1999, Eldorado do Carajás, PA.

Pietroski, Sidinei, MST militant, September 19, 1999, Hulha Negra, RS.

Portes, Gilberto, member, MST National Directorate, April 28, 2000, Brasília, DF.

Pretto, Adão, federal deputy (PT-RS), September 2, 1999, Porto Alegre, RS, April 27, 2000, Brasília, DF, and June 27, 2005, Brasília, DF.

Procópio, Felinto, MST militant (former member, MST State Directorate), May 15, 2000, Teodoro Sampaio, SP.

Renan, José Luiz, member, MST State Directorate, February 2000, Arapiraca, AL.

Ribeiro, Carivaldo, president, Agricultural Union of Marabá, November 1999, Marabá, PA.

Ribeiro, Leonildo Dionísio, MST militant, May 20, 2000, Promissão, SP.

Ribeiro, Maria de Fátima Miguel, member, MST National Directorate, March 2, 2000, Natal, RN.

Rocha, Sebastião Neves, secretary for land and environmental policy, CONTAG, May 2, 2000, Brasília, DF.

Rodrigues, Isabel, member, MST State Directorate (former member, MST National Coordination), October 1999, and July 15, 2005, Marabá, PA.

Rodrigues, Jorge Evandro de Araújo, first secretary, CUT-Pará, November 1999, Belém, PA.

Rohrig, Otávio, vice president, CUT-RS, September 20, 1999, Porto Alegre, RS.

Rui, José, chief, Settlement Division, INCRA-RS, March 24, 1998, and September 3, 1999, Porto Alegre, RS.

Russo, Osvaldo, former president, INCRA, April 25, 2000, Brasíla, DF.

Sampaio, Plínio de Arruda, former federal deputy (PT-SP), March 31, 2000, and April 3, 2000, São Paulo, SP.

Santa Cruz, Marcelo, human rights lawyer, May 1998, Recife, PE.

Santino, José Cicero, MST militant, February 2000, Atalaia, AL.

Santos, Cristiano dos, member, MST State Directorate, February 2000, Atalaia, AL.

Santos, Joaquim Ribeiro dos, MST activist (former member, MST National Coordination), October 9, 1999, Parauapebas, PA.

Santos, Paulo Fernando dos, state deputy (PT), June 3, 1998, and February 2000, Maceió, AL.

Santos, Roosevelt Roque dos, former president, UDR, April 4, 2000, Presidente Venceslau, SP.

Santos, Silas Machado Junior dos, MST militant, February 1999, Joaquim Gomes, AL.

Schiochet, Dilei Aparecida, member, MST State Directorate (former member, MST National Commission), February, 2000, Bananeiras, PB.

Schwengber, Angela, former MST militant, November 1997, São Paulo, SP.

Severo, José Ricardo, technical advisor, CNA, April 26, 2000, Brasília, DF.

Silva, Antonio Vitorino da, president, Federation of Workers in Agriculture of the State of Alagoas (FETAG-AL), February 28, 2000, Maceió, AL.

Silva, Edesio Paixão da, member, MST State Directorate, May 19, 1998, Lagoa Grande, PE.

Silva, Edilson Pereira da, accountant for the MST, February 2000, João Pessoa, PB.

Silva, Hernandes Aparecido da, MST militant, May 20, 2000, Promissão, SP.

Silva, João Batista Romão da, member, MST State Coordination, May 12, 1998, Ribeirão, PE.

Silva, José Carlos da, member, MST State Directorate, February 2000, Joaquim Gomes, AL.

Silva, Marcos Antônio da, member, MST National Coordination, May 27, 1998, and March 17, 2000, Maceió, AL.

Silva, Maria Aparecida, MST militant, May 20, 2000, Promissão, SP.

Silva, Ricardo Fernando da, member MST State Directorate, February 2000, Sapé, PB.

Silva, Sandoval José da, member, MST State Coordination, February 2000, Atalaia, AL.

Silva, Valmor da, MST militant, September 19, 1999, Hulha Negra, RS.

Silva, Vaquimar Nunes da, MST militant, May 15, 2000, Presidente Prudente, SP.

Silva, Vilmar Martins da, member, MST State Coordination, March 11, 1998, Ronda Alta, RS.

Silva, Zelitro Luz da, MST activist (former member, MST National Coordination), May 16, 2000, Teodoro Sampaio, SP.

Siqueira, Advonsil Cândido, president, CUT-PA (former member, MST National Coordination), November 5, 1999, Belém, PA.

Siqueira, José Alberto, former bank workers' union activist, March 19, 1998, Jóia, RS.

Soares, Albino, member, MST State Directorate, February 2000, Delmiro Gouveia, AL.

Soares, Maurílio, MST activist (former member, MST State Directorate), October 16, 1999, Eldorado do Carajás, PA.

Souza, Claudio de, Anglican pastor and MST militant, February 2000, João Pessoa, PB.

Souza, Diolinda, Alves de, MST militant (former member, State Directorate), May 15, 2000, Teodoro Sampaio.

Souza, Francisco Gomes de, member, MST State Coordination, October 1999, Parauapebas, PA.

Souza, Glaydson Barbosa de, member, MST State Directorate, October 6, 1999, Belém, PA.

Souza, Maricélia de, member, MST State Directorate, February 2000, João Pessoa, PB.

Souza, Nilza Pessoa de, former member, MST National Coordination, João Pessoa, PB, February 2000.

Souza, Raimundo Nonato Coelho de, member, MST National Coordination, November 7, 1999, Belém, PA.

Souza, Valdemir Agostino de, member, State Commission, Movimento dos Trabalhadores (MT), February 21, 2000, Maceió, AL.

Stedile, João Pedro, member, MST National Directorate, December 15, 2000, São Paulo, SP.

Stival, David, PT activist (former CPT activist), March 16, 1998, Porto Alegre, RS.

Tallagnol, Friar Wilson, coordinator, CPT-RS, March 4, 1998, Porto Alegre, RS.

Teixeira, Volney, former president, UDR-RS, September 10, 1999, Santa Maria, RS.

Ten Caten, Bernadete, superintendent, INCRA–Southeastern PA, July 14, 2005, Marabá, PA.

Tonin, Ivanete, member, MST State Directorate, March 21, 1998, Ibirubá, RS, and September 9, 1999, Porto Alegre, RS.

Torriani, Edna, MST militant, May 16, 2000, Teodoro Sampaio, SP.

Tortelli, Altemir, vice president for training, CUT, April 15, 2000, São Paulo, SP.

Trajano, Severino José, MST militant, February 2000, Pitimbu, PB.

Treccani, Girolamo, professor of agrarian law, Federal University of Pará (former CPT activist), November 6, 1999, Belém, PA.

Trocate, Charles, member, MST National Directorate, July 13, 2005, Marabá, PA.

Ubiratan, Paulo, PT activist, May 23, 1998, Recife, PE.

Valdecir, member, MST State Directorate, May 10, 1998, Ribeirão, PE.

Vendovatto, Isaias, MST militant (former member, MST National Directorate), March 10, 1998, Ronda Alta, RS.

Viana, Ricardo Romero dos Santos, INCRA agricultural extension agent and MST militant, February 2000, João Pesso, PB.

Vieira, Cleonice, MST militant, May 18, 1998, Lagoa Grande, PE.

Vitória, Ricardo, superintendent, INCRA-AL, June 5, 1998, and February 15, 2000, Maceió, AL.

Wagner, Carlos, reporter, *Zero Hora,* September 4, 1999, Porto Alegre, RS.

Wambergue, Emmanuel, Agricultural and Environmental Center of the Araguaia-Tocantins (CAT) and former CPT activist, October 11, 1999, and July 14, 2005, Marabá, PA.

Xavier, Carlos, president, Agricultural Federation of the State of Pará (FAEPA), November 7, 1999, Belém, PA.

BIBLIOGRAPHY

Government Documents

IBGE (Brazilian Institute of Geography and Statistics). 1960. *Censo agropecuário.*
———. 1970. *Censo agropecuário.*
———. 1975. *Censo agropecuário.*
———. 1980. *Censo agropecuário.*
———. 1985. *Censo agropecuário.*
———. 1992. *Pesquisa nacional por amostra de domicílios (PNAD).*
———. 1993. *Pesquisa nacional por amostra de domicílios (PNAD).*
———. 1995. *Pesquisa nacional por amostra de domicílios (PNAD).*
———. 1996. *Pesquisa nacional por amostra de domicílios (PNAD).*
———. 1997. *Pesquisa nacional por amostra de domicílios (PNAD).*
———. 1998. *Pesquisa nacional por amostra de domicílios (PNAD).*
———. 1999. *Pesquisa nacional por amostra de domicílios (PNAD).*
———. 2000. *Censo demográfico.*
———. 2001. *Pesquisa nacional por amostra de domicílios (PNAD).*
———. 2002. *Pesquisa nacional por amostra de domicílios (PNAD).*
———. 2003. *Pesquisa nacional por amostra de domicílios (PNAD).*
———. 2004. *Pesquisa nacional por amostra de domicílios (PNAD).*
———. 2005. *Pesquisa nacional por amostra de domicílios (PNAD).*
INCRA (National Institute for Colonization and Agrarian Reform). 1998. "Balanço da reforma agrária: Governo FHC (1995/1998)."
———. 1999. INCRA: Um instrumento de governo para a execução da reforma agrária.
———. 2000a. *Estudo prospectivo da demanda por terra: Cenários possíveis para a reforma agrária.* Prepared by Sônia Bergamasco, Maristela Simões do Carmo, Julieta Teresa Aier de Oliveira, Valéria Comitre, and Nelly. M. S. de Figuereido.
———. 2000b. *O livro branco da grilagem de terras no Brasil.*
———. 2000c. *Relatório de atividades do INCRA 1995–1999.*
———. 2002. *Balanço global de gestão: Relatório final.*
———. 2004. *Relatório de gestão. Exercício 2003. INCRA.*
———. 2005. *Relatório de gestão: Exercício 2004.*
———. 2006. *Relatório de gestão 2005.*
———. n.d. *Resumo das atividades do INCRA—1985/1994*
IPEA (Institute for Applied Economic Research). 2003. *Políticas sociais: Acompanhamento e análise.* No. 6.
———. 2006. *Políticas sociais: Acompanhamento e análise.* No. 12.

MDA (Ministry of Agrarian Development). 2006. *Relatório da Ouvidoria Agrária 01/ 2006 (dados relativos ao período de 01/01/06 a 31/03/06).*

MEC/MDA (Ministry of Education/Ministry of Agrarian Development). 2005. *Pesquisa nacional da educação na reforma agrária.*

Documents Published by Nongovernmental Organizations

CONCRAB (National Confederation of Agrarian Reform Cooperatives of Brazil). 1996. *Método de trabalho popular.* Caderno de formação 24.

———. 1997. *Sistema cooperativa dos assentados.* Caderno de cooperação agrícola 5.

———. 1998a. *A emancipação dos assentamentos: Os direitos e os cuidados que os assentados devem ter.* Caderno de cooperaçao agrícola 6.

———. 1998b. *Enfrentar os desafios da organização nos assentamentos.* Caderno de cooperação agrícola 7.

———. 1998c. *Organicidade e núcleos de base.*

———. 1999. *A evolução da concepção de cooperação agrícola do* MST (1989 a 1999). Caderno de cooperação agrícola 8.

CONTAG (National Confederation of Workers in Agriculture). 1998a. *Anais do VII Congresso Nacional de Trabalhadores Rurais.*

———. 1998b. *Desenvolvimento e sindicalismo rural no Brasil.*

———. 1999. *Reforma agrária.* Serie experiências 10. Projeto de pesquisa e formação social, October.

CPT (Pastoral Commission on Land). 1986. *Conflitos de terra no Brasil 1985.*

———. 1987. *Conflitos de terra no Brasil 1986.*

———. 1988a. *A ofensiva da Direita no campo.*

———. 1988b. *Conflitos no campo—Brasil 1987.*

———. 1989a. *Conflitos no campo—Brasil 1988.*

———. 1989b. *Rompendo o cerco e a cerca.*

———. 1990. *Conflitos no campo—Brasil 1989.*

———. 1991. *Conflitos no campo—Brasil 1990.*

———. 1992. *Conflitos no campo—Brasil 1991.*

———. 1993a. *Conflitos no campo—Brasil 1992.*

———. 1993b. *Inserção e prática pastoral das igrejas nos acampamentos e assentamentos: Desafios para a* CPT. Cadernos de estudo 6.

———. 1994. *Conflitos no campo—Brasil 1993.*

———. 1995. *Conflitos no campo—Brasil 1994.*

———. 1996a. *Conflitos no campo—Brasil 1995.*

———. 1996b. *Perspectivas para o campo e inserção da* CPT. Seminário CPT 20 anos: Desafios e compromissos.

———. 1997. *Conflitos no campo—Brasil 1996.*

———. 1998. *Conflitos no campo—Brasil 1997.*

———. 1999. *Conflitos no campo—Brasil 1998.*

———. 2000. *Conflitos no campo—Brasil 1999.*

———. 2001. *Conflitos no campo—Brasil 2000.*

———. 2002. *Conflitos no campo—Brasil 2001.*

————. 2003. *Conflitos no campo—Brasil 2002.*

————. 2004. *Conflitos no campo—Brasil 2003.*

————. 2005. *Conflitos no campo—Brasil 2004.*

————. 2006. *Conflitos no campo—Brasil 2005.*

————. n.d. *Estrutura organizativa da* CPT. Debate & formação. Caderno 2.

MST (Movement of Landless Rural Workers). 1986a. *A luta continua.* Cadernos de formação 10.

————. 1986b. *Construindo o caminho.*

————. 1986c. *Elementos sobre a teoria da organização no campo.* Caderno de formação 11.

————. 1986d. *Reunião da Executiva Nacional do Movimento.*

————. 1987. *Terceiro Encontro Nacional.* Caderno de formação 12.

————. 1988a. *Resoluções do IV Encontro Nacional.*

————. 1988b. *Normas gerais do Movimento dos Trabalhadores Rurais Sem Terra—de caráter nacional.*

————. 1989a. *Normas gerais do* MST.

————. 1989b. *Plano nacional do* MST, 1989 a 1993. Caderno de formação 17.

————. 1990. *Manual de organização dos núcleos.*

————. 1991. *Como organizar a massa.*

————. 1992. *Disciplina.*

————. 1993a. *Alianças.*

————. 1993b. *Debate sobre a estrutura sindical no campo.*

————. 1994a. *A força que anima os militantes.* Prepared by Ranulfo Peloso.

————. 1994b. *Como organizar os assentados individuais.*

————. 1994c. *Documento básico do* MST.

————. 1994d. *Reforma agrária e as eleições.*

————. 1995. *Vamos organizar a base do* MST.

————. 1996. *A reforma agrária e a sociedade brasileira.* Prepared by Ademar Bogo.

————. 1998a. *Mística: Uma necessidade no trabalho popular organizativo.* Caderno de formação 27.

————. 1998b. *Os desafios atuais do* MST: Ocupar novos espaços na sociedade. Prepared by Ademar Bogo.

————. 1998c. *Como implementar na práctica os valores do* MST: Sugestões recolhidas no IX Encontro Nacional do MST—Vitoria.

————. n.d. *Política de finanças.*

NERA (Center for Studies, Research and Projects on Agrarian Reform)/Facultade de Cienciâs e Tecnologia/ Departamento de Geografia/Universidade Estadual Paulista. 2000. *Dataluta. Relátorio preliminar do banco de dados da luta pela terra.* December.

PT (Workers' Party). Liderança da Bancada na Câmara dos Deputados/Secretaria Agrária Nacional. 1998. *A reforma agrária virtual do governo FHC: Una análise crítica ao caderno de campanha do candidato FHC.* Assessoria Técnica. Prepared by Gerson Teixeira and Rolf Hackbart.

————. 1999. *A nova (anti) reforma agrária.* Assessoria Técnica. Prepared by Gerson Teixeira and Rolf Hackbart.

————. 2000. *Um perfil da agricultura e da reforma agrária no Brasil entre 1995 e 1999.* Assessoria Técnica. Prepared by Gerson Teixeira.

————. 2001. *Por um projeto democrático, popular e soberano para o agrário brasileiro.* Prepared by Gerson Teixeira.

———. 2002. *A realidade das metas, e o fracasso da estratégia política do programa de reforma agrária do governo FHC*. Assessoria Técnica. Prepared by Gerson Teixeira. Colaboration: Maria Thereza Pedroso.

Online Databases

IPEADATA. Pobreza—pessoas pobres. http://www.ipeadata.gov.br/ipeaweb.dll/ipeadata?65370046.
———. Produto interno bruto (PIB): Variação real annual, http://www.ipeadata.gov.br/ipeaweb.dll/ipeadata?65370046.
———. Taxa de desemprego aberto nas rms (referência: 30 dias). http://www.ipeadata.gov.br/ipeaweb.dll/ipeadata?65370046

Periodicals

Caros Amigos
Clarín
Estado de São Paulo
Folha de São Paulo
Jornal Sem Terra
Latin American Brazil Report
Veja

Books and Articles

Adriance, Madeleine Cousineau. 1995. *Promised Land: Base Christian Communities and the Struggle for the Amazon*. Albany: State University of New York Press.
Almeida, Lúcio Flávio de, and Félix Ruiz Sánchez. 1998. "Um grão menos amargo das ironias da história: O MST e as lutas sociais contra o neoliberalismo." *Lutas Sociais* 5:77–92.
Alvarez, Sonia, Evelina Dagnino, and Arturo Escobar, eds. 1998. *Cultures of Politics/ Politics of Cultures: Re-visioning Latin American Social Movements*. Boulder, Colo.: Westview.
Amenta, Edwin, and Yvonne Zylan. 1991. "It Happened Here: Political Opportunity, the New Institutionalism, and the Townsend Movement." *American Sociological Review* 56 (April): 250–65.
Andrade, Manuel Correia de. 1964. *A terra e o homem no nordeste*. São Paulo: Brasiliense.
Azevêdo, Fernando Antonio. 1982. *As ligas camponesas*. Rio de Janeiro: Paz e Terra.
Bacha, Edmar L., and Herbert S. Klein, eds. 1989. *Social Change in Brazil, 1945–1985: The Incomplete Transition*. Albuquerque: University of New Mexico Press.

Baer, Werner. 1995. *The Brazilian Economy: Growth and Development.* 4th ed. Westport, Conn.: Praeger.

————. 2001. *The Brazilian Economy: Growth and Development.* 5th ed. Westport, Conn.: Praeger.

Baer, Werner, and Mavio Filizzola. 2005. "Growth, Efficiency, and Equity: The Impact of Agribusiness and Land Reform in Brazil." Working Paper 05–0109, University of Illinois at Urbana-Champaign, College of Business.

Banck, Geert A., and Kees den Boer, eds. 1991. *Sowing the Whirlwind: Soya Expansion and Social Change in Southern Brazil.* Amsterdam: Centre for Latin American Research and Documentation (CEDLA).

Bastos, Elide Rugai. 1984. *As ligas camponesas.* Petrópolis, Brazil: Vozes.

Benford Robert D., and David Snow. 2000. "Framing Processes and Social Movements: An Overview and Assessment." *Annual Reviews of Sociology* 26:611–39.

Benincá, Elli. 1987. "Conflito religioso e práxis: A ação política dos acampados da Encruzilhada do Natalino e da Fazenda Anoni." Master's thesis, Pontifícia Universidade Católica de São Paulo.

Borges, Maria Stela Lemos. 1997. *Terra: Ponto de partida, ponto de chegada; Identidade e luta pela terra.* São Paulo: Anita Garibaldi.

Branford, Sue, and Oriel Glock. 1985. *The Last Frontier: Fighting over Land in the Amazon.* London: Zed Books.

Branford, Sue, and Jan Rocha. 2002. *Cutting the Wire: The Story of the Landless Movement in Brazil.* London: Latin America Bureau.

Brenneisen, Eliane Cardoso. 2002. *Relações de poder, dominação e resistência: O MST e os assentamentos rurais.* Cascavel, Brazil: Edunioeste.

Brockett, Charles D. 1991. "The Structure of Political Opportunities and Peasant Mobilization in Central America." *Comparative Politics* (April): 253–74.

Brumer, Anita, and José Vicente Tavares dos Santos. 1997. "Tensões agrícolas e agrárias na transição democrática brasileira." *São Paulo em Perspectiva* 11 (April–June): 3–14.

Bruno, Regina. 1997. *Senhores da terra, senhores da guerra: A nova face política das elites agroindustriais no Brasil.* Rio de Janeiro: Forense Universitária.

Bussinger, Vanda Valadão. 1994. "Assentamentos e sem-terra no Espírito Santo: A importância do papel dos mediadores." Master's thesis, Universidade Federal do Rio de Janeiro.

Cadji, Anne-Laure. 2000. "Brazil's Landless Find Their Voice." *NACLA Report on the Americas* 33 (March/April): 30–48.

Camarano, Ana Amélia, and Ricardo Abramovay. 1999. "Êxodo rural, envelhecimento e masculinização no Brasil: Panorama dos últimos 50 anos." Brasília: IPEA, Ministério do Planejamento, Orçamento e Gestão.

Campanhola, Clayton, and José Graziano da Silva, eds. 2000. *O novo rural brasileiro: Uma análise nacional e regional.* Vol 1. Jaguariúna, Brazil: EMBRAPA.

Cardoso, Ruth Corrêa Leite. 1994. "A trajetória dos movimentos sociais." In *Anos 90 Política e Sociedade no Brasil,* edited by Evelina Dagnino, 81–90. São Paulo: Brasiliense.

Carnasciali, Carlos H., et al. 1987. "Consequências sociais das transformaões tecnológicas na agricultura do Paraná." In *Os impactos sociais da modernização agrícola,* edited by George Martine and Ronaldo Coutinho Garcia, 125–67. São Paulo: Caetés.

Carneiro, Francisco Galrão. 2000. "Brazil: An Assesment of Rural Labor Markets in the 1990s" Document prepared for the World Bank. http://www.dataterra.org.br, file//A:World Bank Paper.htm (accessed June 18, 2001).

Carter, Miguel. 2002. "Ideal Interest Mobilization: Explaining the Formation of Brazil's Landless Social Movement." Ph.D. diss., Columbia University.

Carvalho, Cícero Pericles de Oliveira. 2000. *Análise da reestructuração produtiva da agroindústria sucro-alcooleira alagoana.* Maceió, Brazil: EDUFAL.

Castells, Manuel. 1982. "Squatters and Politics in Latin America: A Comparative Analysis of Urban Social Movements in Chile, Peru and Mexico." In *Toward a Political Economy of Urbanization in Third World Countries,* edited by Helen Safa, 249–82. New Delhi: Oxford University Press.

Cehelsky, Marta. 1979. *Land Reform in Brazil: The Management of Social Change.* Boulder, Colo.: Westview.

CELAM. 1968 [1970]. *The Church in the Present-Day Transformation of Latin America in the Light of the Council.* Medellín, Columbia: CELAM.

CESOP. 1996. "Tendências: Encarte de dados de opinião pública; Reforma agrária (1962–1995)." *Opinião Pública* 4 (April): 5–17.

CNA. 2003. "Agronegócio cresceu 8,37% e PIB chega a R$424,32 bi." *Indicadores Rurais* 44 (January–February): 1–2.

———. 2006a. "PIB cai 9,79% e produtores perdem R$ 16,6 bi." *Indicadores Rurais* 44 (January–February): 1–2.

———. 2006b. "VBP deve cair 2,1% em 2006." *Indicadores Rurais* 66 (January–February): 3–4.

Coelho, Carlos Nayro. 2001. "70 anos de política agrícola no Brasil (1931–2001)." *Revista de Política Agrícola* 10 (July/August/September): 3–58.

Corrêa, Angela M. C. Jorge. 2000. "Evolução do rendimento médio, desigualdade e pobreza entre as pessoas na agricultura brasileira: Uma análise regional do período 1981–1998." Paper presented at the Séminario desafios da pobreza rural no Brasil, Rio de Janeiro (NEAD).

Costain, Anne N. 1992. *Social Movements as Interest Groups: The Case of the Women's Movement.* Boulder, Colo.: Westview.

Davies, James C. 1962. "Toward a Theory of Revolution." *American Sociological Review* 27:5–19.

De Janvry, Alain. 1981. *The Agrarian Question and Reformism in Latin America.* Baltimore: John Hopkins University Press.

De Janvry, Alain, and Elisabeth Sadoulet. 2002. "Land Reforms in Latin America: Ten Lessons Toward a Contemporary Agenda." Paper prepared for the World Bank's Latin American Land Policy Workshop, Pachuca, Mexico, June 14.

de la Peña, Guillermo. 1994. "Rural Mobilizations in Latin America Since c. 1920." In *The Cambridge History of Latin America,* edited by Leslie Bethell, 379–482. Cambridge: Cambridge University Press.

Del Grossi, Mauro Eduardo, and José Graziano da Silva. 2000a. "Evolução da renda das famílias agrícolas e rurais: Brasil: 1992–1997." In *O novo rural brasileiro: Uma análise nacional e regional,* vol 1, edited by Clayton Campanhola and José Graziano da Silva, 79–100. Jaguariúna, Brazil: EMBRAPA.

———. 2000b. "Ocupação nas famílias agrícolas e rurais no Brasil: 1992–1997." In *O novo rural brasileiro: Uma análise nacional e regional,* vol 1, edited by Clayton Campanhola and José Graziano da Silva, 67–78. Jaguariúna, Brazil: EMBRAPA.

D'Incão e Mello, Maria da Conceição. 1975. *O bóia-fria: Acumulação e miséria*. Petrópolis, Brazil: Vozes.

Doimo, Ana Maria. 1995. *A vez e a voz do popular: Movimentos sociais e participação política no Brasil pós-70*. Rio de Janeiro: ANPOCS.

Dorner, Peter. 1992. *Latin American Land Reforms in Theory and Practice: A Retrospective Analysis*. Madison: University of Wisconsin Press.

Eckert, Cordula. 1984. "Movimento dos Agricultores Sem-Terra no Rio Grande do Sul." Master's thesis, Universidade Federal Rural do Rio de Janeiro.

Eckstein, Harry. 1975. "Case Study and Theory in Political Science." In *Handbook of Political Science*. Vol. 7, *Strategies of Inquiry*, edited by Fred Greenstein and Nelson Polsby, 79–138. Reading, Mass.: Addison-Wesley.

Eisinger, Peter. 1973. "The Conditions of Protest Behavior in American Cities." *American Political Science Review* 81:11–28.

El-Ghonemy, M. Riad. 2001. "The Political Economy of Market-Based Land Reform." In *Land Reform and Peasant Livelihoods: The Social Dynamics of Rural Poverty and Agrarian Reform in Developing Countries*, edited by Krishna B. Ghimire, 105–33. London: ITDG.

Faria, Vilma. 1989. "Changes in the Composition of Employment and the Structure of Occupations." In *Social Change in Brazil, 1945–1985: The Incomplete Transition*, edited by Edmar L. Bacha and Herbert S. Klein, 141–70. Albuquerque: University of New Mexico Press.

Farias, Marisa de Fátima Lomba de. 1997. "Acampamento America Rodrigues da Silva: Esperanças e desilusões na memória dos caminhantes que lutam pela terra." Master's thesis, Universidade Estadual Paulista.

Fernandes, Bernardo Mançano. 1996. *MST: Formação e territorialização*. São Paulo: HUCITEC.

———. 1998. *Gênese e desenvolvimento do MST*. São Paulo: MST.

———. 1999. "Contribuçao ao estudo do campesinato brasileiro: Formação e territorialização do Movimento dos Trabalhadores Rurais Sem Terra-MST 1979–1999." Ph.D. diss., Universidade de São Paulo.

———. 2000. *A formação do MST no Brasil*. Petrópolis, Brazil: Vozes.

Ferreira, Angela Duarte Damasceno. 1987. "Movimentos sociais rurais no Paraná: 1978–1982." In *Movimentos sociais no campo*, edited by Anamaria Aimoré Bonim, 9–50. Caracas: Nueva Sociedad.

Figueiredo, Nelly Maria Sansígolo de, and Angela Maria Cassavia Jorge Corrêa. 2006. "Tecnologia na agricultura brasileira: Indicadores de modernização no início dos anos 2000." Texto para discussão, no. 1163. IPEA.

Filho, José Luliano de Carvalho. 1997. "Política fundiária: Oportunidades perdidas, revoluç/ão cultural e Lampedusa." *São Paulo em Perspectiva* 11 (April–June): 26–34.

Fireman, Bruce, and William Gamson. 1979. "Utilitarian Logic in the Resource Mobilization Perspective." In *The Dynamics of Social Movements: Resource Mobilization, Social Control, and Tactics*, edited by Mayer N. Zald and John D. McCarthy, 8–44. Cambridge, Mass.: Winthrop.

Franco, Mariana C. Pantoja. 1992. "Xagu: de sem-terra a assentado." Master's thesis, Universidade Federal do Rio de Janeiro.

Freeman, Jo. 1973. "The Origins of the Women's Liberation Movement." *American Journal of Sociology* 78:141–53.

Furtado, Celso. 1963. *The Economic Growth of Brazil: A Survey from Colonial to Modern Times.* Translated by Ricardo W. de Aguiar and Eric Charles Drysdale. Berkeley and Los Angeles: University of California Press.

Gaiger, Luiz Inácio Germany. 1987. *Agentes religiosos e camponeses sem terra no Sul do Brasil.* Petrópolis, Brazil: Vozes.

Gamson, William. 1975. *The Strategy of Social Protest.* Homewood, Ill.: Dorsey.

Gamson, William A., and David S. Meyer. 1996. "Framing Political Opportunity." In *Comparative Perspectives on Social Movements: Political Opportunities, Mobilizing Structures, and Cultural Framings,* edited by Doug McAdam, John D. McCarthy, and M. N. Zald, 275–90. Cambridge: Cambridge University Press.

Garcia, Afrânio Raul, Jr. 1989. *O Sul: Caminho do roçado: Estratégias de reprodução camponesa e transformação social.* São Paulo: Marco Zero.

Gasques, José Garcia, and Carlos Monteiro Vila Verde. 2003. "Gastos públicos na agricultura, evolução e mudanças." Texto para discussão, no. 948. IPEA.

Giambiagi, Fabio. 2005. "Rompendo com a ruptura: O Governo Lula (2003–2004)." In *Economia brasileira contemporânea (1945–2004),* edited by Giambiagi, Fabio, André Villela, Lavínia Barros de Castro, and Jennifer Hermann, 196–217. São Paulo: Editora Campus.

Giambiagi, Fabio, André Villela, Lavínia Barros de Castro, and Jennifer Hermann, eds. 2005. *Economia brasileira contemporânea (1945–2004).* São Paulo: Editora Campus.

Goes, Cesar Hamilton Brito. 1997. "A Comissão Pastoral da Terra: História e ambivalência da ação da igreja no Rio Grande do Sul." Master's thesis, Universidade Federal do Rio Grande do Sul.

Gohn, Maria da Glória. 1991. *Movimentos sociais e luta pela moradia.* São Paulo: Edições Loyola.

———. 1997. *Os sem-terra, ongs e cidadania.* São Paulo: Cortez, 1997.

Gomes da Silva, José. 1987. *Caindo por terra: Crises da reforma agrária na Nova República.* São Paulo: Busca Vida.

———. 1989. *Buraco negro: A reforma agrária na Constituinte.* São Paulo: Paz e Terra.

———. 1997. *A reforma agrária brasileira na virada do milênio.* Maceió, Brazil: EDUFAL.

Goodman, David. 1989. "Rural Economy and Society." In *Social Change in Brazil, 1945–1985: The Incomplete Transition,* edited by Edmar L. Bacha and Herbert S. Klein, 49–98. Albuquerque: University of New Mexico Press.

Goodman, David, B. Sorj, and J. Wilkinson. 1984. "Agro-Industry, State Policy, and Rural Social Structures: Recent Analyses of Proletarianisation in Brazilian Agriculture." In *Proletarianisation in the Third World,* edited by H. Finch and B. Munslow, 189–215. London: Croom Helm.

Goodwin, Jeff, and James M. Jasper. 1999. "Caught in a Winding, Snarling Vine: The Structural Bias of Political Process Theory." *Sociological Forum* 14 (1): 27–52.

———, eds. 2004. *Rethinking Social Movements: Structure, Meaning, and Emotion.* Lanham, Md.: Rowan and Littlefield.

Görgen, Sérgio Antônio. 1987. *Os Cristãos e a questão da terra.* São Paulo: FTD.

———. 1998. *A resistência dos pequenos gigantes: A luta e a organização dos pequenos agricultores.* Petrópolis, Brazil: Vozes.

Graziano, Francisco. 1996. *Qual reforma agrária? Terra, pobreza e cidadania.* São Paulo: Geração, 197–221.

Graziano da Silva, José. 1982. *A modernização dolorosa*. Rio de Janeiro: Zahar.

———. 1995. "A industrialização e a urbanização da agricultura brasileira." In *Brasil em artigos*, 197–221. São Paulo: SEADE.

———. 1999. *Tecnologia e agricultura familiar*. Porto Alegre, Brazil: Editora Universidade/UFRGS.

———. 1999. *O novo rural brasileiro*. 2d ed. Campinas, Brazil: UNICAMP.

Graziano da Silva, José, Otávio Valentim Balsadi, and Mauro Eduardo del Grossi. 1997. "O emprego rural e a mercantilização do espaço agrário." *São Paulo em Perspectiva* 11 (April–June): 50–64.

Graziano da Silva, José, and Mauro Eduardo del Grossi. 2001. "Rural Non-farm Employment and Incomes in Brazil: Patterns and Evolution." *World Development* 29 (3): 443–53.

Grindle, Merilee S. 1986. *State and Countryside: Development Policy and Agrarian Politics in Latin America*. Baltimore: Johns Hopkins University Press.

Grzybowski, Cândido. 1991. *Caminhos e descaminhos dos movimentos sociais no campo*. Petrópolis, Brazil: Vozes.

Guimarães, Alberto Passos. 1981. *Quatro séculos de latifúndio*. 5th ed. Rio de Janeiro: Paz e Terra.

Gurr, Ted Robert. 1970. *Why Men Rebel*. Princeton: Princeton University Press.

Hammond, John L. 1999. "Law and Disorder. The Brazilian Landless Farmworkers' Movement." *Bulletin of Latin American Research* 18:469–89.

———. 2001. "The MST and the Media: Competing Images of the Landless Farmworkers' Movement." Paper presented to the Seminar on Contentious Politics, Columbia University, New York.

Helfand, Steven M., and Luis F. Brunstein. 2001. "Policy Reform and the Changing Structure of the Brazilian Agricultural Sector: Evidence from Alternative Data Sources." Paper presented at the Twenty-third International Congress of the Latin American Studies Association, Washington, DC.

Helfand, Steven, and Gervásio Castro de Rezende. 2001. "The Impact of Sector-Specific and Economy-Wide Policy Reforms: The Case of Brazilian Agriculture, 1980–1998." University of California Riverside and Universidade Federal Fluminense. Typescript.

Heredia, Beatriz, Leonilde Medeiros, Moacir Palmeira, Rosângela Cintrão, and Sérgio Leite. 2002. "Os impactos regionais da reforma agrária: Um estudo sobre áreas selecionadas." Typescript.

Hipsher, Patricia L. 1996. "Democratization and the Decline of Urban Social Movements in Chile and Spain." *Comparative Politics* 28 (April): 273–97.

———. 1998. "Democratic Transitions as Protest Cycles: Social Movement Dynamics in Democratizing Latin America." In *The Social Movement Society*, edited by Sidney Tarrow and David S. Meyer, 153–72. Lanham, Md.: Rowman and Littlefield.

Hirschman, Albert O. 1982. *Shifting Involvements: Private Interest and Public Action*. Princeton: Princeton University Press.

Hobson, Barbara. 2003. Introduction to *Recognition Struggle and Social Movements: Contested Identities, Agency, and Power*, edited by Barbara Hobson. Cambridge: Cambridge University Press.

Hochstetler, Kathryn. 2000. "Democratizing Pressures from Below? Social Movements in the New Brazilian Democracy." In *Democratic Brazil: Actors, Institutions, and Processes,* edited by Peter R. Kingstone and Timothy J. Power, 162–82. Pittsburgh: University of Pittsburgh Press.

Hoffman, Helga. 1989. "Poverty and Prosperity: What Is Changing?" In *Social Change in Brazil, 1945–1985: The Incomplete Transition,* edited by Edmar L. Bacha and Herbert S. Klein, 197–231. Albuquerque: University of New Mexico Press.

Hoffman, Rodolfo. 1988. "Distribuição de renda na agricultura." In *Os principais problemas da agricultura brasileira: Analise e sugestões,* edited by Antonio Salazar P. Brandão, 11–48. Rio de Janeiro: IPEA/INPES.

———. 1993. "Distribução da renda e pobreza na agricultura paulista." *São Paulo em Perspectiva* 7:107–15.

Houtzager, Peter Pim. 1997. "Caught Between State and Church: Popular Movements in the Brazilian Countryside, 1964–1989." Ph.D. diss., University of California, Berkeley.

———. 1998. "State and Unions in the Transformation of the Brazilian Countryside, 1964–1979." *Latin American Research Review* 33 (2): 103–42.

———. 2005. *Os últimos cidadãos: Conflito e modernização no Brasil rural (1964–1995).* São Paulo: Editora Globo.

Huber, Evelyne, and Frank Safford. 1995. *Agrarian Structure and Political Power: Landlord and Peasant in the Making of Latin America.* Pittsburgh: University of Pittsburgh Press.

Huizer, Gerrit. 1972. *The Revolutionary Potential of Peasants in Latin America.* Lexington, Mass.: Lexington Books.

Hunter, Wendy. 2003. "Brazil's New Direction." *Journal of Democracy* 14 (2): 151–62.

Jenkins, J. Craig, and Craig M. Eckert. 1986. "Channeling Black Insurgency: Elite Patronage and Professional Social Movement Organizations in the Development of the Black Movement." *American Sociological Review* 51 (December): 812–29.

Jenkins, J. Craig, and Charles Perrow. 1977. "Insurgency of the Powerless: Farm Worker Movements (1946–1972)." *American Sociological Review* 42 (April): 249–68.

Kay, Cristóbal. 1995. "Rural Latin America: Exclusionary and Uneven Agricultural Development." In *Capital, Power, and Inequality in Latin America,* edited by Sandor Halebsky and Richard L. Harris, 21–51. Boulder, Colo.: Westview.

Keck, Margaret E. 1992. *The Workers' Party and Democratization in Brazil.* New Haven: Yale University Press.

———. 1995. "Social Equity and Environmental Politics in Brazil: Lessons from the Rubber Tapers of Acre." *Comparative Politics* 27 (July): 409–24.

Kingstone, Peter R. 2000. "Muddling Through Gridlock: Economic Policy Performance, Business Responses, and Democratic Sustainability." In *Democratic Brazil: Actors, Institutions, and Processes,* edited by Peter R. Kingstone and Timothy J. Power, 185–203. Pittsburgh: University of Pittsburgh Press.

Kingstone, Peter R., and Timothy J. Power, eds. 2000. *Democratic Brazil: Actors, Institutions, and Processes.* Pittsburgh: University of Pittsburgh Press.

Kornhauser, William. 1959. *The Politics of Mass Society.* New York: Free Press.

Kotscho, Ricardo. 1982. *O massacre dos posseiros: Conflitos de terras no Araguaia-Tocantins.* São Paulo: Brasiliense.

Kurzman, Charles. 1996. "Structural Opportunity and Perceived Opportunity in Social Movement Theory: The Iranian Revolution of 1979." *American Journal of Sociology* 61:153–70.

Landsberger, Henry A. 1969. *Latin American Peasant Movements.* Ithaca: Cornell University Press.

Lapp, Nancy D. 2004. *Landing Votes: Representation and Land Reform in Latin America.* New York: Palgrave Macmillan.

Laurenti, Antonio Carlos, and Mauro Eduardo del Grossi. 2000. "A evolução das pessoas ocupadas nas actividades agrícolas e nao-agrícolas nas areas rurais do Brasil." In *O novo rural brasileiro: Uma análise nacional e regional,* vol 1, edited by Clayton Campanhola and José Graziano da Silva, 15–66. Jaguariúna, Brazil: EMBRAPA.

Leite, Sérgio. 1999. "Políticas públicas e agricultura no Brasil: Comentários sobre o cenário recente." In *O desmonte da nação,* edited by Ivo Lesbaupin, 153–79. 2d ed. Petrópolis, Brazil: Vozes.

Leroy, Jean-Pierre. 1991. *Uma chama na Amazônia.* Rio de Janeiro: Vozes.

Lisboa, Teresa Kleba. 1988. "A luta dos sem-terra no oeste catarinense." Florianópolis, Brazil: Editora UFSC/MST.

Lunardon, Maurício Tadeu. 2000. "Aspectos da agropecuária paranaense: Algodão." http://www.pr.gov.br/seab/aspectos/algodao.html (accessed February 27, 2002).

Mainwaring, Scott. 1986. *The Catholic Church and Politics in Brazil, 1916–1985.* Stanford: Stanford University Press.

———. 1989. "Grassroots Popular Movements and the Struggle for Democracy: Nova Iguaçu, 1974–1985." In *Democratizing Brazil: Problems of Transition and Consolidation,* edited by Alfred Stepan, 168–204. New York: Oxford University Press.

———. 1999. *Rethinking Party Systems in the Third Wave of Democratization: The Case of Brazil.* Stanford: Stanford University Press.

Malin, Mauro. 2002. "Agriculture e reforma agrária." In *A era FHC: Um balanço,* edited by Bolívar Lamounier and Rubens Figueiredo, 179–241. São Paulo: Cultura.

Marcon, Telmo. 1997. *Acampamento Natalino: História da luta pela reforma agrária.* Passo Fundo, Brazil: Universidade de Passo Fundo.

Martine, George. 1987a. "A modernização agrícola e a panela do povo." In *Os impactos sociais da modernização agrícola* edited by George Martine and Ronaldo Coutinho Garcia, 81–95. São Paulo: Caetés.

———. 1987b. "Êxodo rural, concentração urbana e fronteira agrícola." In *Os impactos sociais da modernização agrícola* edited by George Martine and Ronaldo Coutinho Garcia, 59–79. São Paulo: Caetés.

———. 1991. "A trajetória da modernização agrícola: A quem beneficia? *Lua Nova* 23 (March): 7–37.

Martine, George, and Ronaldo Coutinho Garcia, eds. 1987. *Os impactos sociais da modernização agrícola.* São Paulo: Caetés.

Martins, José de Souza. 1981. *Os camponeses e a política no Brasil.* Petrópolis, Brazil: Vozes.

———. 1991. *Expropiaçãao e violênca.* São Paulo: HUCITEC.

———. 1999. "Reforma Agrária: O impossível diálogo sobre a história possível." *Tempo Social* 11 (February): 97–128.

Marx, Gary T., and James L. Wood. 1975. "Strands of Theory and Research in Collective Behavior." *Annual Review of Sociology* 1:363–428.

Maybury-Lewis, Biorn. 1994. *The Politics of the Possible: The Brazilian Rural Workers' Trade Union Movement, 1964–1985*. Philadelphia: Temple University Press.

McAdam, Doug. 1982. *Political Process and the Development of Black Insurgency, 1930–1970*. Chicago: University of Chicago Press.

———. 1983. "Tactical Innovation and the Pace of Insurgency." *American Sociological Review* 48 (December): 735–54.

———. 1996. "Conceptual Origins, Current Problems, Future Directions." In *Comparative Perspectives on Social Movements: Political Opportunities, Mobilizing Structures, and Cultural Framings*, edited by Doug McAdam, John D. McCarthy, and M. N. Zald, 23–40. Cambridge: Cambridge University Press.

McAdam, Doug, John D. McCarthy, and M. N. Zald. 1988. "Social Movements." In *Handbook of Sociology*, edited by Neil J. Smelser, 695–738. Newbury, Calif.: Sage.

———. eds. 1996. *Comparative Perspectives on Social Movements: Political Opportunities, Mobilizing Structures, and Cultural Framings*. Cambridge: Cambridge University Press.

———. 1996. "Introduction: Opportunities, Mobilizing Structures, and Framing Processes; Toward a Synthetic, Comparative Perspective on Social Movements." In *Comparative Perspectives on Social Movements: Political Opportunities, Mobilizing Structures, and Cultural Framings*, edited by Doug McAdam, John D. McCarthy, and M. N. Zald, 1–20. Cambridge: Cambridge University Press.

McAdam, Doug, Sidney Tarrow, and Charles Tilly. 1997. "Toward an Integrated Perspective on Social Movements and Revolutions." In *Comparative Politics: Rationality, Culture, and Politics*, edited by Mark Irving Lichbach and Alan S. Zuckerman, 142–73. New York: Cambridge University Press.

McCammon, Holly J. 2001. "Stirring Up Suffrage Sentiment: The Formation of the State Woman Suffrage Organizations, 1866–1914." *Social Forces* 80 (2): 449–80.

McCarthy, John D., and M. N. Zald. 1973. *The Trends of Social Movements in America: Professionalization and Resource Mobilization*. Morristown, N.J.: General Learning.

McClintock, Cynthia. 1989. "Peru's Sendero Luminoso Rebellion: Origins and Trajectory." In *Power and Popular Protest*, edited by Susan Eckstein, 61–101. Berkeley and Los Angeles: University of California Press.

Medeiros, Leonilde Servolo de. 1989. *História dos Movimentos Sociais no Campo*. Rio de Janeiro: FASE.

Medeiros, Leonilde Servolo de, and Sérgio Leite, eds. 1999. *A formação dos assentamentos rurais no Brasil*. Porto Alegre, Brazil: Editora da Universidade/UFRGS.

———. 2004. *Assentamentos rurais: Mudança social e dinâmica regional*. Rio de Janeiro: MAUAD Editora.

Medeiros, Leonilde Servolo de, Maria Valéria Barbosa, Mariana Pantoja Franco, Neide Esterci, and Sérgio Leite, eds. 1994. *Assentamentos rurais: Uma visão multidisciplinar*. São Paulo: Editora da UNESP.

Merrick, Thomas J. 1989. "Population Since 1945." In *Social Change in Brazil, 1945–1985: The Incomplete Transition*, edited by Edmar L. Bacha and Herbert S. Klein, 15–48. Albuquerque: University of New Mexico Press.

Meyer, David S. 1990. *A Winter of Discontent: The Nuclear Freeze and American Politics.* New York: Praeger.

————. 2004. "Protest and Political Opportunities." *Annual Review of Sociology* 30:125–45.

Meyer, David S., and Debra Minkoff. 2004. "Conceptualizing Political Opportunity." *Social Forces* (4): 1457–92.

Michiles, Carlos, Emmanuel Gonçalves Vieira Filho, Francisco Whitaker Ferreira, João Gilberto Lucas Coelho, Maria da Glória da Veiga Moura, and Regina de Paula Santos Prado. 1989. *Cidadão constituinte: A saga das emendas populares.* Rio de Janeiro: Editora Paz e Terra.

Migdal, Joel. 1974. *Peasants, Politics, and Revolution: Pressures Toward Political and Social Change in the Third World.* Princeton: Princeton University Press.

Moore, Barrington, Jr. 1966. *Social Origins of Dictatorship and Democracy: Lord and Peasant in the Making of the Modern World.* Boston: Beacon Press.

Navarro, Zander. 1988. "Acampamentos: A experiência dos colonos no Sul do Brasil. *Tempo e Presença* 231 (June): 6–8.

————. 1995. "A longa caminhada: Classes populares e democracia em areas rurais do Brasil (com ênfase no caso do estado do Rio Grande do Sul)." Paper presented at the Nineteenth International Congress of the Latin American Studies Association, Washington, D.C.

————. 1996a."Democracia, cidadania e representação: Os movimentos sociais rurais no estado do Rio Grande do Sul, Brasil, 1978–1990." In *Política, protesto e cidadania no campo: As lutas sociais dos colonos e dos trabalhadores rurais no Rio Grande do Sul,* 62–105. Porto Alegre, Brazil: Editora Universidade/UFRGS.

————. ed. 1996b. *Política, protesto e cidadania no campo: As lutas sociais dos colonos e dos trabalhadores rurais no Rio Grande do Sul.* Porto Alegre, Brazil: Editora Universidade/UFRGS.

————. 1996c. "Políticas públicas, agricultura familiar e os procesos de democratização em areas rurais brasileiras (Com enfase para o caso do Sul do Brasil). Paper presented at the annual meeting of the Associaçao Nacional de Pós-graduaçao e Pesquisa em Ciências Sociais, Caxambú, Minas Gerais, Brazil.

————. 2000. "Breaking New Ground: Brazil's MST." Translated by Judy Rein. *NACLA Report on the Americas* 33 (March/April): 36–39.

Navarro, Zander, Maria Stela Moraes, and Raul Menezes. 1999. "Pequena história dos assentamentos rurais no Rio Grande do Sul: Formação e desenvolvimento." In *A formação dos assentamentos rurais no Brasil: Processos sociais e políticas públicas,* edited by Leonilde Servolo de Medeiros and Sérgio Leite, 19–68. Porto Alegre, Brazil: Editora da Universidade.

Neri, Marcelo. 2006. "Miséria, desigualdade e estabilidade: O segundo real." Resumo. Fundação Getúlio Vargas. Centro de Políticas Sociais.

Neri, Marcelo, José Marcio Camargo, and Maurício Cortez Reis. 2000. "Mercado de trabalho nos anos 90: Fatos estilizados e interpretações." Texto para discussão, no. 743. IPEA.

Neto, José Ambrosio Ferreira. 1999. "Lideranças sindicais e ação coletiva. A FETAMAG e a luta pela terra em Minas Gerais." Ph.D. diss., Universidade Federal Rural do Rio de Janeiro.

Novaes, Regina Reyes. 1997. *De corpo e alma: Catolicismo, classes sociais e conflitos no campo.* Rio de Janeiro: GRAPHA.

Novicki, Victor de Araújo. 1994. "Governo Brizola, movimentos de ocupação de terras e assentamentos rurais no Rio de Janeiro (1983–1987)." In *Assentamentos
rurais: Uma visão multidisciplinar,* edited by Leonilde Servolo de Medeiros,
Maria Valéria Barbosa, Mariana Pantoja Franco, Neide Esterci, and Sérgio
Leite, 69–86. São Paulo: Editora da UNESP.

Oberschall, Anthony. 1973. *Social Conflict and Social Movements.* Englewood Cliffs,
N.J.: Prentice Hall.

———. 1994. "Rational Choice in Collective Protests." *Rationality and Society* 6
(January): 70–100.

———. 1996. "Opportunities and Framing in the East European Revolts of 1989."
In *Comparative Perspectives on Social Movements: Political Opportunities, Mo-
bilizing Structures, and Cultural Framings,* edited by Doug McAdam, John D.
McCarthy, and M. N. Zald, 93–121. Cambridge: Cambridge University Press.

———. 2000. "Social Movements and the Transition to Democracy." *Democratization* 7 (Autumn): 25–45.

O'Donnell, Guillermo, and Philippe C. Schmitter. 1986. *Transitions from Authoritarian Rule: Tentative Conclusions About Uncertain Democracies.* Baltimore:
Johns Hopkins University Press.

Offe, Claus. 1985. "New Social Movements: Challenging the Boundaries of Institutional Politics." *Social Research* 52: 817–68.

Oliveira, Edélcio Vigna de. 1996. "Impeachment, mobilização social e aprovação da
lei agrária." Master's thesis, Universidade de Brasilia.

———. 1999. "Bancada ruralista na Câmara dos Deputados: A banca ruralista (1)—
Legislatura 1999/2002." http://www.dataterra.org.br/Documentos/BANC-
ARUR99.htm.

Oliveira, Lúcia Lippi. 1987. "O movimento operário em São Paulo: 1970–1985." In
Movimentos sociais na transiçao democrática, edited by Emir Sader, 24–52.
São Paulo: Cortez.

Oliveira, Marcos Antonio de. 1998. "Notas sobre a crise do novo sindicalismo brasileiro." *São Paulo em Perspectiva* 12 (January–March): 24–29.

Oliver, Pam, and Gerald Marwell. 1993. *The Critical Mass in Collective Action: A Micro-
social Theory.* Cambridge: Cambridge University Press.

Olson, Mancur, Jr. 1965. *The Logic of Collective Action.* Cambridge: Harvard University Press.

Ondetti, Gabriel. 2006a. "Lula and Land Reform: How Much Progress?" Paper prepared for delivery at the meeting of the Latin American Studies Association,
March 15–18, San Juan, Puerto Rico.

———. 2006b. "Repression, Opportunity, and Protest: Explaining the Takeoff of
Brazil's Landless Movement." *Latin American Politics and Society* 48 (2):
61–94.

———. 2007. "An Ambivalent Legacy: Cardoso and Land Reform." *Latin American
Perspectives* 34 (5): 9–25.

Ondetti, Gabriel, Emmanuel Wambergue, and João Batista Gonçalves Afonso. Forthcoming. "From *Posseiro* to *Sem-Terra:* The Impact of MST Land Struggles in the
State of Pará." In *Challenging Inequality: The Landless Rural Workers Movement (MST) and Agrarian Reform in Brazil,* edited by Miguel Carter. Durham:
Duke University Press.

Osa, Maryjane, and Cristina Corduneanu-Huci. 2003. "Running Uphill: Political Opportunity in Non-democracies." *Comparative Sociology* 2 (4): 605–29.

Ozorio de Almeida, Anna Luiza. 1992. *The Colonization of the Amazon.* Austin: University of Texas Press.

Pereira, Anthony W. 1997. *The End of the Peasantry: The Rural Labor Movement in Northeast Brazil, 1961–1988.* Pittsburgh: University of Pittsburgh Press.

———. 2003 "Brazil's Agrarian Reform: Democratic Innovation or Oligarchic Exclusion Redux?" *Latin American Politics and Society* 45:41–65.

Perz, Stephen G. 2000. "The Rural Exodus in the Context of Economic Crisis, Globalization, and Reform in Brazil." *International Migration Review* 34 (3): 842–81.

Petras, James. 1997. "Latin America: Resurgence of the Left." *New Left Review* 223 (May/June): 17–47.

———. 1998. "The Political and Social Bases of Regional Variation in Land Occupations in Brazil." *Journal of Peasant Studies* 25 (July): 124–33.

Piven, Frances Fox, and Richard Cloward. 1977. *Poor People's Movements: Why They Succeed, How They Fail.* New York: Pantheon Books.

Pochmann, Marcio. 2006. "Gasto social e seus efeitos recentes no nível de emprego e na desigualdade da renda do trabalho no Brasil." Manuscript.

Polletta, Francesca, and Edwin Amenta. 2001. "Conclusion: Second That Emotion? Lessons from Once-Novel Concepts in Social Movement Research." In *Passionate Politics: Emotions and Social Movements,* edited by Jeff Goodwin, James M. Jasper, and Francesca Polletta, 303–16. Chicago: University of Chicago Press.

Popkin, Samuel L. 1979. *The Rational Peasant: The Political Economy of Rural Society in Vietnam.* Berkeley and Los Angeles: University of California Press.

Power, Timothy J. 2000. "Political Institutions in Democratic Brazil: Politics as a Permanent Constitutional Convention." In *Democratic Brazil: Actors, Institutions, and Processes,* edited by Peter R. Kingstone and Timothy J. Power, 17–35. Pittsburgh: University of Pittsburgh Press.

Power, Timothy J., and J. Timmons Roberts. 2000. "A New Brazil? The Changing Sociodemographic Context of Brazilian Democracy." In *Democratic Brazil: Actors, Institutions, and Processes,* edited by Peter R. Kingstone and Timothy J. Power, 236–62. Pittsburgh: University of Pittsburgh Press.

Prado, Caio Junior. 1978. *História econômica do Brasil.* 21st ed. São Paulo: Brasiliense.

———. 1999. *A revolução brasilera: Perspectivas em 1977.* São Paulo: Brasiliense.

Priestley, George. 1986. *Military Government and Popular Participation in Panama: The Torrijos Regime, 1968–1975.* Boulder, Colo.: Westview.

Rezende, Gervasio Castro de. 2006. "Labor, Land, and Agricultural Credit Policies and Their Adverse Impacts on Poverty in Brazil." Texto para discussão, no. 1180. IPEA.

Reydon, Sebastián P., and Ludwig A. Plata. 1998. "Politicas de mercados de tierras en Brasil." In *Perspectivas sobre mercados de tierras rurales en América Latina : Informe técnico,* 56–92. Washington, D.C.: Inter-American Development Bank.

Ricci, Rudá. 1999. *Terra de ninguém: Representação sindical rural no Brasil.* Campinas, Brazil: Editora Unicamp.

Rodrigues, Leôncio. 1995. "O sindicalismo nos anos 80: Um balanço." In *Brasil em Artigos,* 131–56. São Paulo: SEADE.

Rudé, George. 1964. *The Crowd in History.* New York: John Wiley and Sons.

Ruscheinsky, Aloisio. 1989. "Terra e política: O movimento dos trabalhadores sem terra no oeste de Santa Catarina." Master's thesis, Pontífica Universidade Católica.

Sader, Eder. 1988. *Quando novos personagens entraram em cena*. São Paulo: Paz e Terra.

Sallum, Brasilio, Jr., and Eduardo Kugelmas. 2004. "Sobre o modo Lula de governar." In *Brasil e Argentina hoje: Política e economia,* edited by Brasilio Sallum Jr., 255–87. Bauru, Brazil: Editora da Universidade do Sagrado Coração (EDUSC).

Schmink, Marianne, and Charles H. Wood. 1992. *Contested Frontiers in Amazonia.* New York: Columbia University Press.

Schmitt, Claudia Job. 1992. "O tempo do acampamento: A construção social e política do colono sem-terra." Master's thesis, Universidade Federal do Rio Grande do Sul.

————. 1996. "A CUT dos colonos: Histórias da construção de um novo sindicalismo no campo no Rio Grande do Sul." In *Política, protesto e cidadania no campo: As lutas sociais dos colonos e dos trabalhadores rurais no Rio Grande do Sul,* 189–226. Porto Alegre, Brazil: Editora Universidade/UFRGS.

Schönleitner, Gunther. 1997. "Discussing Brazil's Agrarian Question: Land Reform Is Dead, Long Live Family Farming?" Typescript.

Scott, James C. 1976. *The Moral Economy of the Peasant: Rebellion and Subsistence in Southeast Asia.* New Haven: Yale University Press.

————. 1977. "Hegemony and the Peasantry." *Politics and Society* 7 (3): 229.

Sigaud, Lygia. 1979. *Os clandestinos e os direitos: Estudo sobre trabalhadores da cana-de-açucar de Pernambuco.* São Paulo: Livraria Duas Cidades.

Silva, Lígia Osorio da. 1996. *Terras devolutas e latifúndio: Efeitos da Lei de 1850.* Campinas, Brazil: Editora Universidade/UNICAMP.

Skidmore, Thomas E. 1967. *Politics in Brazil, 1930–1964: An Experiment in Democracy.* London: Oxford University Press.

————. 1988. *The Politics of Military Rule in Brazil, 1964–85.* New York: Oxford University Press.

Smelser, Neil J. 1963. *Theory of Collective Behavior.* New York: Free Press of Glencoe.

Smith, Christian Stephen. 1996. *Resisting Reagan: The U.S. Central America Peace Movement.* Chicago: University of Chicago Press.

Smith, William C., and Nizar Messari. 2001. "Democracy and Reform in Cardoso's Brazil: Caught Between Clientelism and Global Markets?" In *The Challenge of Change in Latin America and the Caribbean,* edited by Jeffrey Stark, 59–110. Boulder, Colo.: Lynne Rienner.

Snow, David A. 1986. "Frame Alignment Processes, Micromobilization, and Movement Participation." *American Sociological Review* 51 (August): 464–81.

Snow, David, and Robert D. Benford. 1988. "Ideology, Frame Resonance, and Participant Mobilization" *International Social Movement Research* 1:197–217.

Snow, David A., Sarah A. Soule, and Daniel M. Cress. 2005. "Identifying the Precipitants of Homeless Protest Across 17 U.S. Cities, 1980 to 1990." *Social Forces* 83 (3): 1183–210.

Sobhan, Rehman. 1993. *Agrarian Reform and Social Transformation: Preconditions for Development.* London: Zed.

Sorj, Bernardo. 1980. *Estado e classes sociais na agricultura brasileira.* Rio de Janeiro: Zahar.

————. 1998. "A reforma agrária em tempos de democracia e globalização." *Novos Estudos CEBRAP* 50 (Março): 23–40.

Soule, Sarah A., Doug McAdam, John McCarthy, and Yang Su. 1999. "Protest Events: Cause or Consequence of State Action? The U.S. Women's Movement and Federal Congressional Activities, 1956–1979." *Mobilization: An International Quarterly* 4:239–55.

Sparovek, Gerd. 2003. *A qualidade dos assentamentas da reforma agrária brasileira.* São Paulo: Páginas e Letras.

Sparovek, Gerd, Alberto G. O. Pereira Barretto, Rodrigo Fernando Maule, and Sérgio Paganini Martins. 2005. "Análise territorial da produção nos assentamentos." Ministério do Desenvolvimento Agrário/Núcleo de Estudos Agrários e Desenvolvimento Rural (NEAD), Debate 4.

Stanfield, J. David. 1989. "Agrarian Reform in the Dominican Republic." In *Searching for Agrarian Reform in Latin America,* edited by William C. Thiesenhusen, 305–37. Boston: Unwin Hyman.

Stedile, Jõao Pedro, and Bernardo Mançano Fernandes. 1999. *Brava gente: A trajetória do MST e a luta pela terra no Brasil.* São Paulo: Fundação Perseu Abramo.

Stepan, Alfred. 1978. "Political Leadership and Regime Breakdown: Brazil." In *The Breakdown of Democratic Regimes: Latin America,* edited by Juan J. Linz and Alfred Stepan, 110–37. Baltimore: John Hopkins University Press.

Stival, David. 1987. "O processo educativo dos agricultores sem terra na trajetória da luta pela terra." Master's thesis, Universidade Federal do Rio Grande do Sul.

Svampa, Maristella. 2003. "El movimiento piquetero en Argentina: Dimensiones de una nueva experiencia." Paper presented at the Twentieth Annual Latin American Labor History Conference, September 26–27, Duke University, Durham.

Tambara, Elomar. 1983. *RS: Modernização e crise na agricultura.* Porto Alegre, Brazil: Mercado Aberto.

Tarelho, Luiz Carlos. 1988. "Da consciência dos direitos á identidade social: Os sem terra de Sumaré." Master's thesis, Pontifícia Universidade Católica de São Paulo.

Tarrow, Sidney. 1983. *Struggling to Reform: Social Movements and Policy Change During Cycles of Protests.* Western Societies Program Occasional Paper 15. Ithaca, N.Y.: Center for International Studies, Cornell University.

————. 1989. *Democracy and Disorder: Protest and Politics in Italy, 1965–1975.* Oxford: Oxford University Press.

————. 1994. *Power in Movement: Social Movements, Collective Action, and Politics.* Cambridge: Cambridge University Press.

————. 1996. "States and Opportunities: The Political Structuring of Social Movements." In *Comparative Perspectives on Social Movements: Political Opportunities, Mobilizing Structures, and Cultural Framings,* edited by Doug McAdam, John D. McCarthy, and M. N. Zald, 41–61. Cambridge: Cambridge University Press.

Thiesenhusen, William C., ed. 1989. *Searching for Agrarian Reform in Latin America.* Boston: Unwin Hyman.

————. 1995. *Broken Promises: Agrarian Reform and the Latin American Campesino.* Boulder, Colo.: Westview.

Tilly, Charles. 1964. *The Vendée*. Cambridge: Harvard University Press.

———. 1978. *From Mobilization to Revolution*. New York: McGraw-Hill.

Torrens, João Carlos Sampaio. 1991. "O Movimento dos Trahalhadores Rurais Sem Terra no estado do Rio Grande do Sul (1978/90): Teçendo a rede de relações entre os mediadores da luta pela terra." Federaçao de Orgãos para Assistência Social e Educacional. Projeto Democracia e Desenvolvimento Rural na Região do Alto Uruguai. Typescript.

———. 1992. "Alianças e conflitos na mediação política da luta pela terra no Paraná." Master's thesis, Universidade Federal Rural do Rio de Janeiro.

Umbelino de Oliveira, Ariovaldo. 1991. *A agricultura camponesa no Brasil*. São Paulo: Contexto.

———. 1999. *A geografia das lutas no campo*. São Paulo: Contexto.

Veiga, José Eli. 1990. *A reforma que virou suco*. Petrópolis, Brazil: Vozes.

Veltmeyer, Henry, and James Petras. 2002. "The Social Dynamics of Brazil's Rural Landless Workers' Movement: Ten Hypotheses on Successful Leadership." *Canadian Review of Sociology and Anthropology* 39 (February): 79–96.

Voss, Kim. 1996. "The Collapse of a Social Movement: The Interplay of Mobilizing Structures, Framing, and Political Opportunities in the Knights of Labor." In *Comparative Perspectives on Social Movements: Political Opportunities, Mobilizing Structures, and Cultural Framings*, edited by Doug McAdam, John D. McCarthy, and M. N. Zald, 227–58. Cambridge: Cambridge University Press.

Wagner, Carlos. 1988. *A saga do João Sem Terra*. Petrópolis, Brazil: Vozes.

———. 1995. *O Brasil de Bombachas*. São Paulo: L&PM.

Weffort, Francisco Corrêa. 1980. *O populismo na política brasileira*. 4th ed. Rio de Janeiro: Paz e Terra.

Welch, Cliff. 1999. *The Seed Was Planted: The São Paulo Roots of Brazil's Rural Labor Movement, 1924–1964*. University Park: Pennsylvania State University Press.

Weyland, Kurt. 1996. *Democracy Without Equity: Failures of Reform in Brazil*. Pittsburgh: University of Pittsburgh Press.

Wolf, Eric R. 1969. *Peasant Wars of the Twentieth Century*. New York: Harper & Row.

Wolford, Wendy. 2003. "Families, Fields, and Fighting for Land: The Spatial Dynamics of Contention in Rural Brazil." *Mobilization: An International Quarterly* 8 (2): 157–72.

———. 2004. "Of Land and Labor: Agrarian Reform on the Sugarcane Plantations of Northeast Brazil." *Journal of Latin American Perspectives* 31:147–70.

Womack, John. 1968. *Zapata and the Mexican Revolution*. New York, Knopf.

Wood, James L., and Maurice Jackson. 1982. *Social Movements: Development, Participation, and Dynamics*. Belmont, Calif.: Wadsworth.

World Bank. 1982. *Brazil: A Review of Agricultural Policies*. Washington, D.C.: World Bank.

Wright, Angus, and Wendy Wolford. 2003. *To Inherit the Earth: The Landless Movement and the Struggle for a New Brazil*. San Francisco: Food First.

Zald, Mayer N., and Roberta Ash. 1966. "Social Movement Organizations: Growth, Decay, and Change." *Social Forces* 44:327–41.

Zamberlan, Jurandir, and Santo Reni S. Florão. 1989. *Assentamentos: Resposta econômica da pequena propriedade na região de Cruz Alta*. Passo Fundo, Brazil: Berthier.

Zamberlan, Jurandir, and Alceu Froncheti. 1993. *Rincão do Ivaí: Uma história gerando vida*. Passo Fundo, Brazil: Berthier.

Zamosc, Leon. 1986. *The Agrarian Question and the Peasant Movement in Colombia: Struggles of the National Peasant Association, 1967–1981.* Cambridge: Cambridge University Press.

Zimmermann, Neusa de Castro. 1994. "Os desafios da organização interna de um assentamento rural." In *Assentamentos rurais: Uma visão multidisciplinar,* edited by Leonilde Servolo de Medeiros, Maria Valéria Barbosa, Mariana Pantoja Franco, Neide Esterci, and Sérgio Leite, 205–24. São Paulo: Editora da UNESP.

INDEX

Note: All cities, states and regions are located in Brazil unless otherwise noted.

poverty (*continued*)
  reducing, 58, 144, 147, 203, 204, 239
  rural, 62, 64, 92, 172, 182, 205, 217
press. *See* media coverage
Pretto, Adão, 73 n. 21
prices. *See* farmers/farmland, prices of; inflation; land, prices of; stabilization
  plans
private property, 19, 100, 137, 139, 225,
  236–37
  expropriations of, 77–78, 87, 160, 184, 229
privatization, 144, 145, 146, 161, 162, 197
Proálcool (federal program), 59
PROCERA (Special Credit Program for Agrarian
  Reform), 121, 155, 194, 232
Program for Technical, Social and Environmental Advising (ATES), 232
PRONAF (National Program for Strengthening
  Family Agriculture), 155, 214, 232
protests. *See also* demonstrations; grassroots
  protests; land occupations; marches;
  strikes
  aggressive, 42, 154, 196–99
  alternative, 82–83, 91, 128, 191–92, 194
  collective action theory of, 43–46, 160
  cycles of, 13–16, 18, 34–35, 37–38, 51, 56,
    98–99, 107–8, 134
  decline of, 107–8, 131–32, 224
  intensity variation in, 1–6, 16, 23, 27–34,
    42, 46–47, 49, 94–99, 109–13, 168–78,
    200, 220–24
  by landless workers, 49, 96, 113, 128, 142,
    176, 181
  MST, 115, 136, 164, 194–99, 212
  organizational capacity theory of, 8–9,
    28–31
  political opportunity theory, 5, 16–18, 30,
    32, 34–43, 47, 226
  regime change and, 49, 52–57
  responses to, 145, 165–68, 224
  resurgence of, 200–201, 208–14, 217–19
  southern region, 65–82
  takeoff of, 140–43, 172–73, 177–78
  theories of, 23–24
Provisional National Commission of Landless
  Rural Workers, 88–89
public employees' protests, 181
public goods, 43, 45–46, 48, 100, 133–35,
  224–25, 227–28
public opinion, 41
  appealing to, 9, 34, 115, 127
  explosion of, 1–2, 15, 142–43, 155, 162

of land occupations, 67, 79, 96, 140, 164,
  167, 187
regarding massacres, 17, 42, 142, 154, 174,
  176
regarding MST, 160–61, 196–98

Quadros, Jânio, 12

Rainha, José, 131 n. 29, 156, 157 n. 31
ranches, 7, 62–63, 65, 84
Reagan, Ronald, 39
Real Plan, 103, 144, 146, 147, 204, 222
red April. *See* Eldorado do Carajás massacre
reflection groups. *See* ecclesial base communities (CEBS)
regime changes, 9, 40, 52–57, 130. *See also*
  authoritarian regimes; civilian rule; military dictatorship
regions, xx, 7, 19–20. *See also individual regions*
relative deprivation theory, 25–27, 49, 80,
  91, 131, 141, 172, 217
religion, 76, 79, 93, 121–22. *See also* Catholic
  Church; Lutheran Church
repression, 2, 52, 56
  decreasing, 16, 51, 97, 142, 166–67, 174,
    177, 219, 222, 223
  increasing, 18, 43, 106, 115, 179–81, 184–
    85, 187, 197
  overcoming, 30, 114
  provoking, 32, 33, 35, 115
Requião, Roberto, 210
resource mobilization theory, 28–29, 31, 35,
  44
resources, 8–9, 99, 208
  external, 30–31, 32, 50, 93, 131–32, 141
  material, 121–22, 124, 169
  withdrawal of, 180, 194
rightists, 213. *See also* conservatives; leftists
Rio de Janeiro, 56, 83, 87
Rio Grande do Sul, 7, 10, 11
  landless movement in, 70–72, 74–75, 77,
    81–82, 87, 96, 135
  land occupations in, 65, 66, 68–70, 80, 110
road blockages, 5, 114
road-building, 62, 65
Rocha, Sebastião Neves, 173 n. 54
Rodrigues, Leôncio, 108
Ronda Alta occupation, 68–71, 96
Roque dos Santos, Roosevelt, 154 n. 24
Rossetto, Miguel, 214, 215 n. 22
rubber tappers, 34, 107 n. 6
Rui, José, 173 n. 55, 193 n. 23

www.ingramcontent.com/pod-product-compliance
Lightning Source LLC
Chambersburg PA
CBHW021852020426
42334CB00013B/301